Law and Society in Imperial Japan

Law and Society in Imperial Japan

Suehiro Izutarō
and the
Search for Equity

Jason Morgan

Cambria Press
Amherst, New York

Requests for permission should be directed to
permissions@cambriapress.com, or mailed to:
Cambria Press
100 Corporate Parkway, Suite 128
Amherst, New York 14226, USA

Library of Congress Cataloging-in-Publication Data

Names: Morgan, Jason Michael, 1977- author.

Title: Law and society in imperial Japan : Suehiro Izutaro and the search for equity/ Jason Morgan.

Description: Amherst : Cambria Press, 2020

Based on author's thesis (doctoral - University of Wisconsin-Madison, 2016). |
Includes bibliographical references and index. |
Summary: "This is the first monograph on Suehiro in the English language. As the representative figure of the law and society movement in Japan, a study of Suehiro helps us go much deeper into the often-neglected jurisprudential aspects of Japanese history. Far from being a matter of poring over dusty lawbooks and parsing legalese, law-and-society studies helps us see the kaleidoscopic interaction among elites and common people in the roiling 1920s and 30s, greatly complicating and enriching our view of Japanese society (and law) as a whole. Also, Suehiro is our entrepôt into an intellectual history of law-and-society study in Japan. He was in the thick of the social changes of the mid to late Taishō and early Shōwa periods, and was able to translate what he saw around him into the theoretical and legal planes with great fluency. He could translate in the other direction with equal facility. For his time as well as for ours, Suehiro was, and is, an adroit interpreter between society and law, and the addition of his voice to the pageant of Japanese history in English is long overdue"-- Provided by publisher.

Identifiers: LCCN 2019031547 (print) | LCCN 2019031548 (ebook) |

ISBN 9781604979930 (hardcover) | ISBN 9781621964988 (epub)

Subjects: LCSH: Suehiro, Izutarō, 1888-1951. | Law teachers--Japan--Biography. | Law--Japan--Social aspects--History--20th century.

Classification: LCC KNX110.S85 M67 2019 (print) | LCC KNX110.S85 (ebook) | DDC 340.092 [B]--dc23

LC record available at https://lccn.loc.gov/2019031547

LC ebook record available at https://lccn.loc.gov/2019031548

In Memoriam
Ueda Toshio, Nishido Takaaki,
David Lee Morgan, Jr., and
Armand Justin Reixach

Table of Contents

List of Tables

List of Figures

Acknowledgements

A book is like an author: a blending of communion and solitude. The faults of the book are mine alone, but many people helped make the manuscript better. At Cambria, Paul Richardson has been a conscientious and supportive editor. At Waseda, Profs. Asako Hiroshi and Sasakura Hideo taught me legal history and philosophy, Japanese and non-. At Wisconsin, scholars Viren Murthy, Mitra Sharafi, and Rick Keyser provided invaluable comments on the dissertation and MA thesis which are the parent and grandparent of this volume. Dennis, Derek, Ilyas, Michael, and Hye Eun were good friends. A special thanks to the communities at St. Paul's and Holy Redeemer, and to the fine writers at the Madison Speakeasy.

Solitude and community, and also body and soul. Money from these institutions and entities, in the form of scholarships, fellowships, grants, and travel funds, kept body and soul together while I worked on this project both alone and with others: Wisconsin Right to Life, the Fulbright Foundation, Institute for Humane Studies, Intercollegiate Studies Institute (Richard Weaver Fellowship), the Federalist Society, Liberty Fund, the Philadelphia Society, and the Ludwig von Mises Institute in Auburn, Alabama. A warm note of gratitude to the LvMI in particular, which gave me a summer home for, at long last, the unfettered exchange of big ideas.

I now work for a living and understand what I once heard in disbelief, that graduate students have it easy compared with professors. But I wouldn't have it otherwise. Reitaku University is a wonderful place to spend time, and the Moralogy Institute across the street has joined Reitaku in supporting my research and providing a community of real scholars. *Chronicles*, *New Oxford Review*, *The Remnant*, *Public Discourse*, *Seiron*, *WiLL*, the *Sankei Shimbun*, *JAPAN Forward*, *Human Life Review*, *Asia Times*, the *University Bookman*, and *Society* are invaluable fora for trying out new ideas (and occasionally some very old ones). Holy Apostles College and Seminary is where I learn that I don't know anything. Peter Redpath, Timothy Smith, and Randall Colton showed me that *quodammodo anima est omnia*. The Japan Forum for Strategic Studies has the best assembly of political thinkers anywhere. The Rekishi Mondai Ninshiki Kenkyukai has the best historians. Paul de Lacvivier is a brilliant colleague and a fellow follower of truth. There are many good things happening in Chiba and beyond. If there is any happier than I, *c'est bien à mon insu.*

Along the way, I have relied on Ueda Katsutoshi, Chizuko Allen, John Breen, Wilfred McClay, Hata Ikuhiko, Kano Tadashi, Horii Isao, Roger Ames, Kusunoki Shinji, the Komoris, Richard Rice, Hirakawa Sukehiro, Vincent Kato, Sekita Kaoru, Earl Kinmonth, Naito Yasuo, Arimoto Takeshi, Mark Thornton, Takita Makiko, Yumiko Mori, Kawakubo Tsuyoshi, Nagano Reiko, Moriki Midori, Pieter Vree, Inukai Takao, Kaizuka Masae, Fr. John Nariai, Kogure Keiko, Michael Matt, Ōkoshi Masahiro, Fr. Alan Mackey, Uchida Katsuya, Archie Miyamoto, Tamagawa Hirokazu, Al Johnson, Ezaki Michio, Fr. Thomas Onoda, Michael Yon, Ikeda Masaaki, Fr. Charles Merrill, Tsujioka Kenzo, Marshall Wordsworth, the good people in Kashiwa, and a host of others around the world. Aaron Wolf left us far too soon. Kevin Doak, my cousin and intellectual kin, is a prince among men. His imprint is apparent throughout this book, as is the inspired work of an anonymous reviewer. Matsudo is where I have laid up treasure. Chattanooga, San Antonio, and northeast Alabama are whither my mind goes back. Gifu is my New Tennessee. I shall end my labors in New Orleans, someday, where this all began.

Law and Society in Imperial Japan

Introduction

The Enlightenment was essentially the conflation of "European" and "universal." Reason was elevated to the pinnacle of human life and in some places even deified. What was good for Western Europe was thought to be good for everyone everywhere, and a Hegelian spirit of conquering progress invested this Euro-normativity with evangelical zeal. Napoleon, whom Hegel welcomed as the Promethean genius of the Enlightenment, spread this progress by means of a civil code, which was imposed by French forces or adopted by progressivist governments throughout Europe and in North, Central, and South America. It did not matter what laws had existed in a given place before the arrival of the Napoleonic Code. The Enlightenment was seen as nullifying prevenient custom and mores and reconfiguring the culture and mindsets of the people who had been living in pre-Enlightenment anticipation.

But not every Enlightenment thinker was so sure that Western Europe was the only valid social and jurisprudential model. Some philosophers in the eighteenth century (who we now see were the earliest anthropologists) recognized the problems inherent in filtering a given society through the lens of legal codes from very different times and places. In his *l'Esprit des Lois* (1748), for example, the Baron de Montesquieu (1689–1755) observed that each society should have the laws best suited to its particularities. This insight, based in part on Montesquieu's reflections on non-Western traditions such as the Chinese and Persian, was to become the foundation for a new mode of inquiry into how societies and their laws—long separated by scholarly inquiry of a different sort—had interacted in the past, and how they should in the future. It is for this reason that Montesquieu is almost universally credited, in both East and West, with being the founding father of the discipline that scholars would eventually come to call "law and society" or "the sociology of law."

Montesquieu is a good place to start when considering law in Japan. Montesquieuan legal plurality had long been a fact of jurisprudential life in Japan and had grown more salient with the introduction of non-Asian legal ideas after the forceful intervention of the West in the early 1850s. When American commodore Matthew C. Perry visited Japan with his fleet of warships in 1853, Japan soon joined the worldwide rush to throw off old legal practices and adopt some version of the Napoleonic Code. The Meiji leaders who led Japan after the collapse of the Tokugawa bakufu warrior government in the midst of a civil war in 1868 soon invited famed French legal scholar Gustave Boissonade (1825–1910) to Japan, where he spent more than two decades helping legal philosophers like Hozumi Nobushige (1855–1926) write a full civil and criminal code based on French law. In 1873, just five years after the Meiji Restoration had done away with the old Tokugawa order of society and government, Boissonade and his Japanese legal team were trying to build upon that "feudal" legacy (as the Meiji intellectuals deemed it) a solid layer of Western law.[1]

However, the construction of the new code over the old ways created more problems than it solved. A legal plurality accentuates what an apparent legal monoculture conceals: the history of law is, at its most basic, the history of the search for equity. Because laws written down in books can never anticipate, reflect, or fully guide the endless varieties of interactions and events in the real world, it is an equally endless task to find a meet accord between deference to a legal order and flexibility in the name of justice to the people living under it. Too pedantic an adherence to the generalizations and abstractions of black-letter law—too rigid a fixation on what is written "in the code"—can obviate the function of law by causing and exacerbating social disorientation. At the other extreme lies lawlessness. A middle way is needed—equity—to help guide legal reasoning as it slaloms around the unbending pillars of the positive law. This equity is usually nurtured over time and becomes tied up with local custom. Custom is what the Napoleonic Code needed most, especially in Japan, but is also the thing for which such codes inherently maintain the most inherent contempt.

The search for equity within a legal plurality of code and custom was the leitmotif of the life and career of Suehiro Izutarō (1888–1951). A champion of the ideas of Montesquieu,[2] Suehiro was the founder of the Japanese law-and-society movement, a pioneer of Japanese labor law, and the main conduit within Japan for Austrian legal theorist Eugen Ehrlich's (1862–1922) "living law," or the insight that spontaneous social ordering among common people can exist in fruitful tension with the constituted state.[3] Remembered today mainly as the "father of Japanese labor law"—he was involved in the passage of the Trade Union Law, the Labor Relations Adjustment Law, and the Labor Standards Law—Suehiro was, in his earlier career, a protégé, colleague, or mentor of many of the most prominent legal thinkers of Japan of the past century. Briefly a student of Ehrlich's while studying in Switzerland immediately following the First World War, Suehiro returned to Japan to begin his lifelong attempt to bring equitable solutions to bear on the lives of real Japanese people—and not just legal abstractions—in an attempt to find some modus vivendi between antinomian anarchy and jurisprudential rigidity in the context of Japan's unique modernity.

This unique modernity, as it turned out, both helped and hampered Suehiro's search for equity. On the one hand, Japanese law, by the second half of the Taishō Period (1912–1926)—when Suehiro had returned from abroad and began teaching at Tokyo Imperial University—had become a multi-layered arrangement of European legal epistemologies resting uneasily on a much deeper and very different, foundation of older Sino-Japanese understandings of how the law conceptualized individuals within society. Not only did the seeker after equity in interwar Japan have to contend with increasing tension between state and society as he found it, but he also had to peel away the prevailing socio-legal present to get to the non-Western past if he wanted to find a just resolution to most cases. The Western legal dispensations saw individuals, rights, and the state, but the pre-Meiji Tokugawa legal mode privileged a kind of "substantive due process," in which the more common-sense administration of equitable judgments took precedence over any insistence on rights. (Indeed, the word "rights" as understood in the Greco-Roman legal sphere of European Christendom did not exist in Japanese (or Chinese or Korean) until Japanese scholars coined a neologism to translate the term in the late nineteenth century.)

At the same time, there was a turn in the 1920s worldwide against the high liberalism that had helped craft the Napoleonic Code and propelled its exportation across national boundaries. There was a break in Japan, too, between early pro-Western reformers and those who wanted to revisit the older Japanese ways and reassess what had been thrown overboard in the zeal to westernize in the earlier generation. Whereas legal and political thinkers in Japan in the Meiji Period (1868–1912) such as Hozumi Yatsuka (1860–1912) and Nishi Amane (1829–1897) largely abandoned the Tokugawa past, dismissing it as "feudal" and heralding the introduction of Western ideas into Japanese discourse, during the Taishō Period and after there was a *ressourcement* to Japan's pre-Western phase. In literature, for example, Tanizaki Jun'ichirō (1886–1965), once a proponent of Western styles, began to draw on Japanese modes of expression more heavily as he wrote longer and more complex works of fiction. Artist Yokoyama Taikan (1868–1958) was originally interested in Western painting but rediscovered Japanese art later in life and worked on canvases in a Japanese style. Likewise, in law, Suehiro Izutarō, trained in German law, began harkening back to the Tokugawa Period (1603–1868), and in particular to a Tokugawa magistrate, Ōoka Tadasuke, Echizen-no-kami (1677–1752).[4] For Suehiro, Ōoka exemplified the application of what Suehiro called "natural reason" (*dōri*) in order to achieve equitable solutions to even the most sensitive or seemingly intractable cases.[5] Suehiro called trials conducted according to this legal personalism, in which doing justice in the case before the judge takes precedence over political or philosophical distortions, "*menschlich* trials" (*ningen aji no aru saiban*).[6] In his return to Ōoka, Suehiro Izutarō, and the law-and-society movement that blossomed worldwide and in Japan in the years following World War I, recognized the damage done by conceptual jurisprudence (*Begriffsjurisprudenz*) and legal idealism. The Pandekten system, the German species of jurisprudential idealism especially ascendant in Japan during Suehiro's time, was proving unable to address Japan's many social problems, and Suehiro looked back to a native legal philosophy that was much more human in scope.

This human-sized, human-centric vision of law was the essence of Suehirian jurisprudence. For example, in a famous essay from "Yakunin no atama" ("The mind of the bureaucrat"), Suehiro rejected the bureaucratic disregard of people in favor of the "nation," which Suehiro, early in his career, saw as a distortion of the people:

> When they [bureaucrats] represent 'the nation', they forget human sentiment entirely and divorce themselves from the 'taste of humanity'. They think it is enough to become the very personification of 'fairness and impartiality'—or so they say. But they're wrong.[7]

In "Uso no kōyō" ("On the efficacy of lies"), first written for the magazine *Kaizō* in 1917, Suehiro again rejected the inhumanness of jurisprudence, arguing for the recentralization of the human person within the life of the law:

> To my way of thinking, the fundamental defect in prevailing 'law' and 'jurisprudence' is a neglect in researching 'human beings', who are the objects of jurisprudence and law. What's more, there are even points at which law and jurisprudence indiscriminately hypothesize human beings as 'someone'. In other words, I think these are points at which law and jurisprudence frivolously change the values of basically 'unknown quantities'

> into 'known quantities' even though there has been no sufficient empirical investigation.[8]

And in "Kochie ni torawareta gendai no hōritsugaku" ("Modern jurisprudence under the sway of trivialities"), an essay based on a speech titled "Hōritsugaku ni okeru shin-rōmanshugi" ("New romanticism in jurisprudence") Suehiro gave in 1921, Suehiro argues for the human person as the foundation of the law:

> What if we treated human beings not just as possessors of intellect, but as possessors of all psychological processes, and let those as-is human beings have fully play within the law, with the natural human being regulating the law and scholars explaining things on those terms?[9]

These are calls to return to the human element in society and to let the people as individual human persons form the basis for jurisprudence. These are, in other words, fundamentally apolitical sentiments.

However, in the Meiji Period and after, politics was ascendant and was seen by many as the answer to the problems attendant on modernity—labor disputes, landlord and tenant-farmer strife, urban anonymity, family breakdown, social malaise, and the various other ills that rapid industrialization and social liberalism often bring in their wake. Political activists clamored for political solutions—including, most notably, increased suffrage—to problems understood in terms of Western concepts like liberty and popular rights. Suehiro moved in the opposite direction, seeing politics as both the cause and the effect of social dislocation and calling for apolitical solutions to societal ills that he wanted to work out equitably, through the courts, concretely by means of a modified caselaw system.

Suehiro's attempt to find an equitable jurisprudence on the margins of politics was doomed by the imperialization of Japanese life. As the Japanese empire expanded in response to geopolitical pressures, especially following the Bolshevik Revolution in 1917 and the predatory neo-colonialism of the liberal democracies, apolitical solutions to societal fracturing became less and less tenable, and, ultimately, impossible. The empire needed to put as much of society as it could on a war footing in order to meet the threats looming in from abroad. Native equity, which Suehiro advanced as a solution to social discord caused by abstractions such as freedom and rights, succumbed to politics of a different order as the empire recast, with increasing urgency, the relationship between the individual and the state. Equity under empire turned out to be a mirage. By the middle of the 1930s, Suehiro had transitioned away from his earlier, bottom-up individualism and embraced the statism of empire, autarky, and military expansion.

This is the first monograph on Suehiro in the English language, so the questions may be asked, Why Suehiro? Why now? As the representative figure of the law and society movement in Japan, a study of Suehiro helps us go much deeper into the often-neglected jurisprudential aspects of Japanese history. Far from being a matter of poring over dusty lawbooks and parsing legalese, law-and-society studies helps us see the kaleidoscopic interaction among elites and common people in the roiling 1920s and 30s, greatly complicating and enriching our view of Japanese society (and law) as a whole. Also, Suehiro is our entrepôt into an intellectual history of law-and-society study in Japan. He was in the thick of the social changes of the mid-to-late Taishō and early Shōwa periods and was able to translate what he saw around him into the theoretical and legal planes with great fluency. He could translate in the other direction with equal facility. For his time as well as for ours, Suehiro was, and is, an adroit interpreter between society and law, and the addition of his voice to the pageant of Japanese history in English is long overdue.

Historiographically, the study of Suehiro changes the way we should view Japanese law, and also the way we should periodize twentieth-century Japanese history. Legal histories on Japan very often understand the introduction of Western ideas as having fundamentally changed the practice of Japanese law. This holds true for the Meiji Period, as well as the American Occupation from 1945 and the imposition of the present-day Constitution on the defeated nation in 1947, each of which events is seen as the beginning of an increasingly complex interaction among different forms of Western legal thinking and jurisprudence. But the law-and-society movement in Japan, although it was heavily influenced by Western ideas of law, sociology, and politics (Suehiro, making an important distinction, called this influence, not "adoption," but "digestion"), also sought to reintroduce native practices and understandings of equity into Japanese courts and the legal academy. The periodization of Japanese history that articulates once at 1853 with the arrival of American Commodore Matthew Perry to Uraga Bay, again at 1868 with the overthrow of the Tokugawa shogunate in the name of anti "feudal" (the Meiji reformers' favorite adjective for describing the Edo past) Westernization, and, most acutely, at 1945 with the loss of the empire, does not reveal the deeper continuities that run through Japanese law. The Civil Code in effect today, for example, may look very much like a child of the Napoleonic Code and may act very much like the pupil of Anglo-American constitutional theory, but this arrangement has retained much of the Tokugawa-style equity that Suehiro, primarily, preserved and brought forward into today. And the law journal that Suehiro founded, *Hōritsu Jihō*, has continued publication, with a brief interruption at war's end, from the early 1920s to the present.[10] Suehiro's name has remained on the masthead throughout.

Suehiro also underwent, in a very personal way, the *tenkō* (political conversion), surveillance, deunuciation, purge, and reverse course that historians so often discuss as abstract episodes. Having gone deep into the imperial project—becoming involved in leadership roles in law and society surveys in North China, in the Dai Nippon Butokukai imperial-boosting martial arts society, and in the statist Nippon Hōri Kenkyūkai, to name just a few—Suehiro was denounced to the GHQ authorities in 1946 and removed from his teaching and research positions at the University of Tokyo Faculty of Law. Gradually, though, the Americans realized that Suehiro was too valuable to be put out to pasture, so they quietly rehabilitated him, allowing him to travel to the United States on missions to study labor conditions in America and help reduce labor tensions back in Japan. An AP news article copied into Suehiro's SCAP file quotes Assistant Secretary of Labor Philipp Kaiser as stating that "Our success in winning genuine friends of democracy through our programs with German labor officials has convinced us that this plan of study for the Japanese officials can go far toward helping the Japanese understand the United States and its institutions." As a GHQ official scribbled atop Suehiro's letter to SCAP dated February 20, 1947, "This is a pretty good guy, it seems—he has done a lot of good on certain labor boards set up by ESS Labor Division."[11] The Americans purged Suehiro but then realized they couldn't do without him. Suehiro's case thus reminds us that the lines that historians often draw at August 15, 1945, and again with the end of the American Occupation in 1952, were much less distinct to the people living then than those lines appear to us in the present.

At a more philosophical level, this book challenges, and helps us reframe, the way we think about equity. The common law in England developed in the courts of the Norman conquerors, and "equity" in England, which arose as in the Court of Chancery a way to supplement and check the common law, therefore has a precise and historically conditioned definition. But Black's Law Dictionary does not ground the term in a particular place or time: "In its broadest and most general signification, this term [i.e., 'equity'] denotes the spirit and the habit of fairness, justness, and right dealing which would regulate the intercourse of men with men." This is what Suehiro and his legal team sought, and what the Japanese state, in the thrall of Western legal abstractions, could not provide. The question of what equity is and what courts are for runs through the heart of Japanese legal history in the 1920s and 30s, and in this volume I attempt to complicate the use of "equity" as a strictly English common law term of art.[12] Tanaka Kōtarō, the wartime dean of the faculty of law at Tokyo Imperial University (and later Chief Justice of Japan) who recommended to the Occupation authorities that Suehiro be purged, understood equity as part of the natural law, which "recognizes universal applicability and immutability at the level of basic theory; it reserves flexibility when dealing with particulars."[13] Tanaka was a critic of the neo-Kantianism, as he saw it, of Suehiro and his Ehrlichian turn to custom as a form of equity. For Tanaka, equity was not a method, but a working-out of higher principles of justice.[14] Like Tanaka, Suehiro understood people to be the subjects of the law. But whereas Tanaka saw people as human persons, Suehiro said that humans were the "units" (*tan'isha*) of the law.[15] Unlike Tanaka, Suehiro grounded his conception of equity in the procedural parameters of trials and not in the natural law.[16] Must equity have guidance, or is it an art best practiced freehand?

In his student days, Suehiro was fond of sports, and was especially good at kendō, or Japanese fencing. He did not have a strategy for attacking or defending. He just did what he felt was best in the moment, as the spirit moved him. As in sport so in life. He was often criticized for having no logical consistency in his legal philosophy, for never having formulated a system of thought, simply writing down what came into his head. At least one scholar has compared Suehiro's essays and books to a series of fencing bouts, and Kainō Michitaka, one of Suehiro's closest and oldest protégés, assessed his teacher in similar fashion.[17] Suehiro criticized his father, *Daishin'in* justice Suehiro Ganseki, for "having some particular judgment come into his mind during a court case, and then afterwards making that sound logical by finding some precedent or law to fit it."[18] But this was Suehiro Izutarō's way, too. Is equity a feeling, a sense, an intuition? Or is it a matter of logic, principle, and methodological application? By the same token, can one have equity under empire—equity which takes on the coloring of the surrounding political circumstances—or just equity as empirical data, rounded off into a decision by a judge using legal fictions to work around the tight spots of the law? Was Suehiro's call to render "whole-person" decisions in court guidance enough for apolitical equity, or did the ambiguity of the idea open Suehiro's law-and-society movement up to being swayed by forces beyond its control?[19]

These questions about jurisprudence and justice resonate with our own experience today. Societies in liberal democracies are increasingly fracturing along different fault lines, and many parties look to the state as the final—perhaps only—arbiter of social conflict. The debate over activist judges flares up regularly, as well, bringing up the same questions that Suehiro tackled in the 1920s and 30s: What is the proper role of law? How much leeway should judges have in deciding when the law applies and when it should be transcended? Does anything stand behind the laws in lawbooks, or behind the decisions that judges make? Can the state pacify and unify a society, or is society the predecessor and ruler of the state? These are hard questions, and a study of Suehiro's career and writings can help us find answers to them. Just as the lines we draw on the past are invisible to those who lived then, so the line we draw separating the past from the present turns out to be equally imaginary.

NOTES

1. Boissonade brought both positive and natural law insights to bear on his work. Eventually, however, many of the natural law interpretations were rejected or ignored by later jurists in favor of positivist ones.
2. Suehiro considered Montesquieu to be the father of law-and-society study. Cf. *Danchō zengo: ikō to nikki* (Ichiryūsha Press, 1951), 35: "Montesquieu's oeuvre is such that it is acceptable to call him the ancestor of law-and-society studies." From section titled, "Watashi no hōshakaigaku," 31, ff.
3. Suehiro's understanding of "state" changed significantly over time. In his youth and early career, Suehiro understood the state as the government, and largely as being opposed to the interests of the common people. In his mature career, however, Suehiro increasingly indentified the people with the state.
4. See *Rekishi Dokuhon, Tokushū, Tokugawa bakufu no jitsuryokushatachi*, no. 350 (Oct., 1982), 149. Cf. the Song Dynasty magistrate Bao Zheng (999-1062) for a corollary to Ōoka's place within Japanese legal history.
5. For some Ōoka cases see *Ōoka seidan komamonoya Hikobei* (Shōfudaya, 1889).
6. This phrase is taken from the title of Ch. 2 of *Kochie ni torawareta gendai hōritsugaku*, collected in *Uso no Kōyō*, the title essay of which is a celebration of the Ōoka Tadasuke method of jurisprudence. (Tokyo: Kaizōsha, 1923; quote taken from page 170)
7. "Yakunin no atama," reprinted in *Uso no Kōyō*, op. cit., 124.
8. *Uso no Kōyō*, op. cit.
9. Reprinted in *Uso no Kōyō*, op. cit., 164.
10. Guo Wei, *Hō to jōhō kūkan: kindai Nihon ni okeru hōjōhō no kōchiku to henyō* (PhD dissertation, Hokkaido University, 2014), 128.
11. GHQ/SCAP Records (RG 331), Box no. 2275 0, Folder title/number (32), SUEHIRO, Izutaro, Nov. 1946 – Apr. 1950, Classification 021, Type of record z, National Archives of the United States, accessed in microfiche version at National Diet Library, Tokyo, Japan.
12. See Ann Waswo, "In Search of Equity: Japanese Tenant Unions in the 1920s," in Ann Waswo and Nishida Yoshiaki, eds., *Farmers and Village Life in Twentieth-Century Japan* (New York: RoutledgeCurzon, 2003).

13. Tanaka Kōtarō, *Hōritsugaku gairon* (Tokyo: Gakuseisha, 1953), 62-64, cited in Kevin M. Doak, "Tanaka Kōtarō and Natural Law," in Kevin M. Doak, ed., *Xavier's Legacies: Catholicism in Modern Japanese Culture* (Vancouver: University of British Columbia Press, 2011), 70.
14. Ibid., 70-77.
15. Suehiro Izutarō, *Minpō zakkichō*, vol. 1 (Tokyo: Nihon Hyōronsha, 1940), 3.
16. See in particular the section on *jōri* ("reason") in Suehiro Izutarō, *Minpō Zakkichō*, op. cit., 36-43. Suehiro adopts a pragmatic, procedural approach in which, he admits, it does not matter if the law really exists at all. See also Tanaka Kōtarō, "Yuriusu Ofuneru 'Hō to shakai' (Julius Ofner, *Recht und Gesellschaft* (1931, Wien und Leipzig, XXII SS, 308))," in *Hōritsu tetsugaku ronshū*, 2 vols. (Tokyo: Iwanami Shoten, 1942-44).
17. Shichinohe Katsuhiko, "Suehiro Izutarō no seishun: Nitobe Inazo Ikkō kōchō haiseki jiken no sōdōsha," *Hōsei Kenkyū* 82-2-3-148, 439, citing also Kainō Michitaka, et al., "Zadankai: Hozumi hōgaku to Suehiro hōgaku no bunseki to hihan," *Hōritsu Jihō* vol. 23, no. 11, 78, and "Zadankai: Ningen, Suehiro Izutarō wo kataru," *Hōritsu Jihō*, op. cit., 71.
18. Shichinohe Katsuhiko, "Suehiro Izutarō no seishun," op. cit., 406, citing Suehiro Izutarō, "Kyōiku to chokkan," in *Hōsō manpitsu* (Tokyo: Nihon Hyōronsha, 1933). Shichinohe gives Suehiro's father's given name as "Ikashi (Izushi)." Shichinohe, "Suehiro Izutarō no seishun," op. cit., 404. Other reference works give "Ganseki". The *Daishin'in*, or Court of Great Cassation, was the prewar Japanese precursor to the present-day Supreme Court.
19. Shichinohe Katsuhiko, "Suehiro Izutarō no seishun," op. cit., 443, citing Suehiro Izutarō, *Minpō kōwa*, vol. 1 (Tokyo: Iwanami Shoten, 1926), 350 ff.

Chapter 1

From Ōoka Tadasuke to Hozumi Yatsuka

The Emergence of a Legal Crisis in Japan

Legal Fictions and the Emergence of Law-and-Society Study in Japan

The disjunctures and slippages that arise from legal transplants have been a part of the Japanese legal landscape from the beginning of recorded Japanese history. Japan adopted a revised version of the *ritsuryō* legal system from Tang China in the late sixth century, and the Taika Reforms of 645 were a culmination of the Japanese government's attempt to incorporate the Tang legal and political system. But Japanese society was radically different from that in Tang China, and so a *modus operandi* that modulated the strictures of the *ritsuryō* system while also mediating between Japanese society and the modified code began to develop. The compromise was that law in early Japan remained largely formal. It borrowed from China the highly refined hierarchies of courtly ranks and bureaucratic administrations, providing a trellis upon which the increasingly complex Japanese state could climb and spread out. However, the court and society continued to function at the personal level according to custom and propriety, and not in accordance with tomes of regulations written out in formidable classical Chinese.[1] In an even more general sense, government was in the register of the heavenly, not the mundane—the native Japanese word for "government" is *matsurigoto*, which implies propitiating the gods, a far cry from the cut-and-dry bureaucratic nature of law in the Tang.[2] So, the *ritsuryō* system remained more ornamental and referential rather than the standard for the actual administration of the Japanese state.

This arrangement provided broad leeway for accommodating vagaries between law and society. To take one good example, during the Heian period the prerogatives of the court were combined with broad discretion given to the wealthier peasants in the distant provinces tasked with overseeing the nobles' latifundia and sending revenues back to the capital.[3] Whatever disputes arose among the peasantry hardly ever made it back to the owners of the *shōen*, or provincial estates. Justice was administered by the estate managers and enforced by the local strongmen (who would later become the samurai) whom the managers employed in lieu of a centrally controlled military presence. Disputes among the nobles themselves were referred to the elders of the imperial court, or, sometimes, to the emperor himself. There were no specialists at law and no magistrates as in China. Justice was meted out by dint of birth, not by virtue of legal scholarship or by appeal to chapters in a given lawbook. Although the putative law of Heian-era Japan was the *ritsuryō* system adopted from China, the functioning law was a species of benign neglect. *In nuce*, law in Japan until very recently might be summarized as a biplanar system, or perhaps as an ideal (the law) projected like pale movie light onto reality (society). The laws on the books corresponded only analogically to the society paralleling them, standing off from the thinking and doing that had currency in the world.

Eventually, the strongmen who had been commissioned by the estate managers to keep order among the peasants and enforce the will of the distant *shōen* owners gained full control of the estates and their revenue.

These local militias kept martial law among their own ranks, but the peasants living under these military dictators continued, for the most part, to deal with one another based upon longstanding custom.[4] While custom varied from village to village, the *iriai*, or commons, were an important feature of most farming communities. The commons reflect the communal nature of village life—in the end, everyone was in it together. In times of desperation, usually when a crop had failed or some other natural or epidemiological disaster had befallen a given area, the peasantry might rise up against their overseers seeking a redress of their grievances. The leaders of these rebellions were typically executed, but the battle lost was oftentimes the war won because a local ruler, terrified of losing control of his fiefdom should his higher-ups be forced to intervene, could be persuaded to cede to the peasants' demands.

As the warlords vying for control of the Japanese archipelago passed through a long period of brutal internecine fighting, centralized power became ephemeral at best and each daimyō, or feudal satrap, became a law unto himself. The samurai whose fealty he commanded were bound to him by a moral code—heavily Neo-Confucian and increasingly imbued with a Zen Buddhism-inspired resignation to the instant death that might be demanded of a warrior at any moment—that transcended any form of written law. Eventually, Tokugawa Ieyasu (1543–1616) ended the long period of civil war and fossilized the samurai code in the new Edo peace in 1603. The Tokugawa state was an accretion of samurai-centric administrative customs and rules of order meant to prevent underlings from rebelling (or having the resources to consider it) and was as blind and deaf to the peasantry as it had been under the post-Heian samurai jurisprudence (and even, before that, the Heian aristocratic oligarchy). Still, bakufu rule was largely free from ideological ligaturing, and the broad breezeways for maneuvering between law and society ran through the *ritsuryō* era to the nineteenth century.

Such was the divorce between law and practice in the Edo Period, for example, that Luke Roberts has understood the Pax Tokugawa as, at heart, a performance.[5] For example, it was a Tokugawa law that a daimyō had to nominate a successor before he (the daimyō) died or was otherwise incapacitated. In theory, this was to avoid any disagreements—and, potentially, any rebellions—over who the legitimate heir to the ruling daimyō's position was to be. In practice, it was not always possible to designate a successor before a daimyō died or fell ill. In such cases, the following arrangement came to be the norm. The ill daimyō (or his corpse, as it happened) was laid out on his bed behind a folding screen. A Tokugawa official was then summoned to witness the daimyō "sign" the document of succession, nominating his official heir. In the presence of the official, a member of the daimyō's household would manipulate the immobile hand of the daimyō, stretching it out from behind the screen and affixing the daimyō's seal to the document of succession. Everyone, of course, knew that the daimyō was either ill or dead and therefore incapable of signing documents. But society, or the part of it legible and responsible to the law, was obliged to fulfill the law's strictures even when that fulfillment had been rendered completely impossible. It was what would later be called a "legal fiction." The law was satisfied, even if by a transparent lie, and society could go on muddling through as before. The "great peace" had been maintained.

This predominance of the legal fiction during the reign of the samurai extended to other areas of Japanese society, too. In court cases from the time in which peasants came before daimyō-appointed magistrates to answer charges of infringing on the daimyō's absolute prerogatives, for example, it was common to find those magistrates exercising mercy and effecting justice by framing the case in false terms. The semi-legendary master of this method of rearranging fact in order to keep the law from having to bend was Ōoka Tadasuke, Echizen-no-kami (1677–1752). Ōoka's great skill as a judge was in judiciously ignoring what the law told him to do. Ōoka was revered during his own time and thereafter, but then forgotten in the Meiji rush to "modernize" and Westernize. He was subsequently rediscovered in the 1920s by the law and society practitioners in Japan, who saw in his wise judgments the deft navigation of society and law that was lacking in the bureaucratic blindness of Civil Code courts.

Ōoka's courage in defying the law was what made him so good at preserving it. For instance, in one court case brought before Magistrate Ōoka, a woman had plotted to murder a bandit in revenge for his having murdered her husband. Mistakenly, though, she killed the bandit's partner in crime, and only wounded the man actually guilty of her husband's murder. Ōoka, instead of condemning her to death (as the law strictly prescribed, since the woman had not, in fact, been able to avenge her husband's death, which would have been legal, but had instead killed an unrelated party), found that the woman had actually performed a great service to the state. The man the woman killed was guilty of a host of other capital crimes, while the wounded man—the one really guilty of killing the woman's husband—was able to be tried by the state instead of being murdered for blood guilt. This, Ōoka pointed out, was the far more just course of action all around.[6] In setting the law to one side, Ōoka had fulfilled its spirit to overflowing.

By the time of the arrival of Matthew Perry's expeditionary force to Uraga Bay in 1853—the event that would set in motion the forces that would topple the Tokugawa shogunate fifteen years later—the Edo legal system had developed into an extraordinary mix of martial law, affiliated remnants of samurai privilege, status law, the continuously re-kneaded *ritsuryō* system from the Tang, longstanding village practice often differing by location, daimyō prerogative, merchant control of much of the political economy, daimyō control over various aspects of foreign policy and diplomacy, the prerogatives of the cloistered emperors separate from, yet dependent upon, those of the shogunate in Edo, *iriai* rights, trade and fisheries rights, the racketeering activities of the crime syndicates, and the piecemeal adoptions of the newer continental law as prevailing under the Ming and Qing. This arrangement worked very well for Japanese society, but it was also doomed in the new geopolitical context in which Japan found herself. By 1868, the year of the Meiji

Restoration and thus the beginning of a new understanding of law in Japan and of Japan's position within the wider world, this older congeries of laws and traditional practices had begun to give way to the dialectic between law and society renewed in earnest after the period of official legal fiction that had predominated under the Tokugawa administration.

With the fall of the Edo bakufu in the post-Perry tumult and the dispatching of scores of Japanese scouts to the West to learn new modes of government, society, culture, art, and politics came profound changes in every aspect of Japanese life. Perhaps no changes were more jarring than those which irrupted into the life of the law. Law encompassed the full range of philosophical, social, and political implications of Japan's rapid industrialization and concomitant transition to various non-native modalities. In a country long without a civil law of which to speak, the adoption of a *réchauffé* French Code Civil meant that life in Japan began to be lived, little by little, "by the book," and not by the ways of custom. The disjunction between law and society that had always existed in Japan became more difficult to ignore by means of legal fictions.[7] Society was submitted to a Procrustean stretching and cutting to fit to an alien black-and-white law code which was, in its origin and application, very often the opposite of the lived social experience in Japan. The importation of entirely new legal epistemologies unraveled the law-and-society tissue that had held, however imperfectly, the society of late Tokugawa Japan together.

Law also became a liability for Japan in world diplomacy. The Western powers used Japan's so-called "feudal" legal system as a pretext for imposing upon Japan unequal treaties, which conceptualized Japan as a junior partner, at best—a perennial pupil rushing to catch up with the more "enlightened" and "progressive" ways of the West. These unequal treaties, the Western powers promised, would be renegotiated as Japan's mores shifted from legal barbarism to progressive legal enlightenment. And yet, time and again, Japan got to the finish line of legal development only to find that the tape had been moved out of reach, or the game changed altogether. Japanese governments were successively humiliated, and Japan's legal profile was held in derision among the powers that, for her own survival, she was striving to join.

The wholesale importation of an alien legal code,[8] from one episteme wherein law had been abstracted out of society to another episteme wherein legal fictions had long been employed to bridge the gap between social reality and philosophical ideal, shook the fledgling Meiji experiment to its core. At stake was Japan's continued existence as a sovereign power. One by one, Japan's Asian neighbors—Qing strongholds, Hong Kong, Vietnam, the Philippines, Mongolia, India, Indonesia, Burma, and the Korean Peninsula, to name a few—had fallen under Western influence, if not outright mercantilism or colonialism. It was of crucial importance, therefore, that, whatever the social reality in Japan, the law conceive of society as unified, state-centric, and readily interlockable in platoons for the waging of war. This urgent need to retool the very foundations of Japanese life led increasingly to an acceptance of a social and legal Darwinism that provided pseudo-scientific justification for the ruthlessly competitive geopolitics of the nineteenth-century world order. Equity as the apolitical pursuit of justice was giving way to a view of society, not as an ideal of harmonious cooperation, but rather as a struggle for survival. The *iriai* were disappearing, and the labor strike was being born. The loose, socially expansive boulevards of the Edo law should give way to the hard-edged Darwinian absolutism of the Western order.

Hozumi Nobushige and the Rise of Legal Darwinism

This new legal order in Japan was typified by the writings of legal scholar Hozumi Nobushige (1855–1926). In June of 1876, Hozumi had gone to study in England. Three years later, after becoming the first Japanese person to earn a law degree at the University of London, he transferred to Humboldt University in Berlin and finally returned to Japan two years after that, in 1881.[9] While in England, Hozumi had become convinced of the evolutionary theories he found in the works of Charles Darwin (1809–

1882), Herbert Spencer (1820–1903), and Sir Henry James Sumner Maine (1822–1888).[10] After this exposure to the works of these philosophers of John Stuart Mill-style liberalism in, respectively, biology, society, and law, Hozumi combined all three into one overarching theory that law and society were subsets of biology, and therefore fundamentally evolutionary and subject to the same laws of natural selection as were found in nature. Hozumi thereafter "resolved to make it his life's work to apply evolutionary theory to human society."[11] In his incomplete three-volume magnum opus, *On Legal Evolution* (*Hōritsu shinkaron*),[12] Hozumi developed themes found in his (also unfinished) *Legal Evolutionism* (*Hōritsu shinkashugi*) and *Jurisprudential Revolution* (*Hōritsugaku no kakumei*).[13] The titles of the trilogy—from evolution to evolutionism to revolution—give some idea of the beeline progression of Hozumi's neo-Darwinian thought.

The programmatic evolution of Hozumi's legal philosophy was predicated upon the supremacy of the state (*kokka*) over the individual. This, in turn, was made possible by the very divorce between law and society that Hozumi and many other Japanese legal thinkers thought they were working to repair. The organizing principle for the new nation of "Japan" had to be the state, Hozumi believed. It was in the vehicle of the state that Japan as a nation would survive the Darwinian contest. In particular, Hozumi was concerned with re-founding the Japanese state on the "new traditions" of the Meiji reformulation of Japanese society. A Japan strong in society and in custom—even if hastily assembled—was the *sine qua non* of living through an age of rampant neo-colonialism. Hozumi's opposition to the importation of liberal individualism into Japan, for example, was based upon his stanch belief in a rigid Darwinian social model wherein societies lock in pitiless competition for survival on the global stage. Hozumi's attempt to fix social castes as a way to shore up Japan against foreign threats was the conduit for the importation of a totalizing abstract political and legal conceptualization antithetical to the earlier Ōoka style of prudential equity.

Whereas previous Japanese law had allowed for freewheeling social contradictions under the cover of law, the new age of grand systems saw man as fitting into one or another overarching ideology. Law was machine, and men its cogs. In *Jurisprudential Revolution*, for example, Hozumi criticized natural law theory and the doctrine of free will while proclaiming that:

> Jurisprudence is a subset of sociology, and sociology is a subset of biology. All living things are controlled by the grand law (*taisoku*) of evolution. No society formed by the gathering together of human beings is able to avoid [this law]. Everything in society is subject to the fundamental principle (*genritsu*) of natural selection by the struggle for survival. There is no law that does not depend upon this.[14]

Therefore, for Hozumi:

> The task is to strive to collate and categorize all legal facts past and present, East and West, in order to find the universal phenomenon running through as many of those facts as possible. After all, there is no reason why jurisprudential research methods should adhere to any different standards than those of the various physical sciences.[15]
>
> Even if one were able to discover [the principle of social phenomena] qualitatively, it would be a matter of even greater difficulty to ascertain [that principle] quantitatively. [... But] even if knowing the infinitely variegated (*senpen banka*) social phenomena be not a simple matter, there is nevertheless, without a doubt, within [those phenomena] a fixed and unchanging principle. [...] Even though all the laws of all the nations be different and infinitely complex, there exists within them a constant law (*kōki*) spanning all ages unchanged and all nations unswerving.[16]

Hozumi was seeking, through this cerebral program, to strengthen Japan by returning to Japanese "custom," but few things could have been farther from the legal customs of Japan than Hozumi's insistence on the symmetry between society and law.

The "constant law" that Hozumi sought was the neo-Darwinian principle according to which law (and society) developed by fixed stages.[17] Many thinkers in Japan, Europe, and the Americas had long seen society as analogous to the human body,[18] and Hozumi was no exception. For Hozumi, society was an "organic body, whose mechanism never rested for even an instant."[19] "Law is one form of societal force," Hozumi declared. "When law is observed over time, it becomes clear that it must needs be in a state of permanent flux."[20] At stake was jurisprudential anthropology: whether law would see society as a community of individuals bearing inalienable rights or as a phalanx of citizen-subjects subordinate to the demands of the state, locked in an existential evolutionary struggle with other states in the Spencerian geopolitical order.

This turn to the neo-Darwinian was prominent in other Japanese intellectuals' views of their country and region, as well. Fukuzawa Yukichi (1835–1901), for example, appropriated François Guizot's (1787–1874) schema of the development of European civilization to write *Outline of a Theory of Civilization* (*Bunmeiron no gairyaku*) (1875), which posits a three-stage progression of civilizations from barbarism through semi-enlightenment to, finally, civilization. While Guizot putatively indexes these criteria to the degree of individual autonomy within a given civilization, Fukuzawa ends his book by advocating that civilized states engage in conquest. Fuzuzawa's later works largely rejected his initial emphasis on natural rights and focus instead on the prerogatives of the state.[21]

However, over and against this Hegelian notion of the progression of states was the Rousseauian conception of natural rights, according to which, in its Lockean iteration, men formed a society only for their own protection and retained the right to dissolve that society. For the Spencerians in Japan, the Rousseauian vision of atomistic liberalism was particularly threatening, as it seemed to carry the potential to weaken

Japanese society and, by extension, the Japanese nation-state (*minzoku-kokka*), which could ill afford the luxury of weakness given the predations of the colonial powers. In such a jungle-like political environment, the pragmatic search for equity was both a necessity and a liability. There was no time for finding good-enough solutions to social problems, and yet no margin for error if those social problems continued to fester. This view of society as a potential liability led to its reconceptualization as the ribwork of the imperial state and the preclusion of apolitical equity in Japan.[22]

The ie seido

The worsening estrangement between law and society came to a head in the wrangling over the *ie seido*. The *ie seido*, or household system —which some conservatives hailed as the key to preserving Japan's special national polity (or *kokutai*)—became an issue of unprecedented parliamentary contention during the debate over the revision of the Meiji Civil Code in 1898.[23] At issue was whether the law would conceptualize society as a gathering of individuals who had entered into the social contract of their own free will or as a succession of hereditary and ethnic groupings, beginning at the lowest level of the transgenerational family, or *ie*, and culminating in filiation to the emperor as the sovereign head of the national imperial household.[24]

For later law-and-society doyen and Suehiro protégé Kawashima Takeyoshi (1909–1992), the *ie*, as conceived by the Meiji ideologues debating the conceptualization of the family within the Civil Code, had three main facets.[25] First, Kawashima argued, the *ie* was a "lineage group that has nothing to do with domicile, involving a belief in the continuity of its identity despite changes in its membership through deaths, births, and marriages."[26] Indeed, much of this lineage was continued by means of adoption of sons,[27] and is therefore, as Kawashima pointed out, indicative of the extent to which legal fiction had long prevailed in Japan.[28] Although somewhat different than the equity effected by Magistrate Ōoka during the Edo Period (and championed by Suehiro during the late Taishō and early Shōwa), this form of inter-generational legal fiction did help maintain social order by allowing households to obtain heirs peacefully instead of facing ruin for the sake of obeying the formal strictures of the law. Second, Kawashima defined the *ie* as having a *paterfamilias* or *koshu*, whose role as near-absolute sovereign of his household is roughly analogous to the original *paterfamilias* in ancient Rome.[29] Third, Kawashima understood the *ie* as going beyond the first two aspects —namely, those of continuity and (fictive) kinship—and effecting a "sacrali[zation of] the power of the family head, support[ing] it through tradition, and mak[ing] relations of power and subordination outwardly invisible, or outwardly acceptable."[30] The *ie seido* was clearly a legal fiction of lengthy Japanese pedigree. And yet, Hozumi Nobushige and other Meiji neo-conservatives were trying to systematize it in order to make it the foundation for a new, Western-style abstraction: the nation-state.

True to his abstractionist proclivities, Hozumi, citing the German idealist Pandekten system, avowed that Japan still had much work to do before being ready to embark upon the *ie seido* project in earnest:

> Japanese society is now passing *from the stage of family-unit to the stage of individual-unit.* [...] The 'Pandekten-System' is peculiarly suited to this transient state of society, for it provides the rules relating to persons in their capacity as individuals or members of a society in the General Part, and sets apart a distinct place for those rules which relate to persons in their capacity as members of a family. In civilized societies, the rules which regard men as individuals belong to general law, while those which regard men in their family relations belong to particular law. But in less advanced communities, the case is just the reverse; the *family law may be said to form the general law*, the law relating to persons in their individual capacity falling under the category of *particular law.* Japan is now in a transition stage...[31]

For Hozumi, succession passed through three stages: society first conceives of succession as a form of ancestor worship, then of transferal of status, and, finally, as transferal of property. Hozumi saw Japan as moving from the status to property stage, and thus not entirely ready for Boissonade's Code.[32] From an idealist standpoint, Hozumi the Spencerian neo-Darwinian thought Japan was not yet ready for the full ideal of the Code Civil.

Prominent Meiji politician Hozumi Yatsuka was as explicit in grounding the essence of the fledgling Japanese nation-state in the *ie seido* as his brother was in seeing neo-Darwinian notions of social evolution as the organizing principle of human history. For example, Hozumi Yatsuka thought that:

> When children are young, the father is clearly superior both in terms of intellect and physical strength. [...] It is the most clearly discernible standard by which superiority and inferiority are naturally divided. This is to say that the standard has to do with a relationship of power, and that power is the logic involved in issuing a command and compelling obedience. [...] Thus the veneration of parents is a veneration of power.[33]

Or, as he put it more succinctly in 1891, "Our country is a country of ancestor worship. It is a land of the *ie* system. All power, all law is born in the *ie*."[34] Having framed the question in such absolute terms, it is hardly surprising that Hozumi Yatsuka would brook no disagreement over the *ie seido*, which he saw as threatened by the emergence of a Civil Code that he thought did not properly enshrine it. "Upon the emergence of the Civil Code," he thundered in August of 1891, "loyalty and filial piety will disappear."[35]

The Freedom and Popular Rights Movement

These arguments over the *ie seido* and the national essence obscured the fact that there was another way, both in Japan and in Europe and the Americas, of conceptualizing the individual's relationship to society. While theorists, thinkers, and politicians such as Hozumi Yatsuka, Hozumi Nobushige, and anti-Christian philosopher Inoue Tetsujirō (1855–1944) asserted the primacy of the state over the individual—whether considered singly or in the abstract aggregate within the increasingly unquestionable prerogatives of the imperial state—others saw individualism as the proper orientation of the state toward those whom it purported to govern. These notions of the inherent right of man to choose his own government and to decide his own political destiny, minimally fettered by interference from political power, found an intellectual affinity in the writings of Jean-Jacques Rousseau. This French influence continued through the movement toward 'civilization and enlightenment', or *bunmei kaika.*[36] Indeed, when most Meiji thinkers used the term *bunmei kaika*, they meant 'becoming like western Europe.' Liberal Party democrat Baba Tatsui (1850–1888) and legal thinker Ono Azusa (1852–1886) understood human rights from the perspective of the English common law tradition,[37] while with the formation of the Rule of Law Society (*Hōchi kyōkai*) and the Meiji Society (*Meijikai*) in 1892, the Anglo-Continental understanding of law and society began to hold greater sway, especially as propounded by Hosei University founder Ume Kenjirō (1860–1910), in the translations from French legal treatises carried out by Ōi Kentarō (1843–1922), and in the philosophical works of Nakae Chōmin (1847–1901).[38]

The culmination of the individualist strain of Meiji intellectual life was the Freedom and Popular Rights Movement. One of the first uses of the term "popular rights and freedom" comes from a book by democratic revolutionary Ueki Emori (1857–1892), a disciple of Freedom and Popular Rights leader Itagaki Taisuke (1837–1919).[39] Grounding his defense of popular rights firmly in the Rousseauian claim that all government begins with the sovereignty of the individual and the social contract that arises from the necessity of sovereign individuals to live in community, Ueki argues against absolutism—that is, the failure of men to assume their natural right to freedom—as a "sin" and a "disgrace":

> According to Rousseau, man is born free and can be called a free animal. Therefore, although there might be statements that civil freedom comes from social laws, it is nature which endows men with freedom. If people do not assume this natural endowment of

> freedom it is not only a great sin against nature but also a great disgrace to themselves. [...] For the people not to assume their natural right to freedom is [...] a great disgrace![40]

Placing the individual conceptually and politically prior to the state was diametrically opposite to the arguments espoused by the Hozumi brothers and was a clear alternative to the emerging neo-conservative consensus that the *ie seido* was the breastwork standing between civilization and anarchy.

The principled sentiments of Mill and Rousseau did not prevent the Freedom and Popular Rights Movement from devolving into open revolt.[41] Not all Japanese theoreticians of natural right were revolutionaries of course. Baba Tatsui, for instance, preferred to share his potentially revolutionary ideas only with people of the upper class, finding that the "uneducated and illiterate" peasantry and urban dwellers were too unrefined to appreciate the full scope of such ideas.[42] But the Freedom and Popular Rights Movement had extremist tendencies, the very thing that the Meiji conservatives sought to quell. Ueki Emori and Ōi Kentarō, for instance, were instigators and radicals, lecturers to gatherings of the Freedom and Popular Rights movement that were frequently broken up by the police.[43] Ueki even plotted to overthrow the government in the Iida Incident of 1884.[44] Ōi, for his part, organized a plot to foment revolution in Korea, which, it was hoped, would later spread to Japan.[45] Ōi also repeated the familiar anti-establishment strain—found as frequently in Henry George as in François-Noël Babeuf[46]—that the land was to be held in common and exempted from private ownership.

The Freedom and Popular Rights Movement thus seemed virtually to guarantee ongoing social turmoil, while the *ie seido* vision for society froze social relations in place. However, neither course left open the possibility of a real equity for common people. Either the state would be so diminished that courts would hardly be able to function (the anarcho-liberalist model) or so idealized that courts would hardly be necessary (as under the most potent formulations of the kokutai). Either way, law and society were continuing the split that had begun with the rise of politics in the wake of Western imperialism in the middle of the nineteenth century. In the event, with the ascendance of the southern Satsuma-Chōshū *hanbatsu* clique in the factional Meiji government, the Freedom and Popular Rights movement was driven underground, and the *ie seido* vision of state and society won through. The coalescing Meiji state, it was now becoming clear, would maintain as much distance between law and society as was possible without bringing about a complete revolution. This was to be accomplished in large part by denying the majority of Japanese people the right to vote. Promulgated in 1890, the Meiji Constitution enshrined in foundational law a new, Germanic vision of the state, not as a Rousseauian contract among free individuals, but, rather, as a hierarchy of classes and privileges, arrayed around the person of the Emperor.[47] The conditions for the impossibility of an apolitical equity were thus set in constitutional stone. Significantly for the earlier debates over the place of the individual within the state, the constitution was not decided upon after parliamentary deliberation. It was, instead, granted by the sovereign as a gift to his subjects.[48]

The mere act of granting a constitution though did not—contrary to the expectations of some of the *genrō*, or elder statesmen—slake the public's thirst for popular sovereignty, socialism, democracy, and even anarchy. While the newly constituted state moved forward with shoring up power as part of the grand scheme to renegotiate the humiliating unequal treaties, popular discontent among the masses refused to be bottled up by the strictures of the Meiji elite. Sociologist Yoneda Shōtarō (1873–1945) saw this tension between the elite and the surrounding society as the fundamental social problem during the late nineteenth and early twentieth century.[49] Another view of the dilemma comes from constitutional scholar Fujii Shin'ichi:

> Specimen [Meiji] constitutions, which were the result of painstaking investigation and study by numerous intellectuals and were received with unmixed admiration by other intellectuals, fell far short of stimulating and, in any way, influencing the generality

> of the people, who lacked sufficient mental culture and power of understanding. [...] On the other hand, the influence on the people's minds of those petitions and other movements [for the opening of a *kokkai*, or national assembly] was a cause for yet graver concern to the government. The watchwords dear to these petitioners and memorialists were 'Down with the arbitrariness of officials' and 'Give us liberty and the people's rights'. These words were very easy for the people to understand, and pleasing enough to give their whole-hearted support and what was more, they were readily supported by malcontent members of the former military class, now living in obscurity. [...] Constant fear of the ultimate overthrow of the government by these malcontents haunted the minds of Hirobumi Ito, Aritomo Yamagata, and other prominent persons in authority.[50]

Even if the people had the rights for which they were clamoring, in other words, it is not clear that they would have known what to do with them. It was becoming clear that the solution to Japan's social problems would have to be found somewhere other than in politics.

By the time the revised Civil Code was implemented in 1898, these debates about natural rights and their origins had largely been decided, at least for the time being. In the wake of Hozumi Yatsuka's strenuous objection to the importation of the French-style Civil Code on which Boissonade and his assistants had so long labored, Meiji statesman Itō Hirobumi (1841–1909) intervened, ensuring, by their new set of criteria, that the civil code Japan would eventually adopt would be, in the most important respects, radically different from the French one, modeled on individual liberties growing in the Rousseauian garden of natural rights. Indeed, Hozumi Nobushige understood the controversy over the adoption of the Boissonade draft—that is, the draft influenced by the natural law—to have been, "in reality, a contest of the Historical School with the School of Natural Law, resembling in many respects the famous controversy between [Friedrich Carl von] Savigny [1779–1861] and [Anton Friedrich Justus] Thibaut [1772–1840] in the beginning of the same century."[51] Hozumi also understood the controversy to have a second cause: namely, the division within Japan of legal education into two main camps, the French and the Anglo-American (with the German faction quite small at the time, and its members forced to side with either of the two dominant forces).[52] The burden of the Meiji constitution was thus to draw a fractured society into unity in the person of the Emperor —no small task for a country as riven by discord as mid-Meiji Japan.

The backdrop to this momentous consolidation of politics around a constitution was the lingering presence of the unequal treaties. The Freedom and Popular Rights movement and the political parties that spawned the movement and later spun off in its wake had both failed to revise these unequal treaties, whose stubborn persistence seemed to necessitate a more statist solution to the problem of the individual in society in Japan. In 1887, for example, Inoue Kaoru (1836–1915), then prime minister, resigned after failing to effect a suitable revision of the unequal treaties. A resurgence of the Freedom and Popular Rights movement, conservatives feared, would produce endless political chaos at home, thus badly hampering Japan's ability to join the ranks of the great powers.[53] While much of the focus within Japan was naturally on the political station of ordinary citizens, the ratification of the constitution—after the initial jubiliation had worn off—was a tacit reminder that the real heavy lifting of Japanese diplomacy remained undone.

Conversely, much of Japan's failure to change the geopolitical status quo, some scholars argue, was due to its failure to develop a viable public sphere. On this note, contemporary researcher Kyu Hyun Kim interjects an intriguing observation from Hegel's *Philosophy of Right* into the consideration of Meiji politics. "The Meiji state," Kim writes:

> initially aided the growth of the public sphere, as can be seen in its initial support for, and later reluctance to ignore, the discourse of *kōgi yoron* (public opinion or public deliberation). However, state leaders tried their very best to control and limit the development of the public sphere when it began to channel critical discourse

> from civil society and challenged their self-proclaimed primacy over the process of national development.

For Kim, this is distinctly Hegelian:

> [Public opinion], according to Hegel, is 'a repository of ... the eternal, substantive principles of justice, the true content and result of legislation, the whole constitution, and the general position of the state'. Thus it commands respect. At the same time, as public opinion becomes representative of 'concrete arguments about felt wants, public affairs, the organization of the state, and relations of parties within it', it is 'infected by all the accidents of opinion, by its ignorance and perversity, by its mistakes and falsity of judgments'.[54]

The Freedom and Popular Rights Movement might have blossomed into a politically valent public sphere capable of engaging with central state-level decision-making. Failing this, it remained at the level of fractious and endless debates. As long as this continued, the Meiji *genrō* and other conservatives feared, Japan would never clear the unequal-treaty hurdle and achieve parity with the wider world.

Empire, Domestic Disturbance, Taishō Democracy, and the Law-and-Society Problem after 1895

With the Freedom and Popular Rights Movement breaking against the rocks of the Meiji Constitution, the Japanese polity splintered. Just as with later Taishō Democracy, the attempt to effect cultural and social democracy even without political sufferage faltered.[55] Japan was fissioning into disputatious camps with no prevailing centripetal politics to turn the country into a nation-state capable of facing and repulsing the threats from abroad.

When internal processes of state-building break down, one obvious alternative is to engage in foreign adventurism. In 1895, for example, the Japanese military, composed mainly of conscripted peasants, scored a lopsided victory over the hapless Qing Dynasty over the question of the sovereignty of the Chosen court and the Korean peninsula. This war against Japan's perennial rival secured an enormous indemnity for Japan of 200 million taels of silver (7,500 tons).[56] It also shifted the balance of power in East Asia and, most important, added new territory to the burgeoning Japanese empire with the subsequent annexation of the Korean peninsula in 1910.[57] While the Meiji government had officially annexed the Ryūkyū islands in 1879, the Ryūkyūs had been a client state since 1609 of the Satsuma domain under the Tokugawa hegemon, so the formal annexation of what became known as Okinawa did not present a major epistemological challenge to the conceptualization of the Japanese nation-state. The annexation of Formosa, though, meant that the older arguments deployed by Hozumi Yatsuka and other early and mid-Meiji ideologues about the ethnic nature of the Japanese nation would have to be dramatically retooled. Japan was now an empire, and so ideological transcendence of some form would have to be the new organizing principle.[58]

For the time being, at least, the stunning victory in the Sino-Japanese War redounded to the benefit of the centralized state in Tokyo. Patriotic fervor helped salve the old divisions among classes and political parties that had threatened the Civil Code and Meiji Constitution projects just a decade or two before. But this honeymoon period between law and society did not last for long. Ten years after the Sino-Japanese War, the Japanese military was engaged again, this time in a conflict with the much more powerful Russian Empire. National newspapers in Japan seized on the war, many with jingoistic abandon. The national public, too, which had celebrated the Meiji Constitution without knowing what was in it, uncritically supported the war, having been led by the newspapers to believe that a second victory, perhaps even bigger than the toppling of the Great Qing Dynasty in 1895, was in the offing. After having won highly lucrative indemnities in the Sino-Japanese War of 1894–95, the public expected similar financial and geographical gains, with a similar economy of Japanese bloodshed in the Russo-Japanese War ten years later.

Instead, the casualties in the latter war were staggering (many sources estimate around 70,000 war dead on the Japanese side in just one year), and the payoff, after the 1905 Treaty of Portsmouth brokered by President Theodore Roosevelt, was meager. Bitterly disappointed, especially after the sloganeering in the press during the war, the public rioted on September 5, 1905, at Hibiya Park in downtown Tokyo, just outside the gates of the Imperial Palace. These anti-government, anti-press riots spread throughout the country, deeply disturbing the authorities and intensifying suspicion of communist and socialist agitation. The specter of the Freedom and Popular Rights Movement had returned. The mass of common people, shut out of the political process and denied access to equity in the courts, seemed intent on holding their betters accountable in ways other than through regular elections.[59]

The use of imperial expansion as a way to stave off domestic unrest had been dramatically shown, at Hibiya and elsewhere, to be a temperamental gambit. Indeed, Japan's forays into war could have unpredictably negative effects even when Japan's participation had ended relatively well. For example, Japan played a minor role on the Allied side during World War One, with Japanese shipping in high demand as other European and American vessels had been commandeered for the war effort. The good times didn't last, however. The Japanese economy was over-stimulated, and the ensuing inflation, coupled with hoarding and speculating by unscrupulous merchants, drove the price of rice beyond the ability of most people to purchase subsistence amounts. Beginning with disaffected housewives (in a manner eerily reminiscent of the storming of the Bastille), calamitous riots over the skyrocketing price of rice soon affected nearly every region of Japan.[60] The period bracketed by the Hibiya Riots of 1905 and the Rice Riots of 1918 is often called the "Era of Popular Violence" (*minshū sōjō ki*). Nor were Hibiya and the Rice Riots the only irruptions of ideas about the people that conflicted with the vision of state transcendence advanced by those in political power. Radical socialist Kōtoku Shūsui (1871–1911), for example, was executed after being implicated in a plot to assassinate the Meiji Emperor.[61] It is no coincidence that these disturbances at home paralleled the imperial trajectory of a Japan attempting to elbow its way into the already crowded Euro-American neo-colonial project.

Amidst these troublings of the body politic, the relatively neglected courts of law appeared as havens for working out equitable solutions to social problems. This was partly because a tradition of judicial independence and the rule of law was beginning to take hold. In 1891, for example, when Crown Prince Nicholas II was nearly assassinated while visiting Japan, the political and social pressure upon the judiciary to execute the defendant, a policeman named Tsuda Sanzō, was intense. The court ultimately did not execute Tsuda, thus striking a blow for judicial integrity and offering a promising antidote to politicization and the insinuating logic of empire.[62] It was to these same courts that Japan's fledgling law and society practitioners would repair later in the Taishō period and into the early Shōwa, as the rest of Japanese society increasingly seemed to bar any remedies to imperial politics that did not somehow prescribe heavier doses of imperial politics as the cure.

And yet, despite this relative stolidity of the courts, the more basic and ongoing, structural problem facing Japan was the disenfranchisement of the Japanese people. This was especially true at the level of the same courts that had defiantly guarded their independence from party politics and popular frenzy. The reason for this was more procedural than political. Simply put, judges tended to be blind to the idiosyncrasies of people's individual cases and more concerned with protecting the integrity of the statutory law than with dispensing particularized justice. The rigidity of the law and its use in denying equity to the vast majority of the Japanese people was driving the country to the brink of revolution. Still, with political power denied to all but a very few, a court-based apolitical equity remained, for all the procedural shortcomings of the judiciary, the best hope for smoothing over social disaffection and calming the calls for revolt.

For a time, however, and despite—or perhaps, in part, because of—the wave of imperialism-precipitated violence outlined above, Taishō Democracy flowered briefly as a heady season of "visions and arguments" was born, attendant on the first rush of average people to take up political debates in public discussion.[63] But as it became increasingly clear that there was to be no political solution to the problem of the divergence of law and society in Japan, intellectuals, and especially those studying law, began to search for non-political ways to domesticate Taishō Democracy and draw the masses into political participation through means other than party politics and universal suffrage. Just as the Japanese empire was becoming a factor in Japanese political, social, and cultural life, and many in Japan were beginning to link the fate of the Japanese empire with the ongoing existence of Japan as a sovereign country with the autonomy of the Japanese as a people, the law-and-society movement emerged as a way to counter imperial logic and judicial indifference with an injection into the law of a new measure of humanity, flexibility, reality, and jurisprudential common sense.

NOTES

1. See, e.g., Asada Jirō, "Runin dōchūki" (series), *Yomiuri Shimbun*, esp. morning editions for August 15 and 16, 2019 (nos. 397 and 398). My thanks to Kogure Keiko, reference librarian at the Institute for Moralogy, for introducing Asada's work to me, including these two articles.
2. See Kishi Toshio, ed., *Matsurigoto no tenkai* (Tokyo: Chūō Kōronsha, 1986) and Mishina Akihide, *Kodai saisei to kokurei shinkō* (Tokyo: Heibonsha, 1973).
3. See Janet R. Goodwin and Joan Piggott, eds., *Land, Power, and the Sacred: The Estate System in Medieval Japan* (Honolulu: University of Hawai'i Press, 2018).
4. Cf., e.g., Herman Ooms, *Tokugawa Village Practice: Class, Status, Power, Law* (Berkeley: University of California Press, 1996). See also Wagatsuma Sakae, "Minpō sōsoku," in Suehiro Izutarō, ed., *Gendai hōgaku zenshū* (Tokyo: Hyōronsha, 1928).
5. Luke S. Roberts, *Performing the Great Peace: Political Space and Open Secrets in Tokugawa Japan* (Honolulu: University of Hawai'i Press, 2012)
6. See "Keisei Segawa ikken," in Nishino Tatsukichi, tr., *Ōoka seidan* (Tokyo: Kyōikusha Shinsho, 1989), 205-218.
7. Cf. Sasakura Hideo. "Suehiro Izutarō 'Uso no Kōyō' kō: awasete Kurusu Saburō hō to fuikushon ron," in *Waseda Hōgaku*, Vol. 90, No. 2 (2015), 41-74.
8. Nihon Hyōronsha Henshūkyoku, ed. *Nihon no Hōgaku*, op. cit., 3 & 9.
9. Toshitani Nobuyoshi, "Dai ni shō: Nihon hōshakaigaku no rekishiteki haikei, dai issetsu, senzen no hōshakaigaku," 188, in Kawashima Takeyoshi, ed., *Hōshakaigaku kōza 2, hōshakaigaku no genjō* (Tokyo: Iwanami Shoten, 1972). See also Byron Marshall, *Meiji Academic Elite*, op. cit., 73-74.
10. Toshitani, "Dai ni shō," op. cit., 188.
11. Ibid., 188, citing Hozumi Shigeyuki, "Meiji jūnendai ni okeru Doitsu hō no juyō—Tōkyō Daigaku Hōgakubu to Hozumi Nobushige," in Ienaga Saburō, ed., *Meiji kokka no hō to shisō* (Tokyo: Ochanomizu Shobō, 1966), 538.
12. *Hōritsu Shinkaron* (Tokyo: Hozumi Shōgaku Zaidan Shuppan/Iwanami Shoten, Vols. 1 & 2, 1924, Vol. 3, 1926).

13. Toshitani, "Dai ni shō," op. cit., 188, citing the revised and edited edition of Hozumi's work compiled by his nephew, Hozumi Shigetō, 1932-1934.
14. Hozumi Nobushige, *Hōritsugaku no kakumei*, in Hozumi Shigetō, cited in Toshitani, "Dai ni shō," op. cit., 189.
15. Toshitani, op. cit., 189.
16. Ibid.
17. Ibid.
18. See, e.g., Chapter II, Section I, "The Natural-Law Theory of Society during the Period of its Ascendancy," esp. §16, "The General Theory of the Group (Verbandstheorie) in Natural Law," in Otto Gierke, *Natural Law and the Theory of Society, 1500 to 1800* (Boston: Beacon Press, 1957), 95 ff.
19. *Hōritsu shinkaron* (1924), cited in Toshitani, "Dai ni shō," op. cit., 189.
20. Ibid., citing *Hōritsu shinkaron*
21. See, e.g., Fukuzawa, *Datsu-A ron* (1885).
22. See, e.g., Jennifer Pitts, *A Turn to Empire: The Rise of Imperial Liberalism in Britain and France* (Princeton: Princeton University Press, 2005), cited in Mitra Sharafi, *Law and Identity in Colonial South Asia: Farsi Legal Culture, 1772-1947* (Cambridge: Cambridge University Press, 2014), 163.
23. Many Japanese thinkers found the *kokutai* to be *prima facie* irreconcilable with Western modes of political or theologico-anthropological reckoning. Katō Hiroyuki (1836-1916), for example, found Christianity and natural rights to be antithetical to the overall nature of the Japanese state. See, e.g., David Abosch, *Katō Hiroyuki and the Introduction of German Political Thought in Modern Japan: 1868-1883* (Ph.D. dissertation, University of California, Berkeley, 1964).
24. See Emori Itsuo, *Kazoku rekishi no minzokugaku: higashi Ajia to Nihon* (Tokyo: Kōbunsha, 1990).
25. See Ken K. Ito, *An Age of Melodrama: Family, Gender, and Social Hierarchy in the Turn-of-the-Century Japanese Novel* (Stanford: Stanford University Press, 2008), 22, citing Kawashima Takeyoshi, *Ideorogii toshite no ie seido* (Tokyo: Iwanami Shoten, 1957), 33-34
26. Translation in Ito, *Melodrama*, op. cit., from Kawashima, *Ideorogii*, op. cit., 33
27. Or what Kawashima calls a "fictive blood lineage" (*giseiteki kettō*), cited in Ito, *Melodrama*, op. cit., 23
28. Cited in Ito, *Melodrama*, op. cit., 23.
29. Cited in Ito, *Melodrama*, op. cit., 23, citing Kawashima.

30. Ito, *Melodrama*, op. cit., 23-24, citing Kawashima, 34. See also Ueno Chizuko, *Kindai kazoku no seiritsu to shūen* (Tokyo: Iwanami Shoten, 1994).
31. Hozumi, *Lectures on the New Japanese Civil Code*, 52-53. (Emphases in original.)
32. Ibid., 54.
33. Hozumi Yatsuka, "Sosenkyō wa kōhō no minamoto nari," in Uesugi Shinkichi, ed., *Hozumi Yatsuka hakase ronbunshū* (Tokyo: Uesugi Shingō, 1913), cited in Ito, *Melodrama*, op. cit., 24.
34. Cited in Ito, *Melodrama*, op. cit., 23, citing Hozumi, "Minpō idete chūkō horobu," in *Hōritsu Shinpō* (August, 1891).
35. "Minpō idete chūkō horobu," Sekiguchi Yūko, et al., *Nihon kazoku shi* (Tokyo: Kazusa Shuppansha, 1989), 199-219, cited in Ito, *Melodrama*, op. cit., 28.
36. The term was first used by Fukuzawa Yukichi in 1875 in his *Outline of a Theory of Civilization* (*Bunmeiron no gairyaku*). For a fuller discussion of *bunmei kaika*, see, e.g., Ishida Ichirō, *Meiji jidai no rinri shisō—'chūkun,' 'aikoku' no rinri to kindai Nihonjin no seishin kōzō*, esp. Ch. 2, "Bunmei kaika no undō to jishu aikoku no rinri," in Nihon Shisōshi Kenkyūkai, ed., *Nihon ni okeru rinri shisō no tenkai* (Tokyo: Yoshikawa Kōbunkan, 1965), 206-216.
37. Nihon Hyōronsha Henshūkyoku, ed. *Nihon no Hōgaku*, op. cit., 4, remarks by Hirano.
38. Nihon Hyōronsha Henshūkyoku, ed. *Nihon no Hōgaku*, op. cit., 4, remarks by Hirano.
39. Joseph Pittau, SJ, *Political Thought in Early Meiji Japan, 1868-1889* (Cambridge: Harvard University Press, 1967), 65.
40. MBZ, II, 186, quoted in Pittau, *Political Thought*, op. cit., 65-66
41. Bruce R. Bowen, *Rebellion and Democracy in Meiji Japan: A Study of Commoners in the Popular Rights Movement* (Berkeley: University of California Press, 1980), 107-108
42. Bowen, *Rebellion and Democracy*, op. cit., 192, citing Baba as quoted in Ienaga Saburō, *Ueki Emori kenkyū* (Tokyo: Iwanami Shoten, 1960), 363.
43. Bowen, *Rebellion and Democracy*, op. cit., 194; see also Ienaga, *Ueki*, op. cit., 226, and Ike Nobutaka, *The Beginnings of Political Democracy in Japan* (Baltimore: The Johns Hopkins Press, 1950), 109, both cited in Bowen, *Rebellion and Democracy*, op. cit., 194.
44. Bowen, *Rebellion and Democracy*, op. cit., 194-195. See also Kären Wigen, *The Making of a Japanese Periphery, 1750-1920* (Berkeley: University of

California Press, 1995), 205, ff., including fn. 60. Ueki narrowly escaped arrest only when the plot's leader, Muramatsu Aizō, lied to the police in claiming that Ueki was not involved.

45. Bowen, *Rebellion and Democracy*, op. cit., 195; Fukuda Hideko was perhaps the most prominent co-conspirator in this plot. See Sharon Sievers, *Flowers in Salt: The Beginnings of Feminist Consciousness in Modern Japan* (Stanford: Stanford University Press, 1983).
46. Bowen, *Rebellion and Democracy*, op. cit., 200.
47. See Carl Schmitt, tr. Jeffrey Seitzer, *Constitutional Theory* (Durham: Duke University Press, 2008), esp. part one, section one.
48. Lawrence W. Beer, "Constitutional Revolution in Japanese Law, Society and Politics," in *Modern Asian Studies*, Vol. 16, No. 1 (1982), 33-67.
49. See *Gendai chishiki kaikyū undō to narikin to demokurashii* (Tokyo: Kōbundō Shobō, 1919).
50. Fujii Shin'ichi, *The Constitution of Japan: A Historical Survey* (Tokyo: The Hokuseido Press (Kokushikan University), 1965), 113-114.
51. *Lectures on the New Japanese Civil Code as Material for the Study of Comparative Jurisprudence* (Tokyo: Maruzen Kabushiki-Kaisha, 1912), 15-16.
52. See also Richard H. Mitchell, *Justice in Japan: The Notorious Teijin Scandal* (Honolulu: University of Hawai'i Press, 2002), esp. "Development of Personal Rights," 13, ff.
53. See, e.g., Ōkubo Kazushi, ed. *Ana-Boru ronsō* (Tokyo: Dōjidaisha, 2005), and Junji Banno, *Meiji kenpō taisei no kakuritsu: fukoku kyōhei to minryoku kyūyō* (Tokyo: Tokyo University Press, 1971).
54. *Age of Visions and Arguments*, 8, citing G.W.F. Hegel, tr. T. M. Knox, *Philosophy of Right* (Oxford: Oxford University Press, 1952), 204-205
55. I follow here Henry DeWitt Smith, II's distinction "between democracy as a type of social and political structure and Democracy as a set of beliefs and prescriptions." "The Nonliberal Roots of Taishō Democracy," in Harry Wray and Hilary Conroy, eds., *Japan Examined: Perspectives on Modern Japanese History* (Honolulu: University of Hawai'i Press, 1983), 191-198.
56. Zhaojin Ji, *A History of Modern Shanghai Banking: The Rise and Decline of China's Finance Capitalism* (Armonk, NY: M.E. Sharpe, 2003), esp. 52 ff.
57. See June Teufel Dreyer, *Middle Kingdom and Empire of the Rising Sun: Sino-Japanese Relations, Past and Present* (Oxford: Oxford University Press, 2016).
58. I follow closely here Kevin Doak's argument in "Culture, Ethnicity, and the State in Early Twentieth-Century Japan," in Sharon

Minichiello, *Japan's Competing Modernities: Issues in Culture and Democracy, 1900-1930* (Honolulu: University of Hawai'i Press, 1998).

59. For a contemporary account, see Yoshino Sakuzō, "Minshū no seiryoku ni yotte jikyoku mondai wo kaiketsu sen to suru fūchō wo ronzu," in *Chūō Kōron*, April 1, 1914, 101. Cited in Andrew Gordon, "The Crowd and Politics in Imperial Japan: Tokyo, 1905-1918," in *Past & Present*, No. 121 (November, 1988), 144.
60. Andrew Gordon, "The Crowd and Politics," op. cit., 141-170. See also Miyachi Masato, *Nichiro sengo seijishi kenkyū* (Tokyo, 1973), 226-228, cited in Gordon, "The Crowd and Politics," op. cit., 141, and Okamoto Shumpei, "The Emperor and the Crowd: The Historical Significance of the Hibiya Riot," in Tetsuo Najita and J. Victor Koschmann, eds., *Conflict in Modern Japanese History* (Princeton: Princeton University Press, 1982), cited in Gordon, "The Crowd and Politics," op. cit., 142.
61. See, e.g., Robert Thomas Tierney, *Monster of the Twentieth Century: Kōtoku Shūsui and Japan's First Anti-Imperialist Movement* (Berkeley: University of California Press, 2015).
62. See, e.g., George Alexander Lensen, "The Attempt on the Life of Nicholas II in Japan," in *The Russian Review*, Vol. 20, No. 3 (July, 1961), 232-253, and Peter Yong-Shik Shin, *The Ōtsu incident: Japan's hidden history of the attempted assassination of future Emperor Nicholas II of Russia in the town of Ōtsu, Japan, May 11, 1891 and its implications for historical analysis* (PhD dissertation, University of Pennsylvania, 1989). See also, for example, Fujino Hiroko, "Toshi minshū sōjōki no shuppatsu, saikō: Hibiya yakiuchi jiken," in *Rekishigaku kenkyū*, Vol. 792 (Sep. 2004), 1-16.
63. See, e.g., Suehiro Izutarō, "Shihō no ken'i to demokurashii: hōtei bujokuzai shinsetsu no gi ni sesshite," in *Hōsō manpitsu* (Tokyo: Nihon Hyōronsha, 1933), 113-131. See also Matsuo Takayoshi, *Taishō Demokurashii* (Tokyo: Iwanami Gendai Bunko, 2001).

Chapter 2

Suehiro Izutarō and the Founding of the Law-and-Society Movement in Japan

Under the influence of Western political abstractions, a shift from a self-contained political sphere to destabilizing expansionism under the new empire, and the social disorder attendant on capitalist industrialization and the looming existential threat of colonization, Japanese society during the Taishō Period (1912–1926) was the scene of ongoing struggles among a myriad of classes, interests, parties, factions, schools, and groups. Although diverse in manifestation, the political questions of the day revolved around whether there was to be political and economic equality in Japan, or whether some of those older distinctions would perdure into the new political economy. While class and status distinctions have been gradually cleared away with the revision of the registration laws (*koseki hō*) beginning in the 1870s, what was effected on paper was not always mirrored in society at large.[1]

As the unenfranchisement of the common citizen that had been one of the hallmarks of Meiji political life persisted into the first decades of the twentieth century, it became clear to a handful of Japanese legal scholars that equity—the promise of case-by-case justice in courts of law—was a more pressing need, and a more attainable objective, than formal political equality. The political system in Japan was frozen into a reconfiguration of the old privilege system, with almost everyone shut out of democratic representation. Politics was a new topic of debate as the vibrant civil society fostered during the Edo period took up new questions of government and political theory, but government itself was well beyond the reach of those condemned to argue about it from afar.

To be sure, there had been incremental gains in voter participation. But, as Andrew Gordon points out, even as suffrage rates slowly rose, the political parties, ostensibly operating within a parliamentary democracy, allied themselves much more closely with the bureaucratic power-brokers and imperial cabinet than with the voters, and even less so with the men and women in the street for whom the ballot box was out of reach. Politicians, bureaucrats, government officials, and, yes, lawyers and judges almost all emerged from the same chrysalis of elite upbringing, elite education, and elite social networking. Democracy, in the mouths of party politicians playing a cynical game of power-brokering under the guise of the parliamentary system, was as remote from the common citizen as it had ever been.[2] As Max Weber discovered in the nineteenth century and Japan scholar Darryl Flaherty recapitulated in his work on the legal profession in Meiji Japan, intellectuals have a tendency to be co-opted by the state. Young revolutionaries often find themselves with a bureaucratic sinecure in middle age.[3]

While the political parties fought, often with cynical self-interest, over their visions of future political arrangements, a few legal thinkers realized that the mechanism for bringing justice to the disenfranchised was already in place in the Japanese courts. Suehiro Izutarō, one of the founders of the law-and-society movement in Japan, also took a keen interest in these questions. Where Suehiro differed from many of his politically minded contemporaries was in his turn to the law, and not to parties and legislation, to help resolve the social problems pulling Japan apart at the seams. Suehiro saw that, unlike politics—where graft, bribery, and horse-trading dulled to near insignificance whatever measure of influence voters might have brought to bear on the legislative process—the judicial system could be changed efficiently from within by exerting pressure on judges through a promotion of case law. As real social problems emerged into the jurisprudential light by way of individual cases. Suehiro hoped to hold judges accountable for providing the equity inhering in the Civil Code by publicizing judges' decisions and showing how these decisions did—or most often did not—comport with the Code, the facts of the case, and the dictates of natural justice that Suehiro, following Austrian legal scholar Eugen Ehrlich (1862–1922), eventually came to call "the living law." Equity, in other words, could make up for what politics had for decades failed to achieve—the reconciliation of law and society and the amelioration of the social ills plaguing a rapidly Westernizing Japan.

For Suehiro and many others in the early law-and-society movement in Japan, these questions were inextricably bound up with the failure of natural rights—and especially the Freedom and Popular Rights Movement—to take hold in Japan. For Suehiro, this failure was, in turn, attributable in part to Christianity's weak Japanese reception.

> Although we have been told ad nauseam about the Freedom and Popular Rights Movement during the Meiji Period, in the end the failure of [that movement] to put down roots is probably quite deeply related to the lack of Christianity in Japan. In other words, there is an extremely intimate relationship between the democracy that we see in the new [Japanese] constitution, and the Christian idea of respect for the individual.[4]

For others, though, the shallowness of Christian roots in Japan was due to an even deeper cause: namely, the "feudalism" of the pre-Meiji past. For law-and-society scholar Kawashima Takeyoshi, for example, the question came back to the particularities of Japanese feudalism.[5]

Kawashima's fellow law-and-society specialist Suekawa Hiroshi thought "feudal absolutism" was the main factor that prevented the Freedom and Popular Rights Movement, based as it was upon a vision of individual liberty that most Japanese found entirely alien, from establishing a lasting influence on Japanese society:

> I think that the essential point is not whether there was or was not Christianity, but, rather, that the substantial restraints arising from the feudal absolutism that pervaded the very fundamentals of the Japanese social structure did not permit the development of the realization of Freedom and Popular Rights thinking.[6]

These debates over fundamental aspects of society and culture reveal a growing sense among Japanese intellectuals across the political spectrum that the ills of Japanese society could not be helped solely by reference to Western political concepts. Hozumi Nobushige cryogenically preserved the *ie seido* in the cold, evolutionary abstractions of Charles Darwin and Herbert Spencer, but Suehiro Izutarō and the budding law-and-society movement were beginning to look more deeply into the still-fresh Japanese past to understand the living Japanese present.

These insights still lay in the future for Suehiro as he neared the end of his graduate studies in law at the Tokyo Imperial University. As a student of professors of the Hozumi Nobushige and Hozumi Yatsuka generation, Suehiro felt hemmed in by his training in German legal idealism and unable to find a solution to the seemingly permanent divorce of law and society in Japan. While others in his cohort turned to theory—Marx, Engels, Kropotkin, Hans Kelsen, Schopenhauer, and Rousseau, among others—for an explanation of and remedy for Japan's social fracturing—Suehiro sought a solution that would incorporate actual, lived Japanese social life, and not abstract it away into the thickets of Western social models. In 1918, as the First World War was nearing its conclusion, Suehiro went abroad for what had by then become the customary period of apprenticeship to European and American specialists in law. This trip was to provide Suehiro with the clues he would later use to attack the riddle of how to bring Japan's law into closer harmony with its society, and vice versa. The legal philosophy of Eugen Ehrlich, the legal realism of Harvard law professor Roscoe Pound and Chicago law professor James Parker Hall,[7] and the labor struggles surrounding the negotiations leading to the signing of the Treaty of Versailles set the tenor for Suehiro's lifelong attempt to bring equity back into the Japanese judicial system, thereby domesticating Taishō Democracy.

Eugen Ehrlich and the "Living Law" in Japan

Eugen Ehrlich was among the seminal group of law-and-society thinkers at the turn of the twentieth century who launched the sociological turn in jurisprudence and in legal philosophy. Ehrlich, along with German legal thinker Hermann Kantorowicz (1877–1940), founded the *Freirechtsbewegung* (Free Law Movement) in the first decade of the 1900s.[8] Ehrlich and Kantorowicz, following the pioneering lead of German legal anti-historicist Rudolf von Jhering (1818 –1892) and his teacher, Roman-law scholar Georg Friedrich Puchta (1798–1846), along with Max Weber (1864–1920), Sir Henry Maine, Émile Durkheim (1858–1917), Weimar Republic author and social law theorist Hugo Sinzheimer (1875–1945), and Roscoe Pound (1870–1964),[9] formed the nucleus of what would later become known as the law and society movement.[10] The idea of the movement was simple: the law was Aristotelian rather than Platonic. In other words, law was more empirical than metaphysical, and the grounds of the law were in society, not in the law itself, the state, or in some abstracted conception of these. It was a radical privileging of common people over the prerogatives of the state, and as such it presented a serious challenge to the prevailing legal systems of much of the world, which had been premised upon the ideals of mainly German theorists such as Hans Kelsen (1881–1973).[11]

Ehrlich's sparse biography is in keeping with his exile from mainstream European intellectual life over his personal and professional idiosyncrasies. Born into a deracinated Jewish family in Czernowitz (present-day Chernivtsi, Ukraine) in the Austria-Hungarian province of Bukovina, Ehrlich did his Habilitation on Roman law in Vienna in 1894.[12] However, as an ethnic Jew, Ehrlich was never able to rise above the second-rate appointment of rector (1906 to 1907) of Franz-Josef University in Czernowitz.[13] After World War I, he was forced by rising anti-Jewish sentiment in Europe to resign from Franz-Josef University and go into exile in Vienna, where he died.[14] Even today, Ehrlich remains a neglected figure in twentieth-century legal history.

However, Ehrlich's biographical quietism is belied by the pathbreaking nature of his legal philosophy. Unlike his predecessors, Ehrlich was almost indifferent toward the existence of the state within the framework of actually existing legal practice. In an age of high neo-Darwinian and neo-Hegelian nation-statism, Ehrlich took the opposite tack of putting custom and the common people ahead of the state. Ehrlich's turn away from state-bound German legal idealism eventually found expression in his development of the theory of Free-Law. This was nothing less than a repudiation of the legal fiction of the "seamless web" of the legal codes and the washing-out of social facts under the glare of the positive law. German legal theorist Hubert Rottleuthner positions Ehrlich's Free-Law ideas thusly:

> As a Free-Law advocate [...], Ehrlich criticized the ideal of the seamless web of a codified legal order, and made clear that the decision in an individual case could not be understood as a logical derivation from general norms (or even concepts), performed 'with the aid of a hair-splitting machine and a hydraulic press'. Like [Ernst] Fuchs [(1851-1930)], he too emphasized the creative role, the personal moment, in the application of law. However, by this he did not intend that the private intuition of the judge be set free. Rather this is the point where his specific understanding of legal sociology came into play: when the law permits no orientation, the application of law should orient itself on social norms, on the norms of the law which was actually alive in society. In his legal sociology, Ehrlich stressed precisely the central role of society—as the totality of human associations—for the emergence and development of

> law. Legislation, jurisprudence, and judicial decision-making, by contrast, were considered secondary phenomena. The true legal science—understood as legal sociology—had to capture the law that was 'alive' in society. Traditional jurisprudence was blind to this sphere and only took into account laws and the norms of judicial decisions.[15]

This was a sweeping rejection of state-centric law in favor of the people living under law's command.

Ehrlich's thesis was also a challenge to the ideas of Max Weber, who saw capitalism as looming large in the background of the law. For example, while Weber understood a "rational-legal authority" as a hallmark of modern states and a precondition for capitalism, Ehrlich, along with other sociologically minded thinkers (many of whom have also largely been forgotten in Western scholarship), understood law as much more organic and non-state-centric than did Weber.[16] In this, Ehrlich's ideas largely paralleled those of Leon Petrażycki (1867–1931),[17] a Russo-Polish sociologist who argued that law was "intuitive." For Petrażycki, law did not proceed from state-centric legislation but was rather an organic outgrowth of the human condition. Nevertheless, Ehrlich, Petrażycki, legal sociologist Georges Gurvitch (1894–1965), and others who foregrounded the social in the budding law-and-society turn comprised an important new development in the thinking about the interaction between the state and the state's laws, on the one hand, and a given society's comparatively more informal laws, on the other.[18] This was a significant departure from the formalism and structuralism of Max Weber, Karl Marx (1818–1883), and the earlier generation of big-system thinkers who tended to focus on the economy, institutions, and the state.

As an ethnic Jew (albeit a thoroughly Germanized Roman Catholic), Ehrlich may have been more keenly aware than his contemporaries of the "marginality" of the state-centric law, and therefore prone to question claims of the primacy of the state in legal interpretation. Other theories posit the plurality of law in the Bukovina region of Austria-Hungary as the origin of Ehrlich's puzzlement over the gap between what the law in the books said, and what the people in the villages and towns actually did. While interpersonal disputes were meant to be adjudicated according to the Weberian scheme of the state's monopoly of violence, in reality those disputes were often resolved in the outlying area of Bukovina according to customs and practices that often had very little to do with the codified positive law. For Ehrlich,[19] the application of the law involved, not the robotic matching of real-life case to an ethereal and abstracted Civil Code, but, rather, a great deal of human agency floating clear of the legal realm and drawing on norms better understood by the new discipline of sociology.[20] Equity, in other words, was not an ideal imposed from above—by legislatures, for example—but a process of messy discovery taking place in the lower ranks of society below the upper atmosphere of legislative diktat. There was much fodder in these Austro-Hungarian, highly unorthodox legal theories for a young, socially-conscious researcher from Japan.

In 1920, Suehiro, coming to the end of a two-and-a-half-year period of studying abroad, arrived in Switzerland via Italy,[21] and in Berne was able to meet Eugen Ehrlich directly,[22] as the latter had been exiled from Czernowitz but had not yet arrived in Austria.[23] (Suehiro, stranded by bureaucratic complications more than one year after the end of the war, was waiting in Berne for his return to Japan.[24]) While other Japanese students in Suehiro's situation passed the time reading German annotated volumes (*chūshakusho*), Suehiro, who had already read Ehrlich's groundbreaking *Grundlegung der Soziologie des Rechts* (1913) before arriving in Switzerland, encouraged his Japanese compatriots to focus less on reading books in the library and more on going out into society to observe the profound changes underway in the wake of the Reich's defeat in the Great War.[25] During one meeting between the aspiring Japanese socio-legal thinker and the co-founder of the law-and-society movement in Europe, Ehrlich asked Suehiro about farming in Japan and Suehiro found he couldn't answer. This ignorance of his own country's social situation—despite his years of study and his insistence that society be taken into account when thinking about the law—prompted Suehiro to think about investigating the conditions in his own country. The intellectual tide was turning away from the state and toward societies, and Suehiro sensed in Ehrlich a harbinger of this new socio-jurisprudential wave.

In the writings of Eugen Ehrlich, Suehiro, who had been educated at the University of Tokyo in the same idealized Pandekten method of Civil Code jurisprudence[26] against which Ehrlich deployed the controversial idea of "living law" (*lebendes Recht*), had found a way, it seemed, between the Scylla of the state and the Charybdis of the people. Suehiro had once deemed any law not German no law at all, but he had now found a powerful antithesis to rigid German legal idealism.[27] The concept of the living law (*ikeru hō*, as Suehiro translated the German term into Japanese)—premised on Ehrlich's and Kantorowicz's observations that societies organically and spontaneously generate their own legal orders apart from the oversight of a state[28]— set the stage for the entirety of Suehiro's career, both as a legal scholar and as a practitioner of the law.

Suehiro also saw in the living law a method for achieving equity in a polity that was top-heavy with an imperialist state. Where politics had failed to bring Japanese citizens equality vis-à-vis the legislature and elected officials, the living law promised to find equitable solutions *within* the law, thereby effecting an apolitical solution to a set of social problem that politics had done nothing but exacerbate. The Pandekten idealists and strong-state advocates in Europe and Japan, Ehrlich and the young Suehiro agreed, had gotten things backwards. Increasing the power of the state—to legislate, regulate, and control ever-greater swaths of private life and to co-opt ever more non-state institutions through promises of political inclusion—led only to greater corruption and a wider gulf between law and society. Left to their own devices, people tended to fare much better. This rediscovery, courtesy of Ehrlich's notions of *Lebendesrecht*, of society beneath the holograms of legal neo-Platonism was to have a profound effect on Suehiro's legal thinking and practice upon his return to Japan. Instead of fighting the state head-on through politics, Ehrlich's idea of the living law allowed Suehiro to conceive of another strategy: namely, bypassing politics altogether and attempting to domesticate Taishō Democracy by using the courts and not the legislature as the means for bringing equity to bear on the lives of ordinary people cut out of the political process. This tension among law, society, and the state was summed up by Ehrlich in one of the last publications before his death:

> Legislation is commonly considered the oldest, the original, the peculiar task of the state. In reality, however, the state becomes a law-giver only late in its existence. The original state is a purely military center of might and is concerned neither with law nor with courts. The original state, so far as it is not yet Europeanized, knows no legislation. We speak, it is true, of the legislation of Moses, of Zarathustra, of Manu, of Hammurabi, but these are only collections of judicial and juristic laws together with numerous religious, moral, ceremonial and hygienic provisions such as we can see in popular or popular-scientific writings. An oriental despot can, if he pleases, level a city to the earth or condemn a few thousand human beings, but he cannot introduce civil marriage into his kingdom.[29]

This insight was the door to the vistas between law and society that had kept Japan relatively stable, despite periods of intense warfare, for centuries before the coming of the West.

The twentieth century was the age of free rein given to the notion that increasing state centralization could solve the problems that politics had engendered in the first place. Ehrlich's work was a call to revisit and re-question the assumptions of a hyper-politicized age and to re-examine the gulf that had opened between law and society precisely where the codification of the civil law had promised to close it. This disconnect between law and society was especially glaring in Japan where, just two decades after Meiji oligarchs had adopted a Prussian-style constitution at the height of the German legal model's influence, the sand had shifted under their feet and they found themselves confronted with the persistence of the social movements that the Meiji constitution had been carefully crafted to isolate and neutralize. As in Europe and America, the more central planners worked to identify law with society through executive power, the farther law and society drifted apart.

In Japan and elsewhere, this alienation of law and society sometimes led to strange metaphors and epithets for those who diagnosed the chronic drift. For example, Suehiro was pejoratively labeled a "Jew" for having imported Western (i.e., "Jewish") ideas about politics and law into Japan.[30] This epithet was applied to Suehiro by Japanese intellectual Mitsui Kōshi (1883–1953), a member of the Genri Nihonsha to which belonged kokutai-crusader Minoda Muneki, who would go on to launch a public attack against Suehiro in the 1930s.[31] Mitsui was particularly troubled by Suehiro's ideas about land reform, the subject over which Mitsui and Suehiro would spar in print after Suehiro's return to Japan.[32] Uesugi Shinkichi (1878–1929), too, a professor of constitutional law at the Tokyo Imperial University, called Christian liberal Yoshino Sakuzō's quasi-democratic ideas of political organization in an imperial polity "Jewish," and earlier, in 1923, said that "Japan's half-educated leftists imitate Jews by cursing the state."[33]

As Stalinists pushed out Trotsykists in the Soviet Union, as small-state Supreme Court justice Stephen J. Field (1816–1899) and small-government presidents Warren G. Harding (1865–1923) and Calvin Coolidge (1872–1929) gave way to Franklin D. Roosevelt's New Deal, and as National Socialists crowded out international socialists in post-WWI Weimar Republic Germany, the issue of the state emerged as the shibboleth of the twentieth century's middle-third. In Japan, too, the central state was rapidly increasing in power, not least due to the imperial counter-pressure that many Japanese political leaders felt must be applied to the expansionist Soviet Union, United States, Great Britain, and other European states, as well as to control the fallout from the collapse of the Qing Dynasty and the communist and warlord elements vying for the scraps. Amidst all this, Suehiro, following Eugen Ehrlich, began to formulate a legal philosophy that rejected the state in favor of the people. The epithets hurled at him for his heresy revealed the dangers that lay ahead.

SUEHIRO IZUTARŌ, THE "LIVING LAW," AND THE GENESIS OF LABOR LAW IN JAPAN

The question of the state plagued the Versailles negotiations after the armistice which ended World War I in November of 1918. While studying abroad in France, Suehiro had been appointed by the Japanese government to work briefly at the Versailles Peace Treaty negotiations, and what he saw there profoundly influenced his later thinking on the relationship among state, society, and law.[34] In particular, it was during his work at the Versailles conference that Suehiro first saw the importance of labor to the equitable functioning of society. In post-WWI France, where Otto von Bismarck's social and labor reforms had not been carried out as they had been in pre-war Germany, the pressing need was for a labor law able to prevent the Communist revolution that seemed imminent during the war and even more threatening after the war's conclusion.[35] The Bolshevik Revolution, too, which precipitated Russia's early exit from hostilities on the Eastern Front, had been in large part due to the failure of Russian elites to find equitable solutions to the problem of labor in both the Russian cities and countryside. World War I and its aftermath were thus a stark reminder of what could happen when law and society pulled too widely apart.

Based on these experiences, Suehiro learned that labor and labor law would define much of the political, economic, and social realms in post-WWI Japan too. One hardly needed to look too hard to find ample evidence that from 1918 through the early 1920s labor and radicalism were two sides of the same coin and that failing to solve the labor question could easily lead to social upheaval. After Versailles, Suehiro later recounted, there was an "intensification of reactionarism on a global scale," an intensification that only grew from year to year in the early 1920s:[36]

> Nineteen-twenty was a year in which the whole world was deeply affected by reactionary [movements]. The same situation continued into 1921. For a time after the World War armistice in November of 1918 labor movements in the various countries developed exceptionally smoothly. Now, though, we are locked in a bitter battle, and we are hampered by great difficulties.[37]

At Versailles, Suehiro had seen firsthand these "bitter battle[s]" and "great difficulties." The French labor alliance CGT (*Confédération Générale du Travail*) president and future Nobel Peace Prize recipient, Léon Jouhaux (1879–1954), for example, was prosecuted under the "reactionary policies"[38] of French prime minister Alexandre Millerand (1859–1943). Meanwhile, the new CGTU (*Confédération Générale du Travail Unitaire*) broke up under the leadership of labor-leader Gaston Monmousseau (1883–1960) and pro-Soviet communist Marcel Cachin (1869–1958).[39] France had won the war, but this had done nothing to repair the breach between law and society, state and people. If anything, as Suehiro witnessed, the war and subsequent victory had only aggravated the law and society problems that had predated the armed conflict.

The timing of Suehiro's foray into labor law and labor politics exposed him to the risk of being politically labeled a radical or communist, even as he sought apolitical solutions to pressing labor problems.[40] For instance, after the state executed anarchist Kōtoku Shūsui for his alleged role in plotting to assassinate the Emperor—a decision handed down in part by Suehiro's father, who sat on the *Daishin'in* when the verdict was made —a rolling purge of leftists, radicals, and labor organizers had ensued.[41] It soon became not only dangerous, but also illegal to mediate labor disputes apolitically. By 1912, just one year after Kōtoku's execution, Unitarian Suzuki Bunji's (1885–1946) anti-communist Yūaikai ("friendship society"),[42] allied with arch-industrialist Shibusawa Eiichi (1840–1931) (the uncle of Suehiro's law-and-society mentor and partner Hozumi

Shigetō), was the only remaining, legally sanctioned labor organization. Suzuki's program was to make labor the friend of capital (hence the name "friendship society"), but by the end of World War I even the industrialists began to see that the solidarity between "master and retainer"—a vestigial Tokugawa labor ideal—had begun to break down. Society and law (or, in this case, labor and labor governance) were coming apart in this arena, too.

The Western political terms in which modern labor disputes were couched militated against the traditional labor practices that had prevailed in Edo period Japan. As Japan scholar Byron K. Marshall writes:

> In a series of articles and speeches beginning in the final months of 1917, Shibusawa Eiichi added his influential voice to the increasing clamor for a new approach to industrial relations in Japan. Shibusawa had come to believe that the growth of large-scale enterprises, and the changing spirit of the times, necessitated a basic change in management's attitude toward labor. While praising the traditional ethic, he argued that the philosophy of familism or *onjō shugi* was no longer adequate. Factories had grown too large for paternalism to function effectively, and workers were becoming concerned about material security. Moreover, the spread of what he termed 'the mechanistic culture from the Western world' had brought with it the concept of individual rights, and in consequence workers 'naturally' sought to form unions to protect their mutual interests. Thus, Shibusawa concluded in an article entitled 'The Master-Retainer Morality of Old is Bankrupt', 'the times change, and with the influx of Western culture it is only natural that the old master-retainer morality will be destroyed. It is absolutely impossible in today's large enterprises to maintain the close relations between the master and retainer that existed in the past, for spiritual ties are giving way to materialistic negotiations'. Shibusawa [...] advocate[ed] the creation of a central agency [...] to devise and implement new means of ensuring industrial peace.[43]

As old practices proved useless in the face of rapid industrialization and ballooning empire, the absence of the traditional paternalism as a corrective to friction between labor and management meant that a new body of law would have to be devised to take the place of the old, organic norms rooted deeply in Japanese society.[44]

The state considered a further crackdown on left-wing movements, a move that would come with the Peace Preservation Law of 1925. Suehiro waded into the treacherous waters of labor relations as a young government attaché in a foreign, war-torn country only to find that apolitical equity was always already politicized by the demands of empire. There was no way for society to keep up with the exponentially expanding state. Indeed, the logic of empire meant that the state was virtually guaranteed to intervene, partially granting its imprimatur to the vestiges of the former *modus vivendi* and partially devising administrative solutions *de novo*, as the old unwritten laws were crowded out of society by new epistemes of capital, labor, and industrial production as adjunct to imperial expansion. Just as Émile Durkheim had foreseen in his 1893 doctoral dissertation *De la division du travail social*:

> Rules emerge automatically from social conditions as societies become more complex. The division of labour produces different patterns of action corresponding to different functions. [...] The law, which expresses and fulfils the requirements of specialisation and social differentiation, is produced directly by the division of labour itself in an automatic process.[45]

In Japan, however, where status, and not contract, had long governed labor relations, no state-based labor law had emerged. Suehiro returned to Japan with a monumental and potentially very hazardous task before him: to use Eugen Ehrlich's living law insights to broker a permanent solution to the ongoing problems of not only labor specifically, but of social fracturing and the threat of class warfare more generally.

An explanation for the primacy of labor for Suehiro's understanding of law and society comes from Max Weber and Hugo Sinzheimer. For Weber, the bourgeois legal code had no ability to conceive of labor law because labor, as Weber understood it, was inextricably tied up with class.[46] But whereas Weber worried that the incorporation of previously informal, societal-based labor governance into a modern capitalist schema would trap labor within a deadening bureaucratic "iron cage" (*stahlhartes Gehäuse*),[47] Sinzheimer saw that "the class characteristic which is excluded by bourgeois law is taken up into the legal structure through labor law and thus is made into a component of our legal edifice."[48] But labor was virtually invisible to Japanese law. Given these circumstances, there was seemingly unlimited freedom for the labor lawyer in Japan to follow Ehrlich's lead and act as de facto legislator while working through labor cases.[49]

However, and notwithstanding his early debts to the Ehrlichian quasi-stateless conception of the living law, the centrality of the state in labor questions became one of the hallmarks of Suehiro's labor-law philosophy. In 1921, right after returning to Japan from his long study tour of Europe and the United States, Suehiro had jumped immediately into the fray, penning incendiary tracts in support of tenant farmers locked in often violent struggles with landlords in Nagano and elsewhere in the Japanese countryside. Suehiro had even advocated violence in his writings—a mistake that would come back to haunt him when the political mood in Japan darkened considerably in the 1930s. But by 1950, Suehiro had reversed his youthful pronouncements of Ehrlichian indifference to the state and quasi-Marxist defiance of parochial authority in the hinterlands, finding instead that the state was an indispensable element in his dialectical law-and-society approach. In the following passage, for example, Suehiro might even be read as subtly rejecting Ehrlich's key ideas by nuancing them into insignificance:

> I think that, in the study of law and society, the so-called *Lebendesrecht* (living law) corresponds generally to what we know as legal custom.[50] [...] Laws are not necessarily carried out exactly as the state made them; in some cases, laws are constrained by conventional factors handed down within a society for many years, so that, in reality, the scope of the law is entirely different from that of state law. [...] The most important thing to remember when considering this issue is that one must not see either legal custom

> or living law as having a fixed form independent of state law. In point of fact, I believe that the living law exists kinetically in a kind of "broken-line" form, in contact with the particularities of state law and of society. In other words, the living law is a condition of legal instability arising when forces are in contention with one another. I call this the "dynamic structure of the legal order." [...] I first sensed this when I read Ehrlich's *Grundlegung*. But there have been various subsequent misunderstandings on this score, because Ehrlich actually wasn't entirely clear on this point.[51]

For the Suehiro of 1950, the very notion of an emerging labor law opened up untouched vistas of possibility for the law-and-society approach, but within the context of the state. As Weber predicted, intellectuals will become brokers on behalf of the state.[52] While Suehiro continued to view the living law as a corrective to state power, thus leaving open the possibility of apolitical equity within his approach to law and society in Japan, his acceptance of the state as part of a dialectical relationship among labor and law and custom marked a key turning point in his career and thought. This turn came gradually but by the mid 1930s was largely complete. Suehiro would continue thereafter to search for apolitical modes of equity in Japanese society, but the admission of the state into the equation of equity meant that, as the imperial episteme crowded more and more into putatively non-state, apolitical spheres of social activity, the possibilities for apolitical equity in Japan under Suehiro's law-and-society scheme grew increasingly remote.

NOTES

1. On changes in the registration law over time, see David Chapman, "Geographies of Self and Other: Mapping Japan through the Koseki," *The Asia-Pacific Journal*, Vol 9, Issue 29 No 2 (July 18, 2011).
2. See Andrew Gordon, *A Modern History of Japan: From Tokugawa Times to the Present* (New York: Oxford University Press, 2003), esp. Ch. 10, "Democracy and Empire between the World Wars," 161-181.
3. Darryl Flaherty, *Public Law, Private Practice: Politics, Profit, and the Legal Profession in Nineteenth-Century Japan* (Cambridge: Harvard University Press, 2013).
4. Nihon Hyōronsha Henshūkyoku, ed. *Nihon no Hōgaku*, op. cit., 16. Fellow symposium panelist Ukai Nobushige (1906-1987) then clarifies this point by adding: "So, what you're saying is that equality before the law proceeds from the philosophy of equality before God." Nihon Hyōronsha Henshūkyoku, ed. *Nihon no Hōgaku*, op. cit., 16.
5. Nihon Hyōronsha Henshūkyoku, ed. *Nihon no Hōgaku*, op. cit., 16.
6. Nihon Hyōronsha Henshūkyoku, ed. *Nihon no Hōgaku*, op. cit., 16.
7. Hall was the first dean of the University of Chicago Law School (1904-1928).
8. There is some scholarly dispute over the precise year. Hermann Kantorowicz, although widely credited with initiating the movement and coining the term *Freirechtsbewegung* through the publication of his 1906 book on the subject, refused (apparently out of humility) to acknowledge his own importance. Gustav Radbruch disagrees in "In Memoriam Hermann Kantorowicz," *Gesamtausgabe* Bd. 16 (1988), 73. J.M. Kelly divides the founding between Kantorowicz in 1906 and a lecture by Ehrlich in 1903 (*A Short History of Western Legal Theory* (Oxford: Oxford University Press, 1992), 359). Others put Kantorowicz in the center of the emerging Free Law idea. See Vivian Grosswald Curran, "Rethinking Hermann Kantorowicz: Free Law, American Legal Realism and the Legacy of Anti-Formalism," in Annelise Riles, ed., *Rethinking the Masters of Comparative Law* (Oxford: Hart Publishing, 2001), 70 ff.
9. "Roscoe Pound first issued his call for a 'sociological jurisprudence' in 1910." David M. Trubek, "Back to the Future: The Short, Happy Life of the Law and Society Movement" (University of Wisconsin-Madison Institute for Legal Studies Working Papers, Series 4, Madison, Wisconsin,

April, 1990), 5, citing Pound, "Law in Books and Law in Action," 44 *American Law Review* 12 (1910), and "The Scope and Purpose of Sociological Jurisprudence," 24 *Harvard Law Review* 591 (1911), 25 *Harvard Law Review* 140 (1912), 25 *Harvard Law Review* 489 (1912). For Pound, legal history was "the record of a continually wider recognizing and satisfying of human wants or claims or desires through social control; a more embracing and more effective securing of social interests; a continually more complete and effective elimination of waste and precluding of friction in human enjoyment of the goods of existence—in short, a continually more efficacious social engineering." Roscoe Pound, *An Introduction to the Philosophy of Law* (1922) (New Haven: Yale University Press, 1959), 47, cited in Edwin M. Schur, *Law and Society: A Sociological View* (New York: Random House, 1968), 39.

10. Lawrence M. Friedman, "The Law and Society Movement," in *Stanford Law Review*, Vol. 38, No. 3 (Feb., 1986), 763–780. See also Michel Coutu, "Book Review: Living Law: Reconsidering Eugen Ehrlich, by Marc Hertogh (ed)," in *Osgoode Hall Law Journal*, Vol. 47, No. 3 (2009), 587–593, esp. 587-590.
11. Joseph Lazar, "Juridical Perspectives on National Character," *The Annals of the American Academy of Political and Social Science*, Vol. 370, National Character in the Perspective of the Social Sciences (Mar., 1967), 16-22.
12. Coutu, "Review," op. cit., 587 and Hubert Rottleuthner, *Three Legal Sociologies: Eugen Ehrlich, Hugo Sinzheimer, Max Weber* (Madison: University of Wisconsin-Madison Institute for Legal Studies, 1987), 19, ff.
13. Rottleuthner, *Three Legal Societies*, op. cit., 19
14. Coutu, "Review," op. cit., 587, see also Rottleuthner, *Three Legal Societies*, op. cit., 22 ff. for an extended consideration of Ehrlich's Jewishness and its effect on his sociolegal thinking.
15. Rottleuthner, *Three Legal Societies*, op. cit., 5, citing Ehrlich, lecture at *Juristische Gesellschaft*, Vienna, 4/3/1903, reprinted in *Recht und Leben*, Berlin, 1967 (M. Rehbinder, ed.), 196, and Ehrlich, *Grundlegung der Soziologie des Rechts*, 196.
16. Sera Terushirō, "Gendai shakai to hō," in Kawashima Takeyoshi, ed. *Hōshakaigaku kōza 10, rekishi, bunka to hō 2* (Tokyo: Iwanami Shoten, 1973), 13-36.
17. See Adam Podgórecki, "Unrecognized Father of Sociology of Law: Leon Petrażycki: Reflections based on Jan Gorecki's Sociology and Jurisprudence of Leon Petrażycki," in *Law & Society Review*, Vol. 15, No. 1 (1980-1981), 183-202.

18. Because of his intensive focus on the "inner ordering of social groups," some have referred to Ehrlich's legal-sociological conceptualization of the law as "anthropological jurisprudence." F.S.C. Northrop, *The Complexity of Legal and Ethical Experience* (Boston: Little Brown, 1959), 248-249, cited in Edwin M. Schur, *Law and Society: A Sociological View* (New York: Random House, 1968), 37. Cf. Ehrlich: "The centre of gravity of legal development lies not in legislation, nor in juristic science, nor in judicial decision, but in society itself." Eugen Ehrlich, *The Fundamental Principles of the Sociology of Law* (1913), trans. W. Moll (Cambridge: Harvard University Press, 1936), Foreword, cited in Edwin M. Schur, *Law and Society: A Sociological View*, op. cit., 37.
19. As for Ernst Fuchs, see Rottleuthner, *Three Legal Societies*, op. cit., 5.
20. Rottleuthner, *Three Legal Societies*, op. cit. 5.
21. Ushiomi Toshitaka and Toshitani Nobuyoshi, eds., *Nihon no hōgakusha* (Tokyo: Nihon Hyōronsha, 1974), 341
22. For an account, in Suehiro's own words, of his meeting with Ehrlich, see "Kosai Ryōta, corr., Rokumoto Kahei and Yoshida Isamu, eds., Suehiro Izutarō kōgi 'Hōritsu shakaigaku' (1949)," Lecture 1: Foreword, 2/26/1949, in Rokumoto Kahei and Yoshida Osamu, eds., *Suehiro Izutarō to Nihon no hōshakaigaku* (Tokyo: University of Tokyo Press, 2007), 25, ff.
23. For Takayanagi Kenzō's recollections of meeting Ehrlich, see Ushiomi and Toshitani, *Nihon no hōgakusha*, op. cit., 341, citing "Ērurihhi, hōshakaigaku no jo," in *Hōgaku Kyōkai Zasshi*, Vol. 40, No. 1.
24. Ushiomi and Toshitani, *Nihon no hōgakusha*, op. cit., 341.
25. Ushiomi and Toshitani, *Nihon no hōgakusha*, op. cit., 341-342.
26. See Aomi Jun'ichi, *Hō to shakai: atarashii hōgaku nyūmon*, Chūkō shinsho 125 (Tokyo: Chūō Kōron Shinsha, 1967/2007), 154. See also Suehiro, "German law gradually came into prominence beginning in [Meiji] 30 [i.e., 1897]; I graduated university in [Meiji] 45 [i.e., 1912], which was the zenith of German law's flourishing." Nihon Hyōronsha, ed. *Nihon no hōgaku*, op. cit., 38, quoted in Rokumoto and Yoshida, eds., *Suehiro Izutarō to Nihon no hōshakaigaku*, op. cit., 236, fn 9. The "pioneer" of German jurisprudence, Kawana Kaneshirō (1875-1914), died in 1914, the same year that Suehiro was appointed an assistant professor. (Rokumoto and Yoshida, eds., *Suehiro Izutarō to Nihon no hōshakaigaku*, op. cit., 236) In 1917, Ishizaka Otoshirō (1877-1917) also passed away, leaving the new guard of Civil Code scholars—Suehiro, Hatoyama Hideo, and Hozumi Shigetō—in the forefront of legal studies at the University of Tokyo.

Rokumoto and Yoshida, eds., *Suehiro Izutarō to Nihon no hōshakaigaku*, op. cit., 236.

27. Nihon Hyōronsha Henshūkyoku, ed. *Nihon no Hōgaku*, op. cit., 40.
28. Cf. "Pandektenrecht und deutsches Privatrecht," in Hatoyama Hideo, Mitsuma [sic: Miduma] Shinzō, and Suehiro Gentarō [sic: Izutarō], comp., *Zivilrechtliche Lesestücke* (Tokyo: Maruzen, 1916).
29. Eugen Ehrlich, "The Sociology of Law," under the heading "An Appreciation of Eugen Ehrlich," by Roscoe Pound, *Harvard Law Review*, Vol. XXXVI, No. 2, December, 1922, 137, cited in Kahei Rokumoto, ed., *Sociological Theories of Law* (New York, NY: New York University Press, 1994), 101.
30. Christopher W.A. Szpilman argues that Japanese officers first encountered anti-Semitic conspiracy theories during the Siberian Expedition. Szpilman, "Fascist and Quasi-Fascist Ideas in Interwar Japan, 1918-1941," Chapter Three in E. Bruce Reynolds, ed., *Japan in the Fascist Era* (New York: Palgrave Macmillan, 2004), 81. Gerhard Krebs argues, in the same volume, that it was the initial 1883 production of *The Merchant of Venice* that introduced the Japanese, lastingly, to anti-Semitic tropes through the person of Shylock. See Krebs, "The 'Jewish Problem' in Japanese-German Relations," Ch. 4, in Reynolds, ed., *Japan in the Fascist Era*, op. cit., 107. Citing Shiōden [sic: Shiōten] Nobutaka, *Yudaya shisō oyobi undō* (Tokyo: Naigai Shobō, 1941), 59
31. Szpilman, "Fascist and Quasi-Fascist," op. cit., 83. See also Ch. 5 of the present book.
32. Szpilman, "Fascist and Quasi-Fascist," op. cit., 83, citing Mitsui Kōshi, "Yudaya teki Marukusu shisō gekimetsu hōhō," *Kokuhon*, Vol. 5, No. 11 (November, 1925), 17-23.
33. Szpilman, "Fascist and Quasi-Fascist," op. cit., 83, citing Nagao Ryūichi, *Nihon Kenpō shisōshi* (Tokyo: Kōdansha, 1996), 97. For Mitsui, Tokyo Imperial University was a "hotbed of 'Jewish thought' which had to be destroyed for the sake of a powerful Japan." Szpilman, "Fascist and Quasi-Fascist," op. cit., 83, citing citing Mitsui Kōshi, "Yudaya teki Marukusu shisō," op. cit., 21.
34. Ushiomi and Toshitani, *Nihon no hōgakusha*, op. cit., 340-341. On January 10, 1920, Suehiro was appointed by the Japanese Cabinet to work on the Commission on International Labour Legislation that was established on January 18, 1919 following the November, 1918 armistice. See Kudō Seiji, *Shiroku ILO tanjōki* (Tokyo: Nihon Rōdō Kyōkai, 1988), cited in Roku-

moto and Yoshida, eds., *Suehiro Izutarō to Nihon no hōshakaigaku*, op. cit., 21, incl. fn. 54.

35. See, e.g., Nomura Heiji, *Nihon rōdōhō no keisei katei to riron* (Tokyo: Iwanami Shoten, 1957).
36. Ushiomi and Toshitani, *Nihon no hōgakusha*, op. cit., 340-341, citing Suehiro, "Furansu rōdō renmei no dōyō," in *Uso no Kōyō* (1924).
37. Ushiomi and Toshitani, *Nihon no hōgakusha*, op. cit., 340-341, citing Suehiro, "Furansu rōdō renmei no dōyō," in *Uso no Kōyō* (1924), 221.
38. Ushiomi and Toshitani, *Nihon no hōgakusha*, op. cit., 341.
39. Ushiomi and Toshitani, *Nihon no hōgakusha*, op. cit., 341, citing Suehiro, "Furansu," op. cit., 221-222.
40. Suehiro Izutarō, "Chūsan kaikyū no okāsangata he: shijo no kyōiku to shokugyō sentaku tō ni tsuite," *Fujin Kōron*, No. 6 (1932), reprinted in Suehiro Izutarō, *Yakuningaku sansoku: hyōron, zuihitsu* (Tokyo: Nihon Hyōronsha, 1955), 45-50.
41. Byron K. Marshall, *Capitalism and Nationalism in Prewar Japan: The Ideology of the Business Elite, 1868-1941* (Stanford: Stanford University Press, 1967), 78 ff.
42. See Stephen S. Large, "The Japanese Labor Movement, 1912–1919: Suzuki Bunji and the *Yūaikai*," *Journal of Asian Studies*, Vol. 29, No. 3 (May, 1970), 559-579.
43. Byron K. Marshall, *Capitalism and Nationalism*, op. cit., 81, citing *Shibusawa Eiichi denki shiryō* (Tokyo: Shibusawa Seien Ki'nen Zaidan Ryūmonsha, 1955-1963), vol. XXXI, 605-662; "Kyū shujū dōtoku no hassan," in *Chūō Kōron* (December, 1917), 625-626; and Kyōchōkai, eds., *Kyōchōkai jigyō ippan* (Tokyo: Kyōchōkai, 1923), 991-992.
44. "Shihonshugi to rōdōhō," in Nomura Heiji, *Rōdō kihonken no tenkai* (Tokyo: Iwanami Shoten, 1975).
45. Roger Cotterrell, *Émile Durkheim: Law in a Moral Domain* (Stanford: Stanford University Press, 1999), 104.
46. See Max Weber, *Rechtssoziologie*, 2 ed., Neuwied/Berlin, 1967, 16, cited in Rottleuthner, *Three Legal Societies*, op. cit., 29, fn. 87
47. The term "iron cage" is Talcott Parsons' from his 1930 translation of *The Protestant Ethic and the Spirit of Capitalism*, and differs from the literal translation of "steel-hard case/shell". See, e.g., Peter Baehr, "The 'Iron Cage' and the 'Shell as Hard as Steel': Parsons, Weber, and the Stahlhartes Gehäuse Metaphor in *The Protestant Ethic and the Spirit of Capitalism*," in *History and Theory*, vol. 40, no. 2 (May, 2001), 153-169.

48. Rottleuthner, *Three Legal Societies*, op. cit., 30, citing Hugo Sinzheimer, "Wie verhält sich der para.950 BGB zu dem Satz, daß jeder Arbeiter Eigentümer des Arbeitsproduktes werden soll?" (1932), in *Arbeitsrecht und Rechtssoziologie*, vol. 1, Frankfurt/Köln, 1976, 423-426. See also Michel Coutu, "Max Weber on the Labour Contract: Between Realism and Formal Legal Thought," *Journal of Law and Society*, Vol. 36, No. 4 (Dec., 2009), 558-578.
49. For an example of how caselaw has changed the practice of Japanese labor law, see Nomura Heiji, ed., *Hanrei rōdō sōgi* (Tokyo: Ichiryūsha, 1957).
50. See also Suehiro Izutarō, "Hōritsu to kanshū: Nihon hōri tankyū no hōhō ni kansuru hito kōsatsu," in *Zoku Minpō zatsu kichō* (Tokyo: Nihon Hyōronsha, 1949), 312-325, and "Jijitsutaru kanshū," ibid., 42-54.
51. Nihon Hyōronsha Henshūkyoku, ed. *Nihon no Hōgaku*, op. cit., 351-353.
52. Darryl E. Flaherty, *Public Law, Private Practice*, op. cit. Weber foresaw the neo-Kantian technocrat as the ideal bureaucratic statist. See, e.g., James Farganis, *Readings in Social Theory: The Classic Tradition to Post-Modernism* (3E) (New York: McGraw-Hill, 2000), 102, ff.

Chapter 3

The Caselaw Study Group

The Law-and-Society Movement in Theory and Practice

Bringing the Living Law to Japan

In 1921, Suehiro's caselaw revolution quietly got underway. The "gathering of lively youths who had fallen away from formalism" was the kernel of the caselaw revolution that Suehiro hoped to effect in the effort to repair the breach between law and society, jurisprudence and custom, that had opened with the introduction of Western political discourse into the Japanese mainstream in the middle of the nineteenth century. As Suehiro explains:

> Beginning in July of 1921, we met once a week in the Civil Code Research Room at the Law Department of Tokyo Imperial University, where we studied in sequence the Case Record (*hanketsuroku*) of the 1921 session of the Great Court of Cassation (*Daishin'in*) (Vol. 27). We published our findings in *Hōgaku kyōkai zasshi*, beginning in Vol. 39, No. 9 and continuing through Vol. 40, No. 9. [...] We were a gathering of lively youths who had fallen away from formalism.[1]

The caselaw study group started unobtrusively, but it was not long before Suehiro's group got the attention of the legal establishment. In volume after volume of the *Hōgaku kyōkai zasshi*, Suehiro, Hozumi Shigetō, and their acolytes pounded away at the status quo in the Japanese courts, revealing again and again that most *Daishin'in* judges did not pay attention to the facts of the cases brought before their benches. This situation was not in the least ameliorated by the almost universal lack of legal training among *Daishin'in* judges. Political appointments to cronies also helped complicate Suehiro's search for apolitical equity in Japanese courtrooms. In addition to pathbreaking work in the new area of labor law, then, Suehiro also returned to Japan intending to reform the court system and, by extension, the very nature of the interaction between law (conceived capaciously as politics and the state) and society in Japan.

Suehiro's father, Suehiro Ganseki (1858–1922), had been a *Daishin'in* magistrate. However, Suehiro saw his father as an "Oriental-style" judge who wanted to see the Freedom and Popular Rights Movement spread among the Japanese masses. In praising his father for his social awareness, Suehiro linked him with Jeremy Bentham, whom Suehiro saw as having tried to effect the French Revolution in England without appealing to the Revolution's methods.[2]

Suehiro's appeal to the French Revolution points to the radical nature of his attempt to remake Japanese society by recasting Japanese jurisprudence. Like Jeremy Bentham trying to have the ends of the French Revolution without the means, Suehiro wanted to avoid the perils of politics to empower disenfranchised citizens by way of the courts, not the Diet.[3] As Kawashima Takeyoshi, a Suehiro protégé during the caselaw study years, remembered:

> Case law research was not "case law review." The point that must be emphasized in researching cases in the sense of judicial precedents is that those cases cannot be divorced from the facts of the case, and that cases have significance as conclusions corresponding to the facts of the case. [...] I [...] had started from the

> black letter of the law and then engaged in deductive reasoning, finally turning to the case at hand and fitting the deductions to facts of the case. This is how I came up with my conclusions—this was the course of my reasoning. This is how judges write legal arguments in their decisions, but it cannot be the thinking or the logical process followed by a caselaw researcher.[4]

The caselaw method reversed the flow of conceptual, legislatively derived jurisprudence, foregrounding society, and not lawmakers, in judges' decisions.

Suehiro's goal was to bypass the deadlocked Diet in order to bring the regard for liberal individual rights, so often spoken of by elite politicians, into the lives of those most in need of it.[5] This predictability of the law made to operate within the bounds of precedent and due regard for the consequences of judicial decisions is what Suehiro meant when he made "the security of the law" the highest among his hopes for the case-law project that he undertook:

> It is a certainty that those who hold law to form a perennially perfect *Geschlossenheit* [cohesive unity][6] will, of course, deny that legal decisions have the power to create law. [...] The first and most important point we stress in the study of caselaw is not about how a court understands a phrase in a law text in an abstract, scholarly way. Nor is it the formal logic apparent in a decision, nor is it simply the conclusion itself. Judges are people who, when faced with the concrete details of a case, engage, unconsciously, in a complex set of behaviors that goes beyond formal logic and rigid reasoning. The essential point of the study of caselaw is to attempt to arrive at a thoroughgoing, concrete legal security, *Rechtssicherheit*, by discerning fixed principles from within that set of behaviors.[7]

The security of the law (*Rechtssicherheit, hōteki anzen*) was achievable outside the legislative orbit of the Diet through the intervention of judges. Suehiro saw caselaw as the means to provide the due process and governmental restraint that would give common people the benefits of a fully democratic system—in effect domesticating Taishō Democracy—without engaging with the perilous politics of the metastasizing centralized state.

However, just as Suehiro and his team were moving to domesticate Taishō Democracy using the law to provide social security and stability, the state was moving to proselytize Asia and the Pacific with the benisons of civilization and enlightenment. Suehiro was busy integrating the Tokyo proletariat into the new social dispensation while the Japanese state was busy expanding the boundaries of "Japan" far beyond the pre-Meiji limits. This shift to empire, in which the emperor became the embodiment of the Japanese polity, ensured the failure of any apolitical attempt to reach equity apart from the totalizing state. Furthermore, the court system, which might have exerted a measure of supervision over the political and administrative processes *qua* extensions of the imperial person, was also potentially compromised, as cases—even those in which the judicial system was called upon to interpret actions of the legislature—were understood to be adjudicated in the emperor's name.[8] Suehiro had tried to make an end run around politics, but the empire turned the tables on him, making its own end run around society. Apolitical equity via the living law had been checkmated by the ascendancy of Prussian-style conceptions of the relationship between the individual and the state.

In order to ensure that these more global political considerations did not affect the pursuit of justice in courtrooms, Suehiro insisted on specificity, subjectivity, and empiricism. The research group's remit was "to attempt to know the law in a concrete way" (*gutaiteki hōritsu wo shiran to suru*).[9] To this end, it was vital to know what a court was and what really happened at a trial:

> A court is a place where the law is interpreted and applied. It is not a legislative body of government. This is a fact of the constitutional state, and is also called for in the Japanese constitution. But if you look at what actually goes on in the courts, you'll find that they are also continuously engaged in 'creation'. The laws are

> actually made by them [i.e., the courts]. Is what they are doing contradictory? Is it unconstitutional?[10]

The question of constitutionality brought up the further question, for Suehiro, of the divide between the academicians and the people:

> Those who look at the law in an academic way would call what the courts do [i.e., acting as de facto legislative islets] unconstitutional. But the man in the street approves [of what the courts do]. When the courts neglect to 'create' in a manner consistent with the desires of the people, the people ridicule the courts, calling them 'fossils lacking any common sense'. In the end, are the academicians right and the people wrong?[11]

A legal pragmatism percolating up through court cases was to be the empirical ground for incremental social reform.

This populist jurisprudence had a related, linguistic valence, as well. In "The dead-end problem of the Japanese language: the Latin-script movement as a cultural movement,"[12] for example, Suehiro avowed that the "complexities of Chinese characters themselves are the reason" that many Japanese words cannot be pronounced by sight.[13] In effect, the Japanese writing system was indirectly disenfranchising many of the urban poor, who could not afford the years of study required even to learn how to pronounce what was putatively their native language. Suehiro emphasized the social benefits he saw to be gained by a dramatic simplification of the way Japanese was written:

> The societal format in Japan has been completely renewed since the Meiji Period. The feudal society that had regard for native place was swept away, giving way to the Meiji Period of freedom of travel. Ordinary citizens were equally granted freedom of occupation. [...] Because of this, we must never be complacent about letting ourselves get carried away by the force of custom. Characters that are read in certain ways only by certain people, and in particular things like personal names and place names, have already fallen completely out of step with society today. We must seek out

> new letters and a new language for the new world in which we live.[14] [This is because of] the rapid **importation of Western civilization** during the Meiji Period. [...] **The importing of new concepts necessitates the generation of a new language.**[15]

The Japanese language itself was thus a hindrance to people's ability to understand the social context in which they found themselves—a largely foreign landscape whose conceptual landmarks were obscured by the linguistic fog that had settled into Japanese.

Suehiro was concerned about the intelligibility of the Japanese language for more narrowly legal reasons, as well:

> That law [i.e., the Civil Code] has the most intimate relationship to our private lives today. Why is it that, despite each person's being unable to separate himself from the Civil Code for even a moment, the Civil Code has, as always, been poorly understood? It is due to no other reasons than that the statutes and the law books are entirely too difficult to comprehend, are entirely too bland and dry, and because no one has worked to research [how to change it].[16]

The law, for Suehiro, was initially the main focus of his attempt to make the language of the state at least potentially intelligible to the average citizen. This was in keeping with Suehiro's overall drive to bring equity to the common person. For if someone could not understand the law, how could he be expected to defend himself in the courts of the state?

Like someone fighting to save a minority dialect from being absorbed by a surrounding elite-centered language, Suehiro tried to preserve the independence of courts by insulating them from the legislature. On the fundamental question of whether legislation was the exclusive province of legislatures, Suehiro argued that it was not:

> The academicians say that the courts are not legislative organs. But what *is* the meaning of this 'legislation' about which we're speaking? In the end, the issue at hand turns on how we define this word. The constitution is clear about the functions of the organ which crafts laws and fashions imperial edicts and other orders.

> [...] But is the entirety of the law coterminous solely with what such an organ brings forth? No, it isn't. Even if, hypothetically speaking, they [i.e., the legislative body] were to foresee the whole future and arrive at a perfect law, when applied to the infinite variety of the real world, the resulting conclusions would be extremely complex. If we look at how such a theoretical case plays out in reality, we might express it nearly enough by saying that the legislature makes the 'outer walls' of the law, while the courts fill in the 'contents' of those walls. Whether one uses the word 'law' to refer to these 'contents' or not is beside the point. In actual fact, there is no reason to distinguish [these 'contents'] from law. [...] In the end, legislating is human work. It is impossible to make [a law] that will match perfectly the complicated nature of the world. But even if such a thing were possible temporarily, the vicissitudes of the passage of time would soon render [a perfect law] imperfect. If not the courts, who or what will repair the original and subsequent failings of the law and provide standards for the world around?[17]

The key to Suehiro's thinking comes next, when he describes courts as "Peace-maker[s]". The hope for keeping peace in Japanese society lay with the courts, and ultimately with judges, to whom fell the work of navigating between the strictures of law and the expansive particularities of life:

> Courts are not legislatures. But they are also not just simple tools for applying laws. Through ceaseless 'creation' they become 'Peace-maker[s]' [the word is in English in the original] harmonizing life and the law."[18]

A politics of rights, and especially one of disenfranchisement, could not stitch the law and life together—"Peace" had to be kept by judges.

Suehiro proposed to solve this problem by what today might be called "data mining." He wanted to look at specifics of cases and then use those specifics to feed back into the official gestation process of the black-letter law, influencing legislatures and, it was hoped, judges, too:

> First, to try as best as we can to assemble the most detailed possible factual relationships from among the extremely incomplete factual records kept during trials. Second, to summarize in a simple fashion the way in which the court responded to those facts. And last, to add commentaries. [But] our intention in adding commentaries is completely different from that of the critiques of court decisions (*hanrei hihyō*) that other scholars have attempted in the past. [...] In general, these [i.e., our] critiques have looked into the commonalities between the given case and previous cases in order to explain the ways in which concrete changes in the law and its contents, as related to the issue in question, have gradually come about. To be sure, there are differences of opinion among the different members of our group, arising from differences of perspective, but granted this we nevertheless have sought to avoid straying from the concrete facts and into abstract argument.[19]

The rush of data from courts was designed to swamp any abstractions in empirical fact, thus continuously redirecting the focus of the law back on the people.

Unlike many others who reified imagined histories or romanticized mist-shrouded folkways, custom for Suehiro was not just an empty gesture toward the aroma of the past. Suehiro saw custom as living through and in the law:

> One can find at least a double meaning in the phrase, "case study." First, through caselaw research we can come to know the living law. In other words, not only do legal relationships as they arise in society as it actually exists oftentimes assume aspects that cannot be understood thoroughly through academic speculation, but also, sometimes, essentially limited and fixed laws and regulations can give rise to completely unexpected problems. Because caselaw gives material form to the living law in solving, somehow, these kinds of unforeseen circumstances, by studying cases we are able to add a reflective function to theories of interpretation, and are also able to take in important implications about theories of legislation. In this sense, the significance of case study lies in imparting

> the breath of life to jurisprudence, enriching and diversifying jurisprudential content, and deepening and developing its theory. Second, through caselaw research we contribute to the formation of correct caselaw. What I mean by this is that while cases, as discussed above, provide a working legal solution to the complex and novel problems that arise in actual society, this legal engagement, along with theoretical constructions and the conclusions reached thereby, are not necessarily always appropriate in every instance. In order to free trials of the dogmatism of court judges and to secure an objective suitability, there is an absolute need for an exacting critique of caselaw from an academic perspective. In that sense, caselaw research exercises a kind of corrective and guiding function vis-à-vis trials.[20]

A "corrective and guiding function vis-à-vis trials" was surely needed to untangle the skeins of party politics (and fill the void of a disenfranchised electorate). However, legal engagement had grown difficult under the bureaucratization and imperialization of justice, so Suehiro harkened back to the earlier champion of equity Ōoka Tadasuke, whose Tokugawa-era legal training was to override even the Osadamegaki, or Great Tokugawa Decrees, where the application of the Decrees would have resulted in a miscarriage of justice.[21]

In "Uso no Kōyō" ("On the efficacy of lies"), first published in the July, 1922 issue of the progressive mass-circulation magazine *Kaizō*,[22] Suehiro lauds Ōoka's trials as having been "penetrating [in their understanding of] the nuances of human feeling."[23] As before, Suehiro wanted to bring the human element back into courts. But there is a twist to Suehiro's praise: the secret to Ōoka's fairness, Suehiro argued, lay in his skillful use of lies.[24] What Suehiro advocated in "Uso no kōyō" was a return to the use of legal fictions, a device more than a mere legal technicality but, instead, indicative of the extent to which a due regard for individual circumstances and the equitable resolution of specific cases had pervaded Tokugawa law.[25] Suehiro felt that this regard for human-shaped justice had been lost in the abstractions of Western jurisprudence and political science at the advent of the Meiji Period. The question was whether legal fictions were really lies, and whether lies could be the methodology for rescuing jurisprudence and effecting society-saving equity.

Suehiro's assertion was that the discretion to stretch law's truth, formerly carried out by magistrates during the Tokugawa Period, was now in the hands of prosecutors.[26] Suehiro saw the courts as, increasingly, battlegrounds for individuals vested with Lockean rights, and legal fictions as ways to find equitable solutions even to rights-based complaints.[27] As with Suehiro's Caselaw Study Group, the eventual goal was to increase social stability by increasing the trustworthiness (*shinrai*) of the law among the common man (*ippanjin*),[28] for the benefit of whom the law exists in the first place.[29] However, the common man presents a dilemma because he clamors for change and yet is "ridiculously conservative"[30] at the same time. Historically, lies have been shown to be very socially effective[31] in bridging the gap of this paradox: modern man's desire for equality before the law[32] and flexibility in the law. The solution to the contradiction[33] to which these opposing desires give rise was to find a "sliding scale,"[34] "like rubber,"[35] that could accommodate both the stability and the malleability that people had come to expect the legal system to provide. The way to do that was to continually adapt statutory law to social realities by means of case law, using the Ōoka method of the legal fiction (as Suehiro styles it) to smooth over social rough patches with "the efficacy of lies."[36]

True to Ōokian form, in 1921, Suehiro began duly laying out the rationale for his caselaw review project in a way that separated theoretical speculation from practical necessity:

> The time has already passed for arguing over whether caselaw is or is not a source for law. Theoretically speaking, of course, there is room for debate on the subject. However, it is utterly impossible to understand current law without taking caselaw into account. This is not up for debate; this is fact. Not only that, but established fact.[37]

This approach worked. It did not take long for the caselaw study group to see results. In 1923, Suehiro wrote that many who were sympathetic to the importance of caselaw had begun to emerge within the legal profession and then reports his great satisfaction with the *Daishin'in* for beginning publication, presumably under pressure from Suehiro's case law study group, of a case law compendium (*hanreishū*), which contained details of individual cases, unlike the record of judgments (*hanketsuroku*) that the *Daishin'in* had been publishing before Suehiro launched his critique.

Suehiro saw this change of heart as vindication of his analysis and methods:

> Last year, at the beginning of this series, we said that, "The time has already passed for arguing over whether caselaw is or is not a source for law." We still hold the same view today. Not only that, but voices sympathetic to our pronouncement on caselaw have continued to emerge from within the legal community. Our happiness at this is heartfelt. Of course, we do not believe that our pronouncements alone are responsible for this trend. We think that all that has happened is that, that which was bound to come, has come, in a natural form. We are but a single stone that has been thrown into clear, still water—water that, in truth, had been waiting for someone to come along soon and make some waves. The tossed stone has made a ring of beautiful, gentle ripples on the surface of the still water. That ring of ripples will keep getting broader and broader. [...] Why was publication of the *Daishin'in* record of judgments ended? Why did publication of the *Daishin'in* case law compendium commence? We have no way of knowing the detailed reasons. Rumor has it, though, that the main motivation behind this is that officials in the *Daishin'in* have gradually become aware of the value of caselaw, and, at the same time, have come to notice the many flaws in the old record of judgments and have set out to make improvements. If this is true, then we think that the [*Daishin'in*] officials' greatest joy will undoubtedly be to hear the world's evaluation of the new case law compendium.[38]

Suehiro's drive to render equity by forcing an empirical turn within imperial Japanese jurisprudence was already yielding tangible results by as early as 1923.

This success seemed to validate Suehiro in his decision to eschew politics in favor of low-level guarantees of due process. Those who joined Suehiro's group were also attracted to this apolitical approach. For example, Hozumi Shigetō had witnessed firsthand the pitfalls of political attempts to solve societal problems. Hozumi (the son of Baron Hozumi Nobushige and nephew of Hozumi Yatsuka) was on the staff of the 1919 *Rinji Hōsei Shingikai* (Ad Hoc Commission for the Study of Legal Institutions), which was chaired by Hozumi's father and contained such jurisprudential and political heavyweights as preeminent constitutional law scholar Minobe Tatsukichi (1873–1948), future justice ministers Baron Hiranuma Kiichirō (1867–1952), Okano Keijirō (1865–1925) and Suzuki Kisaburō (1867–1940), and Hanai Takuzō (1868–1931), who had been the defense lawyer for novelist and anarchist Kōtoku Shūsui during the sensational Great Treason Trial of 1910.[39]

As an advocate of "conciliation" (*chōtei*, an early form of alternative dispute resolution (ADR)), Hozumi Shigetō was an odd choice for a governmental committee. In many ways, though, his views overlapped with those of the *ie seido* advocates. Hozumi thought that lawyers tended to assert individual rights, which was inimical to hammering out a just resolution that had the "interests of the collectivity at heart."[40] The committee was not without promise for advancing Hozumi Shigetō's non-statist agenda more broadly, as well. Prime Minister Hara Kei, a parliamentary politician who had formed one of the first political parties in Japan, charged the committee with establishing a jury system, which would have had obvious benefits for bottom-up, living law reform.[41] Prime Minister Hara also wanted the committee to change the Civil Code to reflect Japan's "virtuous ways and beautiful customs" (*junpū bizoku*), a mixture of both a practical and a more nebulous approach to incorporating more of the populace within the political process.[42] But in the event, as might have been expected, the committee eventually dissolved after political divisions stymied any progress toward substantial reform of the Code.

Not stylized "virtuous ways and beautiful customs" in a political party's menagerie, then, but Ehrlichian living law—real, lived custom—would be the ground for the new legal science. Suehiro's program for recovering the law through judges instead of the legislature was premised upon allowing custom-wide latitude to influence trials and judicial decisions. As original caselaw study group member Hirano Yoshitarō remembered later:

> Until Prof. Hozumi and Prof. Suehiro came onto the scene, the unwritten rule was that Japanese jurisprudence should focus entirely on statutory law. Everything else, including custom and case law, was held in complete contempt. No consideration had ever been given to the fact that one must pay close attention to legal custom—along with trial parameters which correspond to the scope of actions—due to law's being a function, a cognitive capability, of society, regulating society internally, or to the fact that caselaw would bring the law back to life by completing statutory law. Therefore, there was a total separation between law, on the one hand, and history, culture, and society, on the other. Prof. Hozumi returned to Japan in 1917, right around the First World War, while in November of 1918 Prof. Suehiro took Prof. Hozumi's place abroad, boarding the *Shunyomaru*[43] for the United States. In the summer of 1920, after Suehiro had returned from overseas, he joined Takayanagi [Kenzō], Hatoyama [Hideo] (who had previously lectured on the Civil Code), and Hozumi [Shigetō] to form a coterie of young, up-and-coming professors. They then set about developing many different things, and started the Case Law Research Group in May of 1921. [As mentioned above, the group first met in July of 1921.] This was an epoch-making event.[44]

Unlike many of the developments of the Meiji period, this "epoch-making event" was not predicated upon any political party or platform. Instead, the operating principle was to be custom and not any Western theory of freedom or popular rights. Suehiro's protégé Kainō Michitaka (1908-1975) observed:

> In the past, trials were conducted according to custom. However, when one conducts trials in accordance with custom, there are situations in which the trials will not adhere to local [practice]. In situations where, for instance, someone from Satsuma [in the far southwest of Honshū] was appointed judge in Tōhoku [in the north], it goes without saying that such a problem [of conflicting customs] arose. Also, trials conducted according to custom will produce uneven results. Sometimes, completely different trials will be conducted for the same incident. I think this greatly risks giving the impression that trials have degraded. This is why, whether we are discussing English law or French law or any other kind of law, there must be some kind of objective law and trials must be conducted in order to apply that law. It is for this reason, I think, that both French law and English law were grounded in the natural law.[45]

This emphasis on custom among Suehiro and his protégés continued well after the Caselaw Study Group was founded, such as in 1946 when group members Wagatsuma Sakae (1897–1973) and Nakagawa Zennosuke (1897–1975) formed an ad hoc committee for the revision of the Civil Code. According to one scholar, it was Nakagawa's emphasis upon the customary spirit of mutual-assistance and -support between husbands and wives that led to similar clauses in the current iteration of the Civil Code.[46]

At first glance, Suehiro and his group's attempts to revivify custom and let the "living law" influence trials and court decisions might have appeared relatively easy. After all, the 1898 Civil Code had already enshrined custom as having a nomothetic heft equal to legislated law. For example, the Law for the Application of Laws (*hōrei*), Law No. 10, June 21, 1898. Art. 2, states:

> Customs which are not contrary to public policy shall have the same force as law in so far as they are recognized by the provision

> of a law or an ordinance or relate to matters which are not provided for by laws or ordinances.

And the Commercial Code, Art. 1, says:

> As to a commercial matter, the commercial customary law shall apply if there are no provisions in this Code; and the Civil Code shall apply if there is no such law.[47]

But just as Yanagita Kunio (1875–1962) had found in attempting an apolitical appraisal of Japanese village-folk practice, the reification of custom within a modern episteme already presumed an opposition between the past and the present which, under the Japanese empire, was a profoundly political act. The political strength of nostalgia, which inheres in an advocacy for native custom, was particularly palpable under the imperial politics driving Japan outward into Asia and the Pacific.[48] This politicization of custom by the imperial state in effect co-opted and rebranded the living law, giving it an imperial spin that put it out of sync with what Suehiro and his group were trying to achieve.

There was still something effronterous about elite professors and politicians making so much of the customs of the common man.[49] This high-handed tone is apparent in a newspaper clipping from 1921:

> Professors to Give Lectures in Hopes of Spreading [Knowledge about] the Law
> Judge Also to Make an Appearance
> Today at the Meiji Kaikan
> In order to disseminate knowledge of the law to the masses, Tokyo University professors Niida, Yoshino, Hozumi [Shigetō], and Suehiro will give lectures today (the 24th) in the evening at the Meiji Kaikan in Kanda on such interesting topics as, "New Romanticism of the Law," "The Restoration (*ishin*) of the Law," and "Common Customs toward the Law."[50]

And yet, while "Disseminat[ing] knowledge to the masses" may sound condescending, it must be remembered that condescension was hardly a new strain in Japanese political life. The Japanese term *kanson minpi*, which denotes the ideal of honoring officials and looking down on the people, was the default attitude of the bureaucratized state. Fukuzawa Yukichi had criticized scholars in 1874 for "[k]nowing the art of officialdom but not understanding the private." Officials "know the art of standing at the top of government," Fukuzawa scolded, "but not the ways that exist below government."[51] If members of the new law and society movement in Japan wanted to bridge the gulf between society and law, then they would first have to step into the class breach that existed in society itself.

As if goaded on by Fukuzawa's words, Japan's legal elites had duly gathered at the Tokyo Imperial University Faculty of Law eager to effect social reform. In 1922, Yūhikaku, the publisher of record of legal volumes in Japan, released the 676-page *Hanrei Minpō*, a collection of caselaw and commentaries by Suehiro's caselaw study group. The authors are listed as Suehiro,[52] Nakagawa Zennosuke, Hozumi Shigetō, Hirano Yoshitarō, Wagatsuma Sakae, Azuma Suehiko, and Tanaka Seiji.[53] Azuma and Tanaka were research assistants and did not make substantial contributions to the record, although Azuma, Suehiro's boyhood friend, soon became involved in extensive research into the legal systems of Italy and Germany.[54] With the later additions of Kawashima Takeyoshi and Kainō Michitaka, his group formed the nucleus of the law and society movement in Japan.[55]

Hozumi's expertise in Japanese family practice and family law laid an important foundation for the work of the Caselaw Study Group on the basis of Japanese custom. Many of the cases he selected for the Suehiro case law compendium involve ordinary people who could not have been expected to have more than a superficial knowledge of the complexities of the law. Much of Hozumi's work was dedicated to remedying this situation by, on the one hand, publicizing case law in order to allow lay people to have easier access to the procedural protocols of the courts, and, on the other hand, pointing out instances—unfortunately not uncommon

—of judges' ignoring the plights of plaintiffs and defendants altogether in order to engage in a purely theoretical ratiocination based solely on the positive law.

Hozumi set forth his objectives in publicizing the law in a 1931 lecture. As society has become more complex, Hozumi argued,

> [...] the law has tried to predict what will happen in society, but the law has come to differ from what actually takes place. The law has [therefore] become extraordinarily specialized and difficult, and knowledge of the law has come to be monopolized by certain people [only], legal specialists [such as] government officials, judges, and lawyers. The common man can no longer approach the law. While it works out well [for such officials] to line up regulations and rules with the letter of the law, in doing so the law becomes rigid and codified, [a product of the minds of the men who crafted it decades before].[56]

The law, then, is not a fossil, but a living organism that must, like other living things, move and change over time.

In order to counter the ossification of the law, Hozumi conducted extensive research into different systems of family law worldwide, producing, for example, a more-than-nine-hundred-page book on divorce laws that investigated the history of divorce in England (going as far back as King Æthelbert (560–616) and Canute the Great (ca. 985–1035)); under the Catholic Church; in Japan at the so-called "divorce temples" whither unhappily married women could flee;[57] and in France during the Revolution, as well as divorce laws then currently active in Europe and the United States.[58] As the cases in Hozumi's casefile make plain, the family was in perhaps the most dire need of equitable solutions, and not further politicization.

Nakagawa Zennosuke (1897–1975) was a student of Hozumi Shigetō at Tokyo Imperial University and became an assistant professor there in 1922, specializing in the Civil Code. In 1927, he transferred to Tōhoku University, where he taught until 1961. In 1967 he became chancellor of

Kanazawa University, retired from academia in 1973, and then registered as a lawyer. Within the Civil Code, Nakagawa's area of particular focus was the Family Law, and he worked to dismantle the older *ie seido*. Today he is known as the "father of the current Family Law."[59] Nakagawa instituted the study of "status law" (*mibun hōgaku*), arguing that notions of status had long been more prominent, especially in villages, than notions of law, with traditional mores and status privileges guiding social interaction much more than did knowledge of, or appeals to, the promulgated, black-letter law. Working with fellow Suehiro group member Wagatsuma Sakae in 1946, Nakagawa and Wagatsuma formed an ad hoc committee for the revision of the Civil Code, where Nakagawa's emphasis upon the original spirit of mutual-assistance and -support between husbands and wives led to similar clauses in the current iteration of the Civil Code.[60]

Hirano Yoshitarō (1897–1980) was also a graduate of the Law Department of Tokyo Imperial University. While studying at Frankfurt University from 1927–1930, Hirano became influenced by Marxism, probably because of Hirano's tutelage under then-communist Karl Wittfogel.[61] Hirano was arrested under the Peace Preservation Law during the round-up of communists and communist sympathizers on May 20, 1930 (*Kyōsantō sympa jiken*), and arrested again, but later found not guilty, during the round-up of Kōza-ha leftist intellectuals in 1936 known as the Komu Academy Incident (*Komu akademii jiken*). Hirano wrote widely on capitalism, at first from an explicitly Marxist perspective.[62] Hirano's subsequent enthusiastic support for the Greater East Asia War—which caused a third round of professional troubles for him when he was dismissed from his teaching post after Japan's defeat in 1945—may seem incongruous unless one takes into account Hirano's conversion (*tenkō*) to imperialism while conducting a survey in China in 1937, part of Hirano's deepening interest in that country.[63] He was the head of the China Research Institute (1946–1960) and also the secretary and head of the Modern China Study Association (now, Japan Association for Modern China Studies) from 1951–1960. Although Hirano resigned in protest from the China Research Institute over the excesses of the Cultural Revolution, his earlier affiliation with China had been deeply colored by his desire to rid Asia of colonialism.

Wagatsuma Sakae, born in Yamagata Prefecture in 1897, studied under Suehiro's brother-in-law Hatoyama Hideo (1884–1946), a legal theorist and parliamentarian and a member of the powerful Hatoyama political family. Like Suehiro, Wagatsuma's work also focused on the "living law," although for Wagatsuma this chiefly entailed tempering the capitalistic individualism of the Civil Code by a regard for custom and society. Wagatsuma saw caselaw as the means for softening the capitalist logic of the positive law. Like Hozumi, Wagatsuma was also interested in the place of the family within the Japanese Civil Code, and in particular the effects of war on the family.[64] Sent after the 1923 earthquake by legal scholar Takayanagi Kenzō to the United States along with Nakagawa Zennnosuke to buy books to replenish the ruined Tokyo Imperial University library, Wagatsuma was close to Suehiro before the war.[65] As with Suehiro and Hirano, Wagatsuma eventually found that the imperial project was better suited to implementing the living law than was the academic study of law. Wagatsuma's expertise in the Japanese Civil Code even led to his being commissioned to direct the drafting of a Civil Code in Manchukuo. These imperial associations notwithstanding, after the war Wagatsuma found continued success, becoming chairman of the board of the Japan Association of Private Law (*Nihon Shihō Gakkai*). However, in later years Wagatsuma's involvement with Suehiro virtually disappears from the record. Wagatsuma's biography makes just brief mention of Suehiro although much of Wagatsuma's formative years were spent in Suehiro's tutelage.[66]

The Cases

The *Hanrei Minpō*'s Table of Contents[67] shows that Suehiro's aim was to invert jurisprudence through a systematic regrounding of the practice of law in cases and customs instead of in legislation. The book itself is not laid out in a fully schematic way. Each case is given a master number, following sequentially from one to one hundred and ninety-four, but beyond this the book seems to consist simply of each edition of the group's journal compiled "end to end," with no internal re-arrangement according to categories. The table of contents, though, is an attempt to impose retroactive order on the group's weekly scholarship. After a miscellany of reflections on the nature of law, specific legal doctrines (for example, "ignorance of the law is no excuse for breaking the law"), and the courts and their judgments, the table of contents divides the cases up into six "books" (*hen*): namely, 1/ General Provisions, 2/ Real Rights, 3/ Credit, 4/ Family Relations, 5/ Succession, and 6/ Compulsory Execution.

Between books 5 and 6, there is a long interlude in the table of contents covering specific laws, with cases related to those individual laws listed under the rubric of the name of the law itself. In this interlude, there are eight additional sections labeled "books" (*hen*), although these "books" are organized as subsets of the discourses on the individual laws. For example, under the un-numbered section labeled Commercial Law, there are five sub-books: 1a/ General Provisions, 2a/ Companies, 3a/ Commercial Activity, 4a/ Instruments of Payment, and 5a/ Maritime Commerce. Each of these sub-books is further subdivided into chapters, just as are the six main books, but all five of the sub-books here fall under the heading of Commercial Law and so are unrelated to the other book-based organization system of the rest of the *Hanrei Minpō*. Likewise, there are three sub-books under a section titled Civil Lawsuits Law: namely, 1b/ General Provisions, 2b/ Lawsuit Procedures in Courts of First Instance, and 3b/ Appeals. This sub-book system, like the other, ends abruptly.

The *Hanrei Minpō* thus mirrors the codified law. However, many of the cases listed in the *Hanrei Minpō* are posed in the form of a question, a further inversion of the declarative certainty of the positive law. Whereas laws passed by legislative bodies are closed systems that also seek to close off other events within them, Suehiro's case law approach is the opposite. For Suehiro, each case was unique, and could be fitted sometimes only very awkwardly within the parameters of the codified law. So, for example, instead of saying, "This clause [i.e., on the meaning of 'real estate' under the section titled "Validity of Right of Exclusive Possession"] shall/shall not apply to x," Suehiro *asks* whether it shall, and then answers his own question with case law. In another instance, the question at hand is, "Does this clause apply to someone who chops down a stand of trees that he purchased from someone else who had no right [to sell it in the first place]?"[68] The rhetorical shift, from law as pronouncement to law as question, changes the nature of the law, and opens up space for the law to be modified by its interaction with the world around it.

Overall, the cases present a vivid portrait of an emerging dialectic between law and society by means of individual cases. In the mundane troubles of the proletariat painstakingly detailed in the cases we can see that gap between the grand scale of parliament and party politics, which were forever giving speeches about the common man, and the comparatively tiny concerns of the common people themselves, far too small for the politicians (or even the judges) to notice, but momentous in the individual lives of the people to whom those concerns had come.

In Case 114, for example, a small-business owner, a Mr. Makino Shōsaburō, wrote a promissory note for business expenses using a check bearing the name of his wife. In order to cover the check he had written, Mr. Makino immediately went to the bank and made a deposit in his wife's account, against which the amount of the check would eventually be drawn. However, the bank refused to honor the check, on the grounds that Mr. Makino, who had written it, could not be forced to bear responsibility for it, thereby rendering his action a kind of false utterance of a financial instrument. The amount of the check is not given, but because Mr. and Mrs. Makino were running a store, and the check was written in the course of a "normal transaction,"[69] it cannot have been for an inordinately large sum of money. The case was brought to court in an attempt to force the bank to honor the check.

In this case, the court ruled that the plaintiff, Mr. Makino, must bear the responsibility for having written the check since the person listed on the check, Mrs. Makino, and Mr. Makino were, obviously, not the same person. Mr. Makino had argued that when, in the course of normal business transactions, one person writes a check bearing the name of another person with the same last name (i.e., a wife or husband, or a child or parent), not only does the check writer belong to the same name group as the person whose name appears on the check, but furthermore, and as an interesting twist, the personal name on the check constitutes a kind of trademark, which multiple people in the same business may use to complete transactions on behalf of the business. The court summarily rejected this last line of argument, holding, "the issue of the use of a trademark has no bearing on the fact that the person whose name appears on a check is solely responsible [for checks written in that name]."[70]

Suehiro's interpretation also cuts past the copyright issue, admitting that it may have some dispositive weight in the case, but nevertheless affirming that other case law established clearly that trademarks must be registered and intended to be shorthand abbreviations by which a company is known among the general public.[71] A personal name may be a trademark, but a personal name on a personal check cannot be, as it indicates a single person who, by check-writing conventions, promises the bearer of the check that there are funds sufficient to cover the check in the check-writer's personal bank account. For Suehiro, then, the copyright and trademark law, invoked by the plaintiff himself, is a distraction to the deeper question at issue: Is it legal for someone to write a check by "posing" as a relative who has the same last name?

In this small case, Suehiro saw a question of much bigger importance for Japanese society. "[I]f we were to allow people to write checks in other people's names," Suehiro wrote, "then, as the plaintiff himself says, it might 'deceive people' or 'harm the standard commerce in checks'." The damage potentially suffered by a small businesswoman like Mr. Makino's wife—had her husband a mind to defraud her using her checks—would not have been a social issue in and of itself, but bigger corporations had the potential to do much greater damage. (This, too, the plaintiff allowed to be true.) Therefore, Suehiro would not allow checks written by others under names not their own to be passed like certificates of security. Mr. Makino had argued that doing so was alright as long as such a check was exchanged among acquaintances or business partners, but Suehiro foresaw much room for mischief were this practice to become widespread, and demurred.

It was for precisely this reason, conversely, that Suehiro insisted that, contrary to the plaintiff's assertion, the person responsible for the check he wrote in his wife's name was actually his wife, and not he himself. The reason for this, Suehiro explained, was that, if Mrs. Makino, whose name appeared on the check, could not be held responsible, and if Mr. Makino was technically incapable of being held responsible, the check became a *de facto* fraudulent document. The problem was ultimately with the power of the check to make a fungible representation, a tradable promise of forthcoming funds. Mr. Makino had made such a promise by writing a good check, and his immediate acquaintances and business partners all traded on that promise in good faith. The problem would be if the check were to pass into the hands of a third party who had no knowledge of Mr. or Mrs. Makino. That third party would assume that Mrs. Makino had written the check, when in fact Mr. Makino had. This, Suehiro thought, the law should never allow, because it was a kind of unintended deception. Also possible, Suehiro argued, was a situation in which Mrs. Makino had, overtly or tacitly, allowed her name to be used by Mr. Makino when writing a check. Their business acquaintances might know of the innocent scheme, but third parties would not, so the result would be the same. In a society quickly passing from village to urban life, and from an agricultural to an industrial economy, it was essential that instruments of exchange be based on independently-verifiable criteria.

There is a further concern here. In a patriarchal society, Mr. Makino would have been able to conduct business on his wife's behalf even without her consent. But Suehiro is interested here in creating a new social order, in which women are able to conduct business independently while also free of the elements of *couverture* that had allowed husbands to act as proxies for their wives. As Suehiro explains,

> It is a common thing for a husband to borrow his wife's name when transacting business. Of course, some of these instances are true cases of agency [in which a husband legitimately acts on his wife's behalf], and should be recognized as such. But in many other cases, the husband acts only for his own interests, borrowing his wife's name for his own ends.[72]

Suehiro thus agrees with the *Daishin'in* in finding Mr. Makino's suit to be without merit. However, Suehiro goes one step further. The court found that, even if one were hypothetically to hold that "the name on the check is the wife's, and she must be responsible for the check, therefore the husband is not to be held responsible," it does not follow that the wife is responsible for the check even if the husband is not. The two parties' responsibility is "completely unrelated."[73] For Suehiro, this was not enough. A woman without adequate legal protection was at the whim of her father or husband—one custom that Suehiro was not willing to bring to bear on Japanese jurisprudence.

Like the legal and societal relations between the sexes, land rights were another frequent source of trouble in Taishō Japan. Case Thirty-One in the *Hanrei Minpō*, chosen by Hozumi, involves unclear land ownership after a single household head died intestate and with no relatives or heirs. There are two things that make this otherwise routine case interesting for Hozumi. First, the single household head, whom Hozumi calls "A," died during the Tokugawa Period, eighty-nine years prior to the court date in 1920 (Taishō 9) (i.e., in 1839). Second, the *Daishin'in*'s convoluted and specious ratiocination was, for Hozumi, so irritating that he seemed unable to resist publicizing, and publicly criticizing, the court for its equal devotion to ignorance and arrogance. This case shows the continuities and disjunctures from the Tokugawa to the Taishō and also highlights the need for a more responsive *Daishin'in* attention to the facts.

In 1839, A died without an heir. Thereafter, Y, presumably A's neighbor, began to encroach on A's unused fields. This situation continued for some time, until, during the first decade of the Taishō Period, the central government demanded proof of Y's ownership of the land in question. (Neither the court records nor Hozumi mention one way or another, but judging from the length of time that had elapsed since A's death nearly ninety years prior, it was almost certainly Y's progeny, and not the original Y himself, from whom the government demanded proof of ownership.) In response, Y countersued the government for confirmation of ownership. The government won the first round in court, and Y won the appeal, thus bringing the case to the *Daishin'in* for final judgment. The *Daishin'in* ruled that, according to Tokugawa law (literally, "law under the former *bakufu*"), commoners' land rights had never been absolute, and that, therefore, whenever a landowner died intestate and without heirs, the decedent's land was to "return completely to the national treasury" (*kanzen ni kokko ni kizoku su*). The *Daishin'in* stipulated, though, that Tokugawa law also called for the merits of owning such land to be taken into account before appropriating it. In the third judgment, the highest court wrestled with the possible implications of the country's appropriating a plot of farmland and chided the lower courts for not considering the consequences of the ownership of the land of long-dead A, according to a law that had been superseded for almost fifty years.

Hozumi's response to the muddled findings of the *Daishin'in* is one of barely concealed contempt. Indeed, Hozumi went so far as to call the *Daishin'in*'s decision an "exhibition of defects" (*ketten no chinretsukai*).[74] For Hozumi, there were no fewer than five main points of criticism with this case. First—a common point of criticism among all the members of Suehiro's group—the *Daishin'in* had not bothered to concern itself with the details of the case. None of the details are to be found in the *Daishin'in*'s records. The higher court judges focused solely on the reasoning employed by the appeals court in its decision. In a sense, the court of first instance acted as a kind of genericizing machine, transmogrifying contingency and particularity into clean entities amenable to the generalizing force of positive legislation. Once scrubbed of their individual qualities, "facts" could be subjected to a higher order of logic and reasoning, a process virtually guaranteed to protect the law at the cost of equity.

Second, although the *Daishin'in* spoke at length about Tokugawa law, nowhere did the court cite a single passage from anything but post-*bakufu* law.[75] Just as the court speculated on the case before it without any notion of the details of the dispute, so too did it hold forth on Tokugawa law without an indication of the supporting ordinances upon which it was relying in its decision-making.

Third, and related to the first two criticisms, Hozumi accused the judges of failing to consult related caselaw. Had the judges bothered to look, they would have found no fewer than twenty-three other cases germane to the question at hand, i.e., whether the land of someone who dies intestate and without heirs does or does not revert to state ownership.[76] Several of those precedential cases were decided by the *Daishin'in* and some just a few years prior to the case in question. For example, in a decision handed down by the *Daishin'in* Third Civil Law Division on February 17, 1915, followed by a decision rendered on February 20, 1918, by the Osaka Appeals Court First Civil Law Division,[77] the courts found that individual land rights under the Tokugawa regime had been "rights of general control" (*sōkatsuteki shihaiken*), while just over three months after the Osaka court's decision, on May 24, the *Daishin'in* First Civil Law Division had held that individual land rights under the Tokugawa had been "usufructuary rights" (*shiyō shūeki*). But the *Daishin'in* cited none of those cases in contending that Tokugawa land rights had been "limited ownership rights" (*seigenteki shoyūken*)[78] "none of which [rights] were rights of absolute ownership."[79] Hozumi takes the court to task for this inability to square its findings even with its own judgments, sometimes those as recent as just a few months prior.

Fourth, Hozumi criticizes the court's "leaps of logic" (*ronri ni chōyaku ga aru koto*).[80] First, Hozumi points out, the court sets for itself the premise that land ownership rights under the Tokugawa were limited but then immediately, and without any intervening justification, arrives at the conclusion that any land once belonging to someone who died intestate and without heirs would automatically revert to the national treasury.

Fifth, Hozumi criticizes the court for making a superfluous point seem to be the main point of contention in the case. This is ironic, because Hozumi suspects that the reason the court foregrounded such a minor point, even going so far as to select it as the excerpt that would stand as the case's abstract, was to chastise the lower courts for *their* error in judgment. Hozumi argues that the court gets the important points precisely backwards, loading up the court record with trivialities, thus obscuring the main facts and the issues of law. The gist of the case at hand, Hozumi points out, is that, in both the original judgment and the statement by the court of appeals, the lower courts mistakenly treated a Tokugawa problem as a Meiji problem. Instead of simply pointing this out and moving on to the main facts of the current case, though, the *Daishin'in*, Hozumi shows, indulged in a spree of "obiter dicta"[81].

This fifth and final point is of particular interest. One of the dangers of caselaw is that legislation will spring from the pen of one man, the judge, and not from a chamber of lawmakers through a process of public deliberation. Suehiro foresaw the problem of legislating from the bench by means of obiter dicta, and warned against it:

> That *obiter dict[a]* could give rise to incorrect predictions both constrains the judgment of the lower courts in this case, and also leads future judgments astray. [Obiter dicta] are not just useless. They are harmful.[82]

This is the obverse of the case-law coin. On the one hand, Suehiro and his group wanted judges to know the facts of the case and work within the confines of the case, the law, and precedent. On the other hand, judges might be tempted to make their influence extend too far beyond the proper bounds.

Concerns about obiter dicta notwithstanding, the consequences of societal change without corresponding legal protection are evident perhaps nowhere so much as in family law. Consider, for instance, Case No. 152, "Parental Custody Rights: A Request for the Return of a Child."[83] According to *Daishin'in* records, which were based upon the lower courts' presentation of the case, this was a simple question of child-custody rights requiring nothing more than a quick consultation of the positive law to resolve. In 1917, Y completed a transaction with X whereby Y, the natural parent of A, a nine-year-old girl, transferred guardianship of A to X for a period of ten years. (The parties in this case are anonymized in the original.) In exchange, Y received a payment of seventy yen and a promise by X to pay for the girl's boarding and training during that time, which X estimated would come to one thousand yen in total. Four years later, the natural parent, Y, petitioned the courts for the return of his daughter.

The court records present the case matter-of-factly, in a way that Hozumi describes as "appearing, in abstract form, extremely reasonable."[84] However, the facts of the case significantly complicate this abstraction. As we learn through Hozumi's investigation, the courts refused to accept the premise that the buying and selling of a nine-year-old girl was tantamount to "treating a person like a thing," despite the fact that the biological parent, Y, had sold his daughter to X in the full knowledge that X was running a geisha house and that the small child would immediately start working there as an apprentice geisha (*sūgi*). What's worse, it was not out of remorse for his earlier decision to sell his own child that Y was petitioning the courts to override his contract with X. Rather, Y openly admitted that he wanted A back in order to "sell [her] to another place as a *maiko* or else as a [full-fledged] geisha."[85]

In this case, the facts reveal the kind of society that arises when the law is privileged over empirical equity. The *Daishin'in* found that human trafficking in children was not technically illegal. Hozumi, however, investigated the facts of the case and came to a very different conclusion. If it is true that the father wants his daughter back only in order to resell her for a better price, then Y, Hozumi asserts, is a "highly dubious father." The very fact that someone would enter into such a business deal is, in and of itself, an abuse of parental rights. If "parental rights" includes the right to buy and sell children, then there is no limit to parental rights, and children are nothing but the "prey" (*kuimono*) of their parents.[86] As Hozumi explains:

> From the very beginning, the adoption contract into which X and Y have entered in this case was legally invalid. It is also clear from case law that 'adoptions for the sake of [apprenticing a girl to become] a geisha' are invalid. [...] It goes without saying that, just because someone runs a geisha house it doesn't mean he can't adopt someone. Besides, A clearly seems to be happy. Even if she's happy now, though, it would be entirely just to return her to her father if that father regretted his decision to sell her to a geisha house and wanted her to come home and share in the hardship of his poverty, and the law and the courts would be obliged to bring that eventuality about. [...] On the contrary, though, if the request for the reinstatement of parental rights is made, not out of self-sacrificial love for the child, but out of self-serving regard for one's own personal interests, then it would be an abuse of parental rights to allow [such a parent to regain custody of his child] if it meant that that child would be more unhappy than she were already.[87]

Parenthood, Hozumi explained, cannot possibly include the right to sell one's child.

Hozumi thought that the larger issue here was the definition of rights. Rights could not be absolute—they must be tempered by some larger consideration of consequence:

> Recently, the principle that 'the abuse of rights is not a right' [(*kenri no ranyō wa kenri ni arazu*)] has been recognized precisely in order to save us from losing sight of the true spirit of the law, which

> occurs when [people like] the parties in this case misuse a general definition of rights for their own personal benefit. I would like to see this principle put to use much more often. This is not solely a matter of protecting those who cannot protect themselves; it is also for the purpose of protecting the very concept of rights.[88]

Rights had entered the Japanese lexicon partly through the writings of Rousseau and J.S. Mill but were not seen as absolute in Japan.[89] The question was how to know how rights should be applied. For the Suehiro group, caselaw was the only way to navigate the tension between rights and reality.

Hozumi's protégé, Nakagawa Zennosuke, was also concerned with the position of the family within the Civil Code.[90] Nakagawa's particular focus was on the cooperation of husbands and wives, and he was influential in the drafting of the relevant passages of the new Civil Code. One short case selected by Nakagawa further demonstrates the importance of case law for filling in lacunae in the positive law, using unforeseeable situations as prompts to reconsider the scope of the law and clarify the way in which courts would decide similar cases.

Case 97, "Illegitimate Children—the Right to Request Acknowledgement [of Paternity] after a Father's Death," also brings up a question of rights which is not easily answered by positive law. [91] There are four plaintiffs in this case, and Nakagawa believes all four of them to be the illegitimate children of the same deceased man. Because the alleged father died without acknowledging any children, the children subsequently sued the public prosecutor for recognition of their status as the children of the deceased. According to the children's reasoning, because there was nothing in the Civil Code pertaining to a case such as theirs, in which children were seeking acknowledgement of paternity after an alleged father's death, after the court of first instance dismissed their suit on grounds of insufficient positive law to guide their decision, the children filed suit against the public prosecutor in accordance with Section Two, which stipulated the overturning of an invalidated marriage and the certification of illegitimate children. The *Daishin'in*, however, followed the lower courts in declaring that there was absolutely nothing in the law to guide this case. A father could obviously acknowledge paternity only while alive, and in any event a public prosecutor could not be sued as a way around this legal impasse.[92]

The *Daishin'in* found that:

> in general, because a request for acknowledgement [of paternity] does not involve a child defining his status vis-á-vis his father, the expression of intent [to acknowledge paternity] can be [issued] only while [a father] is alive. Furthermore, no other person can stand in the place [of the alleged father]. Also, the invalidity of a marriage, or the retraction of said invalidity, does not constitute the expression of [the alleged father's] intent, so seeking a declaration of either establishment and announcement or certification (*kakutei matawa sōsetsu no sengen*) [of paternity] is expressly different from the nature [of an acknowledgement of paternity].[93]

The black letter of the law is clear, and yet strict adherence to the law produces an absurdity: children without a father. Nakagawa took a more realistic view. While it was clearly beyond dispute that a dead man can neither confirm nor deny his paternity of a child, there nevertheless remained the fact of a relationship. It is preferable, Nakagawa asserted, to devise some fair method for evaluating the objective fact of a relationship, which would involve a specialized kind of acknowledgement [of paternity] not predicated exclusively upon recognition by the father alone.[94] In the present case, Nakagawa says, the existence of four illegitimate children testifies to the existence of a marital union (*jijitsu kon*, common-law marriage), even if that union was not officially recognized in the eyes of the law. Like Hozumi, Nakagawa further recommends harsh criticism for the courts, both the lower courts and the *Daishin'in*, for pedantically examining only the abstracted logic of the law without taking into account the very real human consequences of the positive law's obvious shortcomings. Not only are four children left fatherless *de facto*, they are also left fatherless *de jure*, and are furthermore effectively disinherited from their biological father's estate.

While family law was of primary importance to Hozumi and Nakagawa, Wagatsuma Sakae was more interested in economic transactions, and how case law could be used to attenuate the logic of capitalism. One of the cases that Wagatsuma selected for inclusion in the *Hanrei Minpō*—Case No. 21, "Leasing: The Rights of a Leaser vis-á-vis an Illegal Occupant: Are Lease Rights Property?"[95]—illustrates not only Wagatsuma's concern that law be better equipped to deal with the complexities of the economy, but also shows how instrumental judges during the Taishō period were in smoothing out discrepancies between the positive law and the real world of uncertain ownership and financing rights.

In this case, Y leased a plot of land from the City of Tokyo, but a certain X already owned a building on that land. After X refused to respond to Y's request for clarification [presumably of X's purported right to build and/or own structures on said land], Y filed suit. The court of first instance agreed with Y's claim, finding that, because lease rights are real rights, Y had the authority directly to remove the offending structures from his property. Furthermore, the court ruled that, even if lease rights are merely credit obligations, X's actions were illegal because they infringed on those obligations, meaning that Y would have the right not only to sue for reparation of any damages incurred thereby, but also to remove the conditions causing said damage.[96]

Not surprisingly after such a lopsided rejection of his claims on two fronts, X appealed. The *Daishin'in* disagreed with the lower courts' interpretation of the law, finding that, on the first point:

> although there are academic theories that lease rights are also, for example, rights of control, according to our [i.e., the Japanese] Civil Code, they are credit obligations, and as the Civil Code is abundantly clear on that point, there is no further need of discussion.[97]

Based upon this finding on the first point of contention, the *Daishin'in* found that lease rights were not absolute, meaning that, if Y had a grievance against X's allegedly occupying a structure on Y's land, Y was not entitled to raze said structure at will. Rather, Y's course of action would be to petition the court for monetary compensation for his losses. As Wagatsuma points out, the lower courts in this case tried "furtively to test out their theory that lease rights are real rights,"[98] an effort that the *Daishin'in* dismissed out of hand. Wagatsuma further explains that, although there seemed to be a loophole in the positive law, allowing a leaser forcibly to re-occupy a structure in which someone else was actively claiming rights of occupation and then petitioning the courts to recognize the legality of having returned the disputed property to its "rightful" owner (regardless of who built the structure), case law had long since cleared up this discrepancy. Wagatsuma closed by hoping that because instances abound in which rights and obligations in the real world are murky and do not readily conform to the generic provisions of the positive law, the courts will take more trouble to come into contact with reality when dealing with cases brought before them.

The Caselaw Turn and its Legacy

The caselaw compendium compiled by Suehiro and his research group from their studies of the *Daishin'in* brings to life for us today the immediacy of the past at street level. And yet, Suehiro and his group's work have been largely forgotten today, relegated to the foonotes of modern history books or else overlooked entirely. In the end, what was the historical legacy of the practice of case law in Japan after Suehiro's intervention? Did Suehiro and his group effect a case law revolution? Or did the project create more heat than light, fizzling out early without bringing about a change in the way law was practiced in Japan? And, even if Suehiro might have reshaped, at least in some small way, the legal culture of prewar Japan, did his contribution to jurisprudence survive the seismic shift of 1945 and the subsequent grand reformation of the Japanese way of law under Allied occupation?

After the ouster of Minobe Tatsukichi in 1934, and the concomitant attacks on left-wing intellectuals by kokutai guardsmen like Minoda Muneki, Suehiro's case law revolution went into a state of abatement until the end of the Pacific War. (See Ch. 5 of the present volume.) Yūhikaku continued publishing the Civil Code caselaw of Suehiro and his group,[99] but until 1947 there was no official report of lower court decisions, with the exception of what few cases were synopsized in the journal *Legal News.*[100] With the American Occupation of Japan, and in particular the drafting of the new constitution in 1947 and the raft of new legislation following in its wake, the composition and procedural protocol of Japanese jurisprudence changed substantially. Alfred Oppler, who oversaw the overhaul of the legal system during the Occupation, was a self-described "evangelical liberal" who, like much of the rest of the GHQ staff, wanted to remake all of Japan in the image of Washington, DC.[101] In a victory for the caselaw method, in 1947 the Japanese government gave tacit acceptance to the by-then longstanding practice of judges' consulting former cases when deciding new ones. Although the new Constitution expressly stated that only the Diet,[102] and decisions rendered by the Supreme Court,[103] were to be considered sources of law, this was an admission that judges had long been referring to other cases in arriving at their decisions.

In Japan today there remains, as before the war, no firm policy of *stare decisis.*[104] However, lawyers and judges alike routinely rely on case law and commentaries to augment their understanding of statutory law. Although "Article 4 of the Court Organization Law [of] 1947 provides that 'a conclusion in a decision of a superior court shall bind courts below in respect of the case concerned'"[105] (thus instituting a kind of mono-directional, ad hoc *stare decisis* system), "Article 76(3) of the [Japanese] constitution provides that judges 'shall be independent in the exercise of their conscience and shall be bound only by this constitution and the laws'."[106] As one authority on Japanese legal practice asserts, the widespread popularity of journals such as *Jurist*, *Hanrei Jihō*, and *Hanrei Times* probably means that lawyers and judges in Japan rely on case law much more than is commonly realized.[107] Even without explicitly citing case law in their decisions, for example, judges are very likely to have read about the appurtenant case law in one of the three journals listed above and thus to have been influenced in their decisions accordingly. One of the shadows cast by Suehiro's law and society intervention into caselaw is the socialization of jurisprudence—judges read one another's decisions, and a consensus is thereby formed, even if the practice is not openly advertised. While Japan remains, in point of fact, a civil-code country, wherein commentaries by scholars are acknowledged to draw much of their weight from the Germanic legal tradition, in actual practice Suehiro's case-law revolution has attained a quiet and enduring victory.

Beyond the jurisprudential ramifications, the work of Suehiro and the caselaw study group helped change the dynamic between society and law. For a brief moment in the early 1920s, the intellectual thrust of Taishō Democracy was pushed past the confines of the legal academy and into wider society. As will be shown in the next chapter, this trend was greatly accelerated by the devastating 1923 earthquake that leveled much of Tokyo, as Suehiro and his team rolled up their sleeves and left offices and courtrooms behind entirely in the attempt to domesticate Taishō Democracy and bring equity to the masses. But the earthquake was also the impetus behind the law-and-society movement's turn to cooperation with empire. Blindsided by the imperial state, the law-and-society movement faltered, and Suehiro and many of his contemporaries chose collaboration as the key to achieving the social cohesion they once sought in the study of cases. In the ongoing dialectic between law and society, the empire turned out to be the synthesis they thought they had been looking for.

NOTES

1. Suehiro, *Hanrei Minpō,* op. cit., 9
2. Nihon Hyōronsha Henshūkyoku, ed. *Nihon no Hōgaku,* op. cit., 13-14.
3. See J.H. Burns, "Bentham and the French Revolution," *Transactions of the Royal Historical Society,* vol. 16 (1966), 95-114.
4. *Aru hōgakusha no kiseki* (Tokyo: Yūhikaku, 1978), 72-73. Kawashima relates that he was "scolded severely" by Suehiro for failing to grasp this essential principle in one of Kawashima's early Minpō Hanrei Kenkyūkai reports. See ibid., 66 ff.
5. See Douglas Howland, *Translating the West: Language and Political Reason in Nineteenth-Century Japan* (Honolulu: University of Hawai'i Press, 2002), and *Personal Liberty and Public Good: The Introduction of John Stuart Mill to Japan and China* (Toronto: University of Toronto Press, 2005).
6. Cf., e.g., Ernest Gellner's *geschlossener Handelstaat,* or "autarchic modern state," in *Nations and Nationalism* (Cornell: Cornell University Press, 1983), 107.
7. Minpō Hanrei Kenkyūkai, *Furoku: Minpō hanrei kenkyūroku* (1922), op. cit., 1877.
8. Especially after the Administrative Justice Act, Meiji 23. See Norikazu Kawagishi, "The birth of judicial review in Japan," *International Journal of Constitutional Law* (2007) 5 (2): 308–331, esp. 314 ff.
9. Suehiro, *Hanrei Minpō,* op. cit., 7
10. Suehiro, *Hanrei Minpō,* op. cit., 1-2
11. Suehiro, *Hanrei Minpō,* op. cit., 2
12. *Nihongo no ikizumari mondai: bunka undō toshite no Ro-maji no undō,* appearing in "Pamphlet no. 5 of the Japan Latin Script Society, From kanji to Latin letters!!" (*Nihon Ro-maji Kai pamphlet, daigo satsu, kanji kara Ro-maji e!!*), npd, but dated "1934" with library stamp on inside cover. ("*Nippongo wo Rōmazi de! Nipponsikino Rōmazi de!*").
13. Suehiro, *Nihongo no ikizumari mondai,* op. cit., 1.
14. Suehiro, *Nihongo no ikizumari mondai,* op. cit., 2.
15. Emphases in original. Suehiro, *Nihongo no ikizumari mondai,* op. cit., 4.
16. From "Minshū no hōritsu," Vol. 5, No. 1 (August, year not specified), (Osaka/Tokyo: Minshū no Hōritsusha), collected in Suehiro, *Minpō kōwa,* Vol. 1, op. cit., 61.

17. Suehiro, *Hanrei Minpō*, op. cit., 1-3. Suehiro also expounds upon these ideas in more detail in a later work, *Hōgaku nyūmon* (Tokyo: Nihon Hyōronsha, 1952), 157-58. See also Hiroshi Itoh, "How Judges Think in Japan," *The American Journal of Comparative Law*, Vol. 18 (1970), 782-785, as cited in Koichiro Fujikura, ed., *Japanese Law and Legal Theory* (New York, NY: New York University Press, 1996), 94-97.
18. Suehiro, *Hanrei Minpō*, op. cit., 4.
19. Suehiro, *Hanrei Minpō*, op. cit., 7-8. Cf. Kobayashi Satoshi, "Suehiro Izutarō no hanrei kenkyū hōhōron to sono genkai," *Hersetec: Journal of Hermeneutic Study and Education of Textual Configuration* 4, 2 (2010), 41-58.
20. Tōkyō daigaku hanrei kenkyūkai, ed., *Hanrei minjihō* (Tokyo: Yūhikaku, 1947), 1.
21. See, for example, Dan Fenno Henderson's "Law and Political Modernization in Japan," Chapter XI of Robert E. Ward, ed., *Political Development in Modern Japan* (Princeton: Princeton University Press, 1968), 387-456. Tokugawa law required judges to override even the Osadamegaki, or great Tokugawa decrees, where application of the decrees would have resulted in a miscarriage of justice.
22. *Uso no Kōyō*, 2, book form (Tokyo: Kaizōsha, 1923).
23. *Uso no Kōyō*, op. cit., 8, also 10.
24. *Uso no Kōyō*, op. cit., 8.
25. See Ishii Shirō, "'Uso no kōyō' to Ōoka sabaki," in *Tosho* 290 (October, 1973), 52-56.
26. Suehiro, *Uso no Kōyō*, op. cit., 12.
27. Ibid., 13, ff.
28. Ibid., 14-15.
29. Ibid., 16.
30. Ibid., 22.
31. Ibid., 28.
32. Ibid., 32.
33. Ibid., 33.
34. Ibid., 43.
35. Ibid., 44.
36. Ibid., 47.
37. Minpō Hanrei Kenkyūkai, *Hanrei Minpō* (Tokyo: Yūhikaku, 1921), 1. Kawashima remembers Suehiro having been undogmatic in his legal reasoning in general. See Kawashima, *Aru hōgakusha no kiseki*, op. cit., 62.

38. Minpō Hanrei Kenkyūkai, "Furoku: Minpō hanrei kenkyūroku, Taishō jūichi nen do (ichi)," Hōgaku kyōkai jimusho, *Hōgaku kyōkai zasshi*, Vol. 40, No. 10 (1922), 1873-1874.
39. See Haley, *Authority without Power: Law and the Japanese Paradox* (Oxford: Oxford University Press, 1991), 85-86.
40. Ronald P. Dore and Ōuchi Tsutomu, "Rural Origins of Japanese Fascism," in J.W. Morley, ed., *Dilemmas of Growth in Prewar Japan* (Princeton: Princeton University Press, 1971), 203, and Hozumi Shigetō, "Chōtei hō," *Gendai hōgaku zenshū*, Vol. 38 (Tokyo: Nihon Hyōronsha, 1931). Cited in Haley, *Authority without Power*, op. cit., 93, fn. 45. See also Dan Fenno Henderson, *Conciliation and Japanese Law: Tokugawa and Modern*, 2 Vols. (Seattle: University of Washington Press, 1965).
41. Suehiro, "Baishin hōan wo yomitaru ato no kansō," *Uso no kōyō*, op. cit., 393-408.
42. *Tōkyō Asahi Shimbun*, July 17, 1919, 2, cited in Haley, *Authority without Power*, op. cit., 86.
43. Some sources give the transliteration as "Shinyomaru". http://www.yokohama-album.jp/picture/detail/5869/ http://homepage3.nifty.com/jpnships/company/toyokisen_meiji.htm
44. Isoda Susumu, et al., "Hozumi hōgaku, Suehiro hōgaku no bunseki to hihan," *Hōshakaigaku* (1952), 53.
45. Nihon Hyōronsha Henshūkyoku, ed. *Nihon no Hōgaku*, op. cit., 5-6.
46. See Law 222, Art. 752 (mutual support) and 760 (sharing of expenses), as cited in Tanaka Shigetō, "Against Intra-Household Exploitation: Philosophy and Policy for Equity within the Family in Japanese Context," East Asian Social Policy Research Network International Conference (Sep., 2007). See also Nakagawa Zennosuke, "Shinzokuteki fuyō gimu no honshitsu," in *Hōgaku shinpō*, 38 (6) (1928), 1-22
47. Cited in Dan Fenno Henderson, "Law and Political Modernization in Japan," Ch. 11, *Political Development in Japan*, ed. Robert E. Ward (Princeton: Princeton University Press, 1968), 438, fn 94. See also Norikazu Kawagishi, "The birth of judicial review in Japan," *International Journal of Constitutional Law* (2007) 5 (2): 308-331, esp. 315-316. "The logic of the Meiji constitution was that the emperor himself limited his power according to the intent and practices of the founder and ancestors. This was an attempt to forge a compromise between traditional Japanese authoritarianism and Western constitutionalism, but it was not constitutional government in any Western sense. [...] Even the emperor himself could not be considered completely free or autonomous

because his status and power were inherited from his ancestors in a lineal succession." (315-316)

48. Marilyn Ivy, *Discourses of the Vanishing: Modernity, Phantasm, Japan* (Chicago: University of Chicago Press, 1995).
49. On class divisions among legal practitioners themselves, see Etō Yoshihiro, "Kakyū hōritsu jitsumuka to jōkyū hōritsu jitsumuka," in Kawashima Takeyoshi, ed., *Hō shakai gaku kōza 8, shakai to hō 2* (Tokyo: Iwanami Shoten, 1973), 362-375.
50. "Hōritsu fukyū no tame hakasetachi ga enzetsu," *Yomiuri Shimbun* (May 24, 1921), 5
51. Fukuzawa Yukichi, *Gakusha no shokubun wo ronzu*, 6, as cited in Flaherty, *Public Law, Private Practice*, op. cit., 157-58.
52. Suehiro's family was elite, and his mother's side "super elite". Shichinohe, "Suehiro Izutarō no seishun," op. cit., 409-10.
53. Minpō Hanrei Kenkyūkai, *Hanrei Minpō*, op. cit., 1. The authors are listed as Hozumi Shigetō, Suehiro Izutarō, Azuma Suehiko, Wagatsuma Sakae, Hirano Yoshitarō, Nakagawa Zennosuke, and Tanaka Seiji. In the introduction (*jo*), Suehiro writes: "The team later included Hatoyama [Hideo], Matsumoto [Jōji], Tanaka Kōtarō, Kikui [Tsunahiro], Fujita [?], Hirai [Tomisaburō?], and Yamao [?]." Ibid., 10-11.
54. See Nihon Daigaku Hōgakkai, "Azuma Suehiko hakase tsuitōgō," *Nihon Hōgaku*, vol. 46, no. 2 (1981) and Azuma Suehiko, pub., *Mita mama kiita mama: meihō Doku-I ni tsukashite* (not for sale, Tokyo: 1942).
55. For a more detailed view of Suehiro's group, especially as they worked to compile case law pertaining to the Civil Code, see Ōkawa Sumio, "Daishin'in (Minji) hanreishū no hensan to Daishin'in hanrei shinsakai," *Ritsumeikan Legal Studies*, Vol. 6, No. 256 (1997), 139 ff., accessed at http://www.ritsumei.ac.jp/acd/cg/law/lex/97-6/okawa.htm
56. Hozumi Shigetō, *Shihō seikatsu*, Ch. 1, "Hōritsu to seikatsu," in *Saishin kōminka shiryō seisetsu, Bunbushō hensan* (Tōkyō: Teikoku Kōmin Kyōiku Kyōkai, 1931), 5.
57. There were two temples in Japan—in Nitta (Mantokuji) and Kamakura (Tōkeiji)—where women could remain for three years in monastic seclusion in order to be considered divorced. See Ishii Ryōsuke, "Enkiridera: Tōkeiji no baai," in *Hōgaku kyōkai zasshi*, Vol. 76 (1959), 401, and Vol. 77 (1961), 127 and 413. Cited in Dan Fenno Henderson, "Law and Political Modernization in Japan," 402, fn 20, in Robert E. Ward, ed., *Political Development in Modern Japan*, op. cit.
58. Hozumi Shigetō, *Rikon seido no kenkyū* (Tōkyō: Kaizōsha, 1924).

59. See, e.g., *Sōzokuhō no shomondai,* (Tokyo: Keisō Shōbo, 1949).
60. See Law 222, Art. 752 (mutual support) and 760 (sharing of expenses), as cited in Tanaka Shigetō, "Against Intra-Household Exploitation: Philosophy and Policy for Equity within the Family in Japanese Context," East Asian Social Policy Research Network International Conference (Sep., 2007). See also Nakagawa Zennosuke, "Shinzokuteki fuyō gimu no honshitsu," in *Hōgaku shinpō,* 38 (6): 1-22. 1928. Nakagawa's views on the nature of the law are summarized in his *Minpō: ikiteiru hanrei,* 1E (Tokyo: Nihon Hyōronsha, 1962).
61. Hirano translated and edited some of Wittfogel's classic early works on China. See Hirano Yoshitarō and Moritani Katsumi, eds. and trans., *Tōyōteki shakai riron* (Tōkyō: Nihon Hyōronsha, 1939).
62. See, for example, his series of short books on Japanese capitalism, titled *Nihon shihonshugi hattatsushi kōza.* See also *Burujoa minshushugi kakumei* (Tōkyō: Hōsei University Press, 1968), part of the series *Nihon shihonshugi kenkyū.* Hirano was still a Marxist as late as 1933. See, e.g., his *Meiji ishin no henkaku ni tomonau atarashii kaikyū bunka to shakaiteki seijiteki undō* (1932) and *Meiji ishin ni okeru seijiteki shihai keitai* (1933) (Tōkyō: Iwanami Shoten), both part of the series *Nihon shihonshugi hattatsushi kōza.* For a contextualization of Hirano's writings within the larger Marxist historiography on the Meiji Restoration, see Germaine A. Hoston, "Conceptualizing Bourgeois Revolution: The Prewar Japanese Left and the Meiji Restoration," *Comparative Studies in Society and History,* Vo. 33, No. 3 (Jul., 1991), 539-581.
63. For an account of Hirano's conversion from Marxism to pan-Asianism, see Mutō Shūtarō, "Hirano Yoshitarō: 'The Historical Basis of Greater Asianism', 1945," Ch. 30 in Sven Saaler and Christopher W. A. Szpilman, eds., *Pan-Asianism: A Documentary History, Vol. 2: 1920-Present* (Plymouth, UK: Rowman and Littlefield, 2011), 271 ff.
64. See, for example, his "Senshisha no tsuma no sōzokuken," Ch. 9, 84 ff., and "Katei to hōritsu," Ch. 24, 275 ff., in *Atarashii ie no rinri* (Tōkyō: Gakufū shoin, 1949).
65. Matsuno Yoshitora, *Wagatsuma Sakae: hito to jidai* (Sendai: Gyōsei, 1993), 337.
66. Ibid.
67. *Hanrei minpō, mokuji,* op. cit., beg. 1.
68. *Hanrei Minpō,* op. cit., Case 22, 65.
69. *Hanrei Minpō,* op. cit., 366.
70. *Hanrei Minpō,* op. cit., 368.

71. Court of Cassation 39-10-4, Civ Code 1-12-1, 203.
72. *Hanrei Minpō*, op. cit., 366.
73. *Hanrei Minpō*, op. cit., 372.
74. *Hanrei Minpō*, op. cit., 86.
75. Specifically, the Grand Council of State proclamation no. 20, Meiji 17 (1884), and the Civil Code, section 239, item 2 (86).
76. *Hanrei Minpō*, op. cit., 87.
77. Ibid.
78. *Hanrei Minpō*, op. cit., 87.
79. *Hanrei Minpō*, op. cit., 87.
80. *Hanrei Minpō*, op. cit., 88.
81. *Hanrei Minpō*, op. cit., 88. Hozumi uses the Latin phrase, preceded by its Sino-Japanese equivalent: "*boron* (*obiter dictum*)".
82. *Hanrei Minpō*, op. cit., 88.
83. *Hanrei Minpō* Case 152, *Shinken—yōji hikiwatashi no seikyū*, 514-518
84. Ibid., 515.
85. Ibid., 516.
86. Suehiro also used this exact word, "prey," in a newspaper article from 1920, in which he advocated making the age of seniority eighteen, because so many children were being "preyed upon" by their parents and legal guardians: "Guardians and people with parental custody are not always entirely concerned with caring [for their children]. On the contrary, there are more than a few cases in which [such people] prey upon [their children] for their own benefit." *Yomiuri Shimbun* (Dec. 22, 1920), 5.
87. *Hanrei Minpō*, op. cit., 517-518.
88. Ibid., 519.
89. See Howland, *Translating the West*, op. cit.
90. See Nakagawa Zennosuke, "Ūzusuko," in *Shinkō kagaku no hata no moto ni*, 1: 68-90, esp. 77. Cited in Kevin M. Doak, "Under the Banner of the New Science: History, Science, and the Problem of Particularity in Early Twentieth-Century Japan," *Philosophy East and West*, Vol. 48, No. 2 (Apr. 1998), 232-256, esp. 243 (& fn 48).
91. "Shiseishi—chichi no shibōgo ni okeru ninchi seikyūken," *Hanrei minpō*, op. cit., 303-305.
92. Ibid., 302-303.
93. Ibid., 303-304.
94. Ibid., 304.

95. "Chintaishaku—fuhō senyūsha ni taisuru chinshakujin no kenri—chinshakuken wa bukken ka?" *Hanrei minpō*, op. cit., 63-65.
96. Ibid., 63-64.
97. Ibid., 64. "Chinshakuken wa tatoi kore wo shihaiken nari to ronzuru gakusetsu aru ni seyo, waga Minpō ni yoreba isshu no saiken naru koto, dōhō no kiteijō meihaku ni shite, imasara tagen no yō nashi"
98. Ibid., 64.
99. See, e.g., *Hanrei Minjihō*, 1935 edition (1936).
100. See Meryll Dean, *Japanese Legal System* (2E) (London: Cavendish: 2002), 135, fn 34: "Prior to 1947, there was no official reporting of lower court decisions, although some of the more important decisions did make it to *Legal News*."
101. See Richard H. Minear, "Review of *Legal Reform in Occupied Japan: A Participant Looks Back*," The *American Historical Review*, vol. 81, no. 5 (December, 1976), 1205.
102. Article 41. The Diet shall be the highest organ of state power, and shall be the sole law-making organ of the State.
103. Article 76. The whole judicial power is vested in a Supreme Court and in such inferior courts as are established by law. No extraordinary tribunal shall be established, nor shall any organ or agency of the Executive be given final judicial power. All judges shall be independent in the exercise of their conscience and shall be bound only by this Constitution and the laws.
104. An important distinction must be made, when discussing stare decisis in Japan, between *ratio decidendi* and *obiter dicta*. At the Common Law, only the former has precedential force; the latter is extraneous. But Japanese judges, not in the habit of citing case law at all even when having consulted it, do not make this distinction; therefore, the entirety of their decisions may become part of the case law, either directly or indirectly. See, e.g., Toshiaki Iimura, Ryu Takabayashi, and Christoph Rademacher, "The Binding Nature of Court Decisions in Japan's Civil Law System, China Guiding Cases Project," June 30, 2015, available at https://cgc.law.stanford.edu/commentaries/14-Iimura-Takabayashi-Rademacher . See also Shigenori Matsui, "Constitutional Precedents in Japan: A Comment on the Role of Precedents," *Washington University Law Review*, Vol. 88, Issue 6, Decision Making on the Japanese Supreme Court, 1669-1680.

105. Dean, *Japanese Legal System*, op. cit., 136. See also Nobuo Yamamoto, "Guide to Japanese Legal Literature," *International Journal of Law Libraries*, vol. 7 (1979), 177.
106. Dean, *Japanese Legal System*, op. cit., 136
107. See Ishida Takashi, "Case Law in Japan," *International Journal of Law Libraries* (1979), 135-48, cited in Dean, *Japanese Legal System*, op. cit.

Chapter 4

Settlement Houses and the Law-and-Society Movement after the Great Kantō Earthquake

The Great Kantō Earthquake

During the first phase of his work after returning to Tokyo Imperial University following a more-than-two-year study abroad visit to Europe and the United States, Suehiro Izutarō, influenced by the legal pragmatism of American jurist Roscoe Pound and the sociological jurisprudence advocated by Austrian legal thinker Eugen Ehrlich, attempted to work within the existing legal institutions of Japan—namely, the courts and the legal profession—to ameliorate Japan's social ills. However, despite Suehiro's search for a truly apolitical form of equity, his project for domesticating Taishō Democracy remained embedded in the court system, discussed in the popular and highbrow press and confined to the halls of his university—one of the most elite institutions in prewar Japan. It was after the Great Kantō Earthquake (*Kantō daishinsai*) on September 1, 1923, that Suehiro, faced with the immediacy of post-earthquake suffering, moved away from institutional case law-based gradualism and Ehrlichian legal custom research and towards the hands-on interventionism of the Settlement House he founded at the Tokyo Imperial University to help the urban poor. This move, in turn, coupled with attacks on him by kokutai crusaders in the academy and the press, precipitated Suehiro's transformation from apolitical activist to proponent of the Japanese empire.

Suehiro's studies with Pound and Ehrlich had led him to believe that the law was capacious and elastic enough to accommodate social problems and provide a venue for solving them. In publications such as "Law and custom: observations on research methods in Japanese jurisprudence" and "Custom as fact,"[1] Suehiro had laid out his rationality and program for bringing the "security of the law" to the common people. After September 1, 1923, Suehiro largely abandoned his earlier, Poundian/Ehrlichian focus on laws and courts and individual cases in favor of a combined approach, sending the law-and-society heuristic out into the streets, as it were, to grapple with the problems which the Japanese legal system by itself was incapable of adequately addressing. For Suehiro, the law-and-society movement, which he and his small band of law-and-society colleagues at the Tokyo Imperial University had brought to Japan from Europe and the United States (as well as rediscovered deep in the Tokugawa legal tradition), would have to be modified, pushed into a more dynamic role and made to engage more directly with political realities.

The impetus for the change can be pinpointed down to the minute. At 11:58 am on September 1, 1923, the capital city of Japan was struck by a magnitude 7.9 earthquake, which wrought massive structural and personal devastation. To give just a few examples, the Asakusa Twelve-Storeys, which had become a popular symbol of Tokyo's ascendancy, was rent in two, its bricks "cascading" downwards as the supporting structure twisted and bent grotesquely in the whiplike convulsions, leaving behind just one uncollapsed wall, "like a thin sword," when all was over.[2] St. Nikolai's Eastern Orthodox Cathedral, a testament to the cosmopolitanism of new Edo, lost its dome to the temblor. Of the Yokohama Specie Bank, only the front door remained standing, the rest of the building a heap of pulverized stone studded with the large steel safes which had collapsed through the disintegrating edifice. Tokyo Bay stood choked with wooden beams and bridge railings. In many places, piles of bodies dwarfed the strewn debris.[3]

Even worse than the earthquake damage was the devastation visited upon Tokyo by the fire that engulfed most of the city almost as soon as the first wave of tremors had passed. As the earthquake struck almost exactly at the beginning of the lunch hour, cooking fires throughout the city were readying the midday repast for the approximately four and a half million people[4] living in the greater Tokyo area.[5] Fires sweeping through Tokyo were nothing new, of course. The "flowers of Edo" that had charred the wood-and-paper city countless times in the past were so commonplace as to have become literary tropes by the end of the Tokugawa Period. But the population density of the industrializing capital, coupled with the gas lines, factories, and warehouses able to add fuel to a conflagration, all combined to turn, virtually overnight, the proudly modern symbol of Japan's new age into a hyper-modern realist portrait of previously unthinkable levels of destruction. So bad and widespread was the damage that the Imperial Household was forced to issue a proclamation on September 12, less than two weeks after the disaster, that, contrary to rumors and anti-Kantō political intriguing, Tokyo would, in fact, remain the imperial capital.[6]

It is not hard to understand why people would have expected the seat of government to be moved, as Tokyo had been virtually annihilated in the first week of September. The *Nihon Denpō* for Sep. 2, 1923, opens with "City of Tokyo Gone," and proceeds to describe the fires raging through the collapsed buildings in vivid detail.[7] The fires burned for two full days, until September 3, and consumed 300,924 households out of a total of 483,000 in the entire city.[8] Every structure in Nihonbashi Ward, at the heart of old Edo and also of the new Tokyo, was completely burned. Almost every structure in Kanda, Asakusa, and Honjo was consumed by the flames, too.[9] In all, some 44 percent of the greater Tokyo metropolitan area was lost to the raging fire. According to a report issued by the Social Bureau of the Ministry of Home Affairs (*Naimushō Shakaikyoku*) in 1926, 91,344 people died (75,953, or some 83 percent, in the post-earthquake inferno), 52,084 people were wounded, and 13,275 people were still listed as missing three years after the disaster. Many of the dead, missing, and wounded were thought to have perished, disappeared, or been injured while attempting to swim into the Sumida River to escape the wall of flames.[10]

Suehiro was with his family in Karuizawa when the earthquake struck. He took the train the next day for Tokyo only to find his research room, books, classrooms, and library in ruin:

> [When Suehiro arrived at Tokyo Imperial University on September 2,] he found his Civil Code Research Room burned to the ground, and the university library also completely destroyed by fire. The Joseph Kohler collection, the sale of which Suehiro was in the process of arranging, was also reduced to ashes.[11]

One can only imagine the dejection with which Suehiro must have gazed upon his entire life's work up to that point turned overnight into a pile of ash and rubble. Suehiro had little time to dwell on his misfortune because "several thousand refugees had gathered inside what had been the campus of the Tokyo Imperial University."[12] Presented with this press of destitute humanity, the university students had "taken the initiative [... and] commandeered a delivery truck to fetch rice and other foodstuffs, which the students distributed [to the refugees]."[13] Suehiro sprang into action, too, "spurred on by his students" and "astonishing" them in turn with his vigor in helping with the relief effort.[14]

One of Suehiro's first tasks was to help at the Tokyo Victims' Information Station (*Tōkyō risaisha jōhōkyoku*), an information-relay station for connecting the droves of people left homeless by the earthquake with the friends and relatives searching for them.[15] On October 1, this initial triage and relief operation came to a halt as the new, much more involved work of caring for the refugees in the long-term began.[16] Suehiro, reflecting wistfully in a speech that month,[17] said that, while he had read Natsume Sōseki's *Gubijinsō*[18] as a high school student, he felt that he had never understood the basics of life [until his work with the earthquake relief effort].[19] Natsume Sōseki had been Suehiro's English teacher at the exclusive First Higher School in Tokyo.[20] Having studied Natsume's works in classrooms, Suehiro was now living them in the streets. The scion of a *Daishin'in* justice and the product of an elite education, which included a two-year sojourn at some of the finest universities in Europe and the United States and a stint at the negotiating table during the proceedings surrounding the drafting of the Treaty of Versailles, Suehiro stumbled onto the ruined campus of the Tokyo Imperial University in early September 1923, to find that, for perhaps the first time in his life, he would have the opportunity actually to live and work among the proletariat.

It was partly due to the inspiration that students took from Suehiro's speech that they decided to set up a Settlement House—a "student movement centered on the person of Prof. Suehiro"[21]—in a slum in Fukagawa in Honjo. [22] The students named their project the "University Settlement," obtaining land in the Fukagawa Sarue-Uramachi area for the purpose.[23] (This is the project that would later be known as the Yanagishima Settlement.[24]) On June 10, 1924, some nine months after the earthquake, the Settlement House in Honjo/Yanagishima was completed, and the first nine residents, known as "settlers," moved in:[25] Uchimura Haruji, Hattori Shisō (1901–1956), Nakatsuka Fumio, Mōri Hideoto (1902–1947), Masutani Tatsunosuke, Nagaya Toshio, Azuma Toshihisa, Nakano Hisao, and Edayoshi Isamu.[26] The money to build the house was provided by four main sources:

1/ 2,500 yen from the Ministry of Culture (Monbushō) as a token of thanks to the Tokyo University Disaster Information Station (Tōdai Shinsai Jōhōkyoku)

2/ 1,000 yen collected from students who had returned to their home provinces

3/ 1,000 yen for the preparation of a map showing the extent of the earthquake damage

4/ 4,000 yen collected in Kyushu by the Tokyo University Shinjinkai

To this was added money donated by Suehiro himself, and money collected from the sale of donated materials such as cloth and lumber, for a total of more than 23,000 yen.

The Settlement residents worked in seven broad areas of social activism, as reflected in the seven different departments into which the settlers divided up their tasks:[27]

1/ Survey Department (chōsabu) This department was tasked with surveying the Yanagishima area to learn the conditions of the local population and then preparing pamphlets reporting these findings.[28]

2/ Laborers' Education Department (rōdōsha kyōikubu) This department conducted classes and seminars for the education of workers on such topics as the system of labor law (an effort led by Suehiro himself). The leftist student-group Shinjinkai[29] was instrumental in staffing the department and also incorporated members of the Society for Social Thought (*shakai shisōsha*).[30]

3/ Citizens' Education Department (shimin kyōikubu) The purpose of this department was to educate the general population, including child laborers working in factories who were unable to attend school with other children.[31]

4/ Medical Treatment Department (iryōbu) This department provided free-of-charge medical services to the people in the neighborhood, a sector of the Settlement activities that also included carrying out censuses of hygienic conditions in Yanagishima. This task was made especially pressing by the fact that Yanagishima was situated in a low-lying area, with the pooled, stagnant water along roadways contributing to the occasional outbreak of diseases such as typhoid fever.[32]

5/ Children's Department (jidōbu) Separate from the Childcare Department (no. 7 below), the Children's Department was tasked strictly with educating children (using "democratic education" (*minshu kyōiku*) methods[33]) and providing them with space to play. Field trips such as picnics were also part of the activities coordinated by this department.

6/ Legal Consultation Department (hōritsu sōdanbu) As the legal profession in Japan grew and the black-letter law (instead of custom or local tribunals) came to regulate increasingly fine-grained areas of daily life and interpersonal interactions, those without access to legal training or counsel were at a distinct disadvantage. This Department was therefore among the most crucial in the entire Settlement House project.

7/ Childcare Department (takujibu) Childcare for laborers was essential in allowing workers to go to their jobs, especially in an urban setting void of the traditional family structures that had provided built-in childcare in the past. This department provided free group childcare for the children of the neighborhood, which included playgrounds and reading rooms for children and consultation offices where parents could inquire about children-related issues.

While all seven of these fields were integral to the Settlement House project and inseparable from the law-and-society movement during the mid-to-late Taishō period, it was in the context of the legal consultation department that Suehiro sought concretely to expand his former court-based search for equity out among the lived experiences of the urban, disenfranchised poor. And in law as in overall posture, the Settlement House was a radical rethinking of the relationship between law and society in Japan.

SETTLEMENT HOUSES AS PART OF RESTRUCTURING JAPANESE SOCIETY: TURNING OF INTELLECTUAL TIDE

The sporadic literature in English tends to view the Settlement House phenomenon in Japan as a descendent of the Hull House movement in Chicago.[34] However, the more voluminous Japanese literature understands the Settlement House pedigree to be much more historically and intellectually complex. For instance, Mutō Chōzō argues that Suehiro and Hozumi acted to build the Settlement House in Tokyo in imitation of the Toynbee Halls that they had both witnessed at Oxford University in England.[35] And, while Suehiro would certainly have known of the Jane Addams Hull House from his time spent in Chicago, he was more likely to cite Welsh philanthropist and utopian socialist Robert Owen (1771–1858) than Jane Addams as the guiding force behind the Tokyo Settlement Project. In full, the Settlement House in Tokyo represented a diverse confluence of views and influences with a wide variety of actors gathering for the general purpose of helping the poor while changing society in Japan.[36]

To be sure, the work of the Yanagishima Settlement House in Tokyo following the 1923 earthquake was inescapably local, but the Settlement House movement overall represented a turning of the intellectual tide in Japan. Reactions to highly abstracted legal positivism and Pandekten-style German idealistic jurisprudence—reactions such as the "living law" set of legal theories developed by Eugen Ehrlich and imported into Japan mainly by Suehiro and Hozumi—flowed into more specifically local Japanese calls for intellectuals to leave the isolation of the academy and interact with surrounding society. Even when we trace the origin of the Settlement Houses back beyond the Chicago Hull Houses to the

Oxfordian Toynbee House on London's East Side, and, even farther, to the rhizomatic socialist movements that informed so much of elite interaction with the burgeoning urban underclasses beginning in the last decades of the nineteenth century in Europe, America, Asia, and Japan, to fully understand these phenomena it remains necessary to situate them more deeply within the seismic shifts in international socio-legal scholarship and praxis that were synchronous with more visible social movements. Law and society were splitting apart the world over, and Suehiro and Hozumi were not alone in trying to find equitable solutions to societal problems attending the rise of the all-politicizing state.

Globally as well as locally, much of this divorce of law and society stemmed from the rise of colonialism, a practice as prone to affect the colonial power's native territory as the lands it oversaw.[37] As Akira Iriye and Pierre-Yves Saunier explain:

> [the] internal consolidation and unification by means of the bureaucratic state apparatus and nationalist ideology were connected to the colonial expansion of the European powers in Africa and Asia and the colonization of North America by the US. [...] Recent scholarship argues that colonial expansion was not peripheral to the project of establishing universal global legal order: on the contrary, the colonial encounter and its consequences have shaped conceptions of public international law, the theory of comparative law and even international private law from the very beginning.[38]

Suehiro and Hozumi, too, understood their Settlement Houses, not only in terms of the social-work model found in Hull Houses and in Toynbee House, but also in terms of more deeply rooted philosophies of the interaction between law and society. Thus, the legal framework legitimating colonization—which is now recognized to have been intimately linked with the emerging global order of the late nineteenth century—also justified, at least in part, Hozumi and Suehiro's benign colonization of the more destitute regions of Tokyo after the Great Kantō Earthquake of 1923.

In addition to this influence of colonialism on the legal *Zeitgeist* in which Hozumi and Suehiro lived and worked, there is also the much more immediately visible problem of how the law was to guide practice and resolve disputes amid the "rapid industrialization and urbanization" that "necessitated the legal regulation of increasing communication and trade across state boundaries," thus leading to "the formation of a class of legal experts who promoted a more encompassing concept of transnational legal order." These legal experts "distanced themselves from the natural law and embraced legal positivism," and thus "advocated [for] the gradual codification of universal legal principles in order to further international peace."[39] In this sense, the Settlement House, as an iteration of an emerging urban-centric internationalism, was already at least partially co-opted by global politics from its very inception.[40]

This shift in the conceptual underpinnings of law from national sovereignty to universal prescripts reintroduced the idea of duty and responsibility into the positive law codes, which had become so abstracted by academic speculation and power politics as to have lost sight almost entirely of law's human subject.[41] This newfound regard for the wellbeing of those without easy access to, or certain standing in, the intricate positive-law legal codes was largely translated into dictums demanding that states exercise due care for their colonial, "native" populations. At the same time, there was also a movement within the legal communities of the industrialized world (including, by that time, Japan) to bring the fruits of the law to the urban poor living, not in far-flung colonies, but often just down the street from the elite institutions of learning within the industrialized nations' burgeoning metropoles.[42] The expansion of the Japanese empire during the Taishō Period temporarily dislocated the nation-state, freeing conceptual space for Suehiro's Ehrlichian focus on non-state law at the bottom, among the vast majority of Japanese people left unenfranchised by the Imperial Constitution.

This multivalent trend away from inflexible doctrine and toward a more democratic framework for the interpenetration of classes found expression in concrete political and policy debates within Japan, as well. For example, as the social classes within industrializing Tokyo pulled farther apart, local and regional governments began to seek ways to bring the benefits of social welfare to those traditionally excluded from the political process. As Kojita Yasunao explains,[43] while the aim of the Kenseikai[44] since the time of the Hara Kei administration (1918–1921) had been to formulate national policies that would:

> have the city councils, or more generally the Diet, play roles as mediators between classes when social problems arose as the result of the expansion of rights under the Society Law, the Seiyūkai and system of metropolitan specialized bureaucracies advocated an integrated approach that attempted to consolidate cities from the top-down by means of specialized bureaucratic administration, all while seeking settlement-type (*rinpo*; also, "neighborhood") cooperation among local bodies such as township administrative councils and guilds, via the mediation of class collaboration, and then taking all of this as the 'purification of the election process'.[45]

Likewise, Suehiro was translating into actual legal practice the legal pragmatism that he learned from advocates such as Roscoe Pound. Elite legal scholars and municipal bureaucrats were doing the same. During an era of rapid imperialization, the Japanese public, for a time, came into much more distinct view in the eyes of local authorities.

Indeed, municipal governments had begun similar projects some five years before the destruction caused by the 1923 earthquake, especially following the Rice Riots of 1918 at the end of the WWI boom economy.[46] Even before this, and as early as the Russo-Japanese War, there were attempts made at various levels of government, but especially at the metropolitan level, to solve social problems by restructuring and reforming urban slums.[47] Institutions in Tokyo such as the Xinhai (Shingai) Relief Society Tenement House (*Shingai kyūsaikai nagaya*) (1911), the Special Tenement House for the Elementary School Support Group (*Tokushu shōgakkō kōenkai fuzoku nagaya*) (1911), and the Tokyo Metropolitan Philanthropic Society Micro-Housing Plan (*Tōkyō-fu jizen kyōkai shōjūtaku keikaku*) (1918) were examples of places where one could take a hot bath, deliver a child, obtain childcare, do laundry, and congregate leisurely in the gardens adjacent to the facilities.[48] And, as early as 1897, when the social problems caused by rapid industrialization and transition to a capitalist society were reaching a crisis point, private-sector efforts such as Katayama Sen's Kingsley House (*Kingusure kan*) had already begun to emerge.[49] The auto-colonialism of big cities by auchthonous elites mirrored much of the transnational drive to "enlighten" the non-Western world in the fallout of imperial acquisition.

It is perhaps a measure of our persistent assumptions on this score that we may be surprised to hear that Osaka, not Tokyo, was the forerunner of the Settlement House-based urban reform and rebuilding work in Japan during the 1920s.[50] Indeed, it was not until 1928, some five years after the Kantō Earthquake, that Tokyo finally opened its first municipally run Settlement House, the Koishikawa Settlement House (*Koishikawa rinpokan*).[51] To further punctuate the importance of Osaka in the municipal Settlement House movement, the seed money for the Tokyo municipal Settlement House in Koishikawa—a gift of 770,000 yen designated as "earthquake disaster relief contributions" (*shinsai kyōen gienkin*)—was provided by the city of Osaka in 1928 after the initial proposal to make a donation toward a Tokyo Settlement House was floated in 1924.[52] Osaka, and not Tokyo, was well ahead of the curve when it came to providing municipal charity, even before the devastation in Tokyo in 1923 overwhelmed whatever municipal services had already been in place.[53]

According to a study carried out by the Social Bureau of the Ministry of Home Affairs (*Naimushō shakaikyoku*) in 1930, the first Settlement House in Japan was founded in Yonezawa in 1887.[54] In 1908, the Salvation Army (*Kyūseigun*) founded a "complete"[55] Settlement House in Tokyo, which was lost to fire just five years later in 1913.[56] After the Yonezawa Settlement opened in 1887, the progression ran thusly:

Table 1. Year-on-Year Increase in Settlement Houses

Year	Number		Year	Number		Year	Number
1887	1		1915	13		1924	49
1891	2		1916	14		1925	60
1899	4		1919	18		1926	71
1900	6		1920	26		1927	82
1905	7		1921	28		1928	94
1909	8		1922	29		1929	102
1911	10		1923	35		1930	**117 (Total)**

As shown in the table,[57] there were some twenty-nine Settlement Houses in Japan *before* the Great Kantō Earthquake, a number which increased dramatically thereafter as individuals and local governing bodies scrambled to respond to the needs of their communities.[58]

Even the post-earthquake Settlement houses, although clustered around the foci of the earthquake damage in Tokyo and Yokohama, were not to be found exclusively in the Kantō region. As often as not, the Settlement houses were to be found far from the new capital, wherever industry and increasingly rootless populations converged.

Table 2. Number of Settlement Houses by City/Region

Place	Number		Place	Number		Place	Number
Hokkaidō	1		Aichi	1		Yamaguchi	2
Tōkyō	57		Shizuoka	1		Wakayama	1
Kyōto	2		Shiga	5		Tokushima	1

The Settlement Houses throughout Japan,[59] especially in areas virtually untouched by the 1923 earthquake, indicate more widespread social dislocation than the sudden and relatively localized damage from a natural disaster, from Hokkaidō in the far north to Fukuoka and Nagasaki in the south.[60] Indeed, the distribution of Settlement houses closely tracks underlying population figures. For example, while Tokyo's fifty-seven Settlements is surely in proportion to the amount of damage caused by the earthquake there, Kanagawa (which includes Yokohama)—just as devastated by the 1923 quake as Tokyo—accounts for a mere seven Settlements out of a total of 105. When controlling for differences in population, this discrepancy in the number of Settlement Houses is in keeping with the expected variation. Dislocation between law and society was not exclusive to Tokyo. Japan's modernity was rending the social fabric nationwide.

LAW IN SOCIETY AT THE YANAGISHIMA SETTLEMENT

Of the seven departments of the Yanagishima Settlement, Suehiro and his group of law students and professors naturally oversaw the legal consultation center (*hōritsu sōdanshitsu*)—really just a room "in the center of which was a large, dirty table with one chair for the professor and three wooden benches on the other sides."[61] The consultation center was relatively unsuccessful at first, but in the fall of 1924 Hozumi Shigetō, Suehiro's partner in law-and-society studies and activism, instituted a reorganization of the center that was widely covered in the newspapers. Many people from the Yanagishima neighborhood and beyond made use of the free legal advice provided mainly by professors and students from the Tokyo Imperial University Faculty of Law.[62] The stated goal of the center was to "provide the poor with knowledge of the law."[63] But this proved far harder than it sounded. Societal conditions—illiteracy, homelessness, ignorance of even the most basic tenets of social life as it was governed by the state—prevented those living in poverty from making much use of the legal knowledge they gained.

This social breakdown, as well as the general confusion of post-earthquake Tokyo, was reflected in the petitions of the consultees. When overseeing the staff of the legal consultation clinic, Hozumi would sit patiently and listen to the legal concerns of those who came for free consultation, struggling to understand their often "incoherent" (*shirimetsuretsu*) stories. Most cases were like "terminal patients," for whom nothing could be done.[64] One consultee, for instance, had calmly loaned his seal out to a pawn shop for a high rate of interest.[65] Another consultee was presented with a compulsory execution and came to the consultation center wondering how it could be "extended."[66] As many Yanagishima residents started to move out and rent properties, they began having trouble with landlords, some of whom even maliciously came to the consultation center posing as tenants in order to gain an unfair advantage over the people renting from them.[67] Perhaps worst of all were the fathers who sold their daughters to geisha houses only to try to buy them back and then re-sell them elsewhere at a higher price.[68] The disenfranchised were flocking to the Settlement House legal clinic asking for relief to a whole range of problems engendered by the disconnection between law and society.

When there were no consultees in the legal consultation center on a given evening, Prof. Hozumi would begin an impromptu lecture, touching briefly on case law before launching into good-humored discourse on kabuki, novels, or other contemporary topics, always rounding out his miscellany with a legal-themed punchline. He was a speaker of great ability, so enrapturing that "the mosquitoes sat still and listened."[69] Afterwards, everyone, Hozumi included, would go to the cafeteria for "paper-thin" slices of pork over curried rice. Self-effacing about his accomplishments, Hozumi maintained that he was simply following in his younger partner's footsteps. "In everything, I just do what Suehiro does," Hozumi said. "The same goes for the Settlement project as well as for the case law research group."[70]

This humility was belied by Hozumi's influence on the legal profession in Japan. Among the professors and students who volunteered to help Hozumi staff were many who would later become famous legal scholars in their own right. For example, Wagatsuma Sakae and Kawashima Takeyoshi would sometimes staff the weekly Tuesday and Friday sessions from five to seven pm.[71] Peace-minded Japanese statesman Hara Yoshimichi (1867–1944), criminal procedure expert Ono Sei'ichirō (1891–1986), and Hirano Yoshitarō were more regularly in attendance, with Hara and Ono putting in the most reliable service.[72] Socialist law and comparative law scholar Fukushima Masao (1906–1989), Kainō Michitaka, public procurator Baba Yoshitsugu (1902–1977), and Chinese law specialist Niida Noboru (1904–1966) also put in stints at the legal consultation center.[73] Suehiro labor law student Kibe Tatsuji (1915–1948) founded the People's University (*shomin daigaku*) in 1946 for the betterment of the laboring masses, and political theorist Maruyama Masao—made famous by Ivan Morris' English translation of some of his essays—was among the volunteer lecturers.[74] Suehiro, for his part, hailed from a priestly *kannushi* lineage in Yamaguchi Prefecture and was related by marriage to the powerful Hatoyama family, occasional occupants of the prime ministership of Japan. In other words, the Tokyo Imperial University Settlement was a gathering of, and training ground for, the upper crust of Japan's social elite.

Hozumi was a member of an even more rarified strata of the social order. Hozumi's grandfather, Shibusawa Ei'ichi, was an enormously wealthy industrialist and was also arguably the most wide-ranging and influential entrepreneur of the Meiji Era, as well as the most generous business tycoon in perhaps the entirety of Japan's post-Tokugawa history.[75] It was from Shibusawa that Hozumi learned the Confucian maxim, "Virtue is never in isolation, but always has neighbors,"[76] which Hozumi was fond of glossing as "*la riche s'obligé.*"[77] Hozumi was especially fond of a copy of the *Analects*, which he had received from his famous grandfather, giving out copies to favored pupils (Fukushima received one after he returned from captivity in the Soviet Union after the war) and also kept a pocket copy with him wherever he went, remarking in letters to friends that reading the *Analects* abroad brought entirely different perspectives on the Confucian classic.[78] Not everyone who came to the legal consultation clinic could read; still fewer could read Confucius, even if they had the time; no one but Hozumi had received a copy of the *Analects* from Shibusawa Ei'ichi.

Whether reading the *Analects* helped the Settlement participants grow in Confucian virtue is hard to say, but in any event the Settlers found themselves growing more socially aware as they dug deeper into their Settlement work. Hirano Yoshitarō remembers students before the earthquake as being individualistic and selfish, concerned only with scoring high enough on exams to get a good job after graduation and having no desire to exert themselves for the betterment of society or the masses around them.[79] This all changed during the Settlement days at Tokyo Imperial University in the aftermath of the earthquake. There were stirrings of this new fluidity between elites and commoners before 1923, to be sure. In his 1920 book *Leave the Ivory Tower* (*Zōge no tō wo dete*), English literature scholar Kuriyagawa Hakuson (1880–1923) argued for the necessity of "leaving the ivory tower and coming into intimate contact with the problems of social survival, no longer blithely carrying on doing art solely for art's sake." Later, Hozumi applied this reformist spirit to the Japanese legal profession, successfully petitioning in 1933 for statutory language limiting the practice of law to males to be excised, four years after he had founded the first law school for women in Japan, the Meiji University Women's College, in 1929.[80] Elites were coming into contact with those outside their usual circles and finding themselves being changed by the society they set out to reform.

Suehiro echoed Kuriyagawa's criticisms of the cloistered university elite when he argued in June of 1924, on the occasion of the founding of the Yanagishima Settlement, that:

> the most tragic failure of society today is the complete divorce between knowledge and labor. The students who, blessed with

> a happy fortune and therefore provided with the opportunity to advance into the top academic institution, are the monopolists of knowledge in society today. I must remark that it would be a tremendous boon for society *and the state* [emphasis mine] if those monopolists, out of gratitude for the good fortune with which Heaven has blessed them, were to find the time each day to share those blessings with the poor, dividing their knowledge up for use by the least among us.[81]

Couching his social commentary in the language of monopoly and casting it in terms redolent of both exoteric lay Buddhism and the Sermon on the Mount, Suehiro seems to have imbibed equal parts progressive anti-capitalism, Japanese folk spirituality, and the Euro-American Social Gospel. This pleading for students and intellectuals to put themselves at the service of society was a constant in Suehiro's life: in 1937, for instance, Suehiro wrote the lyrics to a popular song exhorting young people to sacrifice their own comfort for the sake of the Japanese imperial effort in Manchuria.[82] Suehiro also reiterated his theme of society's need for legally knowledgeable, socially conscious professionals some twenty-seven years after his 1924 pronouncement, in a lecture delivered just five months before his death.[83] The marked change by June of 1924 was that Suehiro, who had advocated violence just two years before in order to extract concessions from landlords in favor of tenant farmers in a labor dispute, was now adding the wellbeing of the state to his list of justifications for the self-sacrifice he was calling on the privileged and educated to make.[84] Where Suehiro had earlier sought an apolitical equity through his caselaw study group, he now found himself having at least to include the political powers within the scope of his advocacy for the disenfranchised at the Tokyo Imperial University Settlement House.

THE "SURVEYING SPIRIT"

Suehiro's openness to the state was part of what Hirano Yoshitarō called his "surveying spirit" (*chōsa seishin*).[85] For Hirano, this "surveying spirit"—

manifested in Suehiro's critiques of the *Daishin'in*—was the same as that which drove the surveys carried out by the legal consultation office under the auspices of the Yanagishima Settlement House. As Hirano recalls Suehiro laying out, the bourgeoisie must expend its energy—and exert itself to the utmost morally, as well—for the sake of the proletariat, an ideal which also motivated Hozumi Shigetō.[86]

However, altruism was not the only motivating factor behind Suehiro's decision to found a legal clinic within the Yanagishima Settlement House. Indeed, for Suehiro, gaining knowledge from the legally ignorant, rather than imparting knowledge about the law to those with little to none, comprised two of the three main objectives in his mission statement for the Yanagishima Settlement House.[87] Writing in 1926, Suehiro stated that the legal consultation department (*hōritsu sōdanbu*) of the Settlement House was created in the hopes of

> 1/ Imparting legal knowledge to the average consultee
> 2/ Having students come to know the contours of the living law practice (*enshū*) thereby
> 3/ Carrying out observations[88] of gaps, defects, and other problems within the legal code that are killed off (*taorisararete iru*) and do not come to the forefront in court.[89]

Suehiro continued to search for apolitical equity, but his "laboratory" setting, as Suehiro called it, objectified and aggregated the people he was trying to see as individual subjects, each with a unique need for equity. This scientism also presumed the existence of a strong state to regulate the lives of those whose data the state had tallied.[90]

Under the (direct and indirect) political pressure of the state, the "surveying spirit" became the conduit for Suehiro's Ehrlichian "living law" approach to change polarity to top-down from bottom-up. As the state expanded its purview over Japanese society, it became easier for Suehiro to seek statist solutions to the tumultuous relationship between the law and surrounding society. By the 1930s, Suehiro was featuring official photographic portraits of Nazi legal theorists in *Hōritsu Jihō* and publishing articles by his associates lauding the efficiency with which National Socialism managed the unruly Volk.[91] The "surveying spirit," it turned out, left the door wide open to a rejection of Ehrlichian custom-based libertarianism in favor of a turn to the dirigisme being proferred worldwide as the antidote to liberal chaos.

THE PERILS OF SCIENTISM IN THE DIVIDE BETWEEN THE 'TRADITIONAL' AND THE 'LEGAL-RATIONAL'

Suehiro modified the Ehrlichian living law into a theoretical justification for observing, as in a "laboratory," the ways in which actual people moved about in the shadow of the law. Suehiro's partial aim in doing this, at least ostensibly, was to empower the marginalized and to make them visible—unignorable—to the entwined apparatus of state jurisprudence and legal scholarship. But by the same token, Suehiro began moving "by slow degrees"[92] to the incorporation of those same people within the imperial project. The perils of Suehiro's approach stemmed from the false distinction, originally theorized by Max Weber, between the people and the law. This Weberian false distinction has been addressed by English philosopher Roger Scruton as follows:

> Among the many dichotomies that have pulverized the modern intelligence, that—due, I suppose to Weber—between legitimacy and legality, between 'traditional' and 'legal-rational' modes of authority, has been the most damaging. Only if law is misunderstood, as a system of abstractions, can legality be regarded as an alternative to—rather than as a particular realization of—legitimacy. But abstract law is, for that reason, without lasting force. [...] The task [...] is to find the grounds of political existence concretely, and to work toward the re-establishment of legitimate government in a world that has been swept bare by intellectual abstractions. Our ultimate model for a legitimate order is one that is given historically, to people united by their sense of a common

> destiny, a common culture, and a common source of the values that govern their lives.[93]

What Scruton lays bare here is the dilemma faced by Suehiro and many other intellectuals in the twentieth century, not only in Japan but throughout the industrialized and industrializing world. The kind of scientistic data-collection that Suehiro saw as conducive to bringing equity to the masses apart from an abstracted, imported politics did not take into account the underlying need for people to belong to a *specific* community, rooted in a given time and place. Suehiro saw himself as a populist, but his proposed top-down remedy makes clear that he had set himself as the people's guide and not their champion.

The American representative of the Settlement House movement, Jane Addams, was firmly against the kind of paternalism of the scientistic social engineer that Suehiro saw as the answer to social fragmentation. For example, writing of the July 1894 Pullman strike, Addams opined:

> After the Pullman strike I made an attempt to analyze in a paper which I called 'The Modern King Lear' the inevitable revolt of human nature against the plans Mr. Pullman had made for his employees, the miscarriage of which appeared to him such black ingratitude. It seemed to me unendurable not to make some effort to gather together the social implications of the failure of this benevolent employer and its relation to the demand for a more democratic administration of industry.[94]

Like a Japanese "Mr. Pullman," Suehiro had begun to see people as data points which central planning could improve en masse.

In a 1931 essay collection, from a section titled "The Individual and Group Life," Hozumi Shigetō shows his own attempt to grapple with the central tension of the 1930s: namely, that between the individual and the collective:

> Up until now, almost everyone, not only in Japan but in countries around the world, has thought of individualism as something,

> ultimately, bad. But this is not really individualism, but, rather, egoism. Individualism develops humanity, and is how we in the human race have progressed thus far. But individualism alone is not enough. When more effort is put into communal living—where individuals gather together collectively to carry out communal life—[it will become clear] that the collective is formed through the formation of individuals. Therefore, it is a mistake to place emphasis on the collective such that the individual gets ignored. It is on this point that today's socialist direction falls into error, focusing on society overall. 'Society is made up of individuals, so placing the emphasis on the individual, as in what is called "individualism," worsens society as a whole.' Nationalism is all well and good as an "-ism," but the state is formed from individuals. The individual is ignored in order to emphasize the state. And it is a difficult thing to try to find ways to bring harmony [*chōwa*] to the individual and the collective.[95]

In attempting to recover the much older paradigm of harmony between individuals and the surrounding society and controlling authorities, Suehiro was also lamenting the upheaval of that old equitable system by the introduction of new, more abstract political philosophies during the Meiji and Taishō eras. In the passage above, Hozumi echoes Suehiro's hopes for an apolitical equity that would bring harmony to a badly politically fractured society.

For Hozumi, the key to solving this problem was citizenship education (*kōmin kyōiku*), which, if done properly, would "turn everyone into citizens" (*subete no hito ga, kōmin ni natte iru*).[96] This, in turn, was to be done by not only raising awareness of the law among citizens, but by also pointing out the affinity between law and morality, which would help group living run smoothly.[97] This would strengthen the collective by strengthening the individual, in effect conflating the two into a spectrum that overcame the distinctions seemingly inherent in a society made up of individual people.[98] The term that Hozumi coined for this new entity that comprised both the individual within the collective and the collective within the individual was "groupman" (*dantaijin*). This is nearly identical to Suehiro's own program for apolitical equity, not an equity of first principles or teleological statecraft, but of people living in groups within the largely alien political schema of the state.[99]

Suehiro had expressed his developing advocacy for top-down solutions via the power of the state as early as just after the Great Kantō Earthquake:

> I have no expectation of lasting world peace insofar as international economic competition among capitalist states continues. Nor can I have any faith in sentimental, superficial, impotent pacifism. Furthermore, I have no trust in bourgeois democratic 'sovereignty' as a vain concept lacking any force. For me, 'sovereignty' is nothing more than a hypothesis, a concept meant to make up for powerlessness. I can conceive of no sovereignty separate from military might, although I still see the prospect of arms reduction and the attack on militarism as entirely separate issues.[100]

For Segawa Nobuhisa, this lack of faith in pacifism, sovereignty, and fundamental rights sprang from Suehiro's experiences at Versailles, where he witnessed the work (much of it following on or predicated upon violence) that underwrote the idealism of the intellectual and political reformers.[101]

But Suehiro was still wavering, like Hozumi attempting to straddle the divide between state and people. Around the same time that he was acquiescing in state power, Suehiro wrote:

> The societally generated laws, which are the results of custom, must always be social norms [with a] societal [valence], irrespective of whether those [societally generated laws] are affirmed by the state or not.[102]

This was because, for Suehiro:

> Legislation is merely an indirect factor [in what law is]. Society itself—whether out of a felt obedience to the law or out of a

> fear of punishment—decides everything, and society itself carries everything out.[103]

While Suehiro never cited "legal pluralism" (*hōritsu tagenron*) in his justifications for taking societal custom as de facto law,[104] his reliance upon Gierke and others who attempted to overcome social problems in a liberal order naturally tended to the overall understanding of the law as growing up out of the soil of society and not descending from the heights of the legislative bodies.[105]

At the same time, Suehiro's concern for the masses also dovetailed with the Japanese government's imperial drive to rid Asia of Euro-American oppression:

> Prof. [Suehiro] was in agreement with the French sociologist [Émile] Durkheim, who thought that society oppressed individuals. [Suehiro] thought that the law was the means by which society oppressed individuals. If one were to replace society with the ruling class, then law would become the means by which the ruling class oppressed the masses. The masses, of their own accord, would undertake collective action in order to rid themselves of this oppression. Politicians would try to control this through the use of power, but the inertia [of the drive to overthrow oppression] cannot be fully stopped. Prof. [Suehiro] understood this and was on the side of the workers. It's a small thing, but it resonates psychologically when resisting oppression.[106]

As Segawa points out, this "estrangement of the law of the state from society" (*shakai to kokkateki hōritsu to no kairi*)[107] would eventually lead Suehiro to abandon the liberal framework underpinning his Settlement House project and embrace the anti-liberal, collectivist elements already coalescing in society as a whole. By the second half of the 1930s, Suehiro had duly shifted from a rights-based view of legal interpretation, to a duties-based formula.[108] In doing so, he was reacting to a great degree to the worsening geopolitical situation of the 1930s, which was also the driving force behind the expansion of the Japanese empire into Asia.

Suehiro was also responding, both directly and indirectly, to sustained attacks against the Tokyo University Law Faculty—and against himself personally—by anti-liberal intellectual Minoda Muneki. Pragmatism is by definition a function of one's circumstances, and Suehiro's pragmatism eventually succumbed to the bare dearth of options in a world of autarky, predatory colonialism, and total war.

Conclusion

As the political situation in Japan worsened and attacks on the universities grew more acute, Suehiro's search for equity in the context of his legal research was increasingly distorted by the pressures of imperial politics. Almost as soon as Suehiro and Hozumi had begun their Settlement House project at the Tokyo Imperial University following the devastating 1923 earthquake, Suehiro's other advocacy work on behalf of tenant farmers caused the authorities to exert political pressure on Suehiro and the Settlement movement. This political pressure became especially acute after Tokyo Imperial University president Onozuka Kiheiji (1871–1944) introduced the Tokyo Settlement House project's legal consultation clinic at the Geneva Convention in 1929.[109] With a high profile came louder calls to root out individualistic or socialistic non-conformity with the kokutai. The Settlement medical team, for instance, had to become more circumspect in dispatching doctors to treat patients, while the Settlement legal clinic was forced to reduce the number of clients taken in for pro bono consultations and the Settlement laborers' school was prevented from taking in new students. Donors to the Settlement House project, too, faced political pressure to discontinue or reduce support for a movement closely affiliated with Suehiro, Hozumi, and the Shinjinkai, all perceived as too leftist or liberal.[110] The political walls were closing in.

By 1934, when Minoda launched his attack against Suehiro, Suehiro had reconfigured his youthful radicalism and come to align more closely with the imperialist state. It was a pragmatic decision. Such pragmatism was, after all, the touchstone of Suehiro's jurisprudence.[111] In 1926, for example, Suehiro complained that traditional jurisprudence had lost applicability to new social phenomena,[112] and by 1940 he wrote:

> Whether we like it or not, our nation at the present time is pressed upon on all fronts—political, economic, cultural, and all others—by a situation that leaves us no choice but to cast off our former system.[113]

The Achilles Heel of apolitical equity was that Suehiro was powerless to articulate alternatives to the prerogatives of state politics, or how there might be individualized justice within the aggressively collectivizing momentum of an empire preparing for, and then waging, total war. By 1940, when Suehiro began his application of the Settlement House methods of social surveying to Japan's new sphere of influence in the north of China, the transition from Taishō Democracy Settlement House pioneer to Shōwa imperialism statist social engineer was complete.

NOTES

1. Suehiro Izutarō, "Hōritsu to kanshū: Nihon hōri tankyū no hōhō ni kansuru hito kōsatsu," collated in *Zoku Minpō zatsu kichō* (Tokyo: Nihon Hyōronsha, 1949), 312-325, and "Jijitsutaru kanshū," ibid., 42-54.
2. Kawabata Yasunari visited the site just two hours after the earthquake, and later wrote up his impressions for *Asakusa Kurenaidan* (1929-1935). Quoted in Edward Seidensticker, *Tokyo Rising: The City since the Great Earthquake* (New York: Alfred A. Knopf, 1990), 9-10.
3. An album of photographs of the destruction in Tokyo is archived in the Dana and Vera Reynolds Collection at Brown University and available for online viewing at http://library.brown.edu/cds/kanto/about.html
4. Based on aggregates from both Tokyo and Yokohama, each computed retroactively within the past few years. Others put the population at half this number: see, e.g., Dahlmann, Joseph, S.J., *The Great Tokyo Earthquake September 1, 1923. Experiences and Impressions of an Eye-Witness* (New York: The America Press, 1924).
5. See Ōnishi Shinji, *Seikyō undō gojūnen: seikyō undō hitosujini, ikita rekishi no shōgen toshite* (Yokohama: Kanagawa ken Seikatsu Kyōdō Kumiai Rengōkai, 1978), 49 ff.
6. See Seidensticker, *Tokyo Rising*, op. cit., 7-8. See also Suehiro, "Shinsai," in *Uso no kōyō*, op. cit.
7. Other issues continue the descriptions. Archived online (in interesting hand-copied format) at: http://dil.bosai.go.jp/disaster/1923kantoeq/denpo/
8. Narita Ryūichi, *Taishō Demokurashii* (Tokyo: Iwanami Shinsho, 2007), 164
9. Ibid., 164.
10. Narita, op. cit., 164-165.
11. Hirano Yoshitarō, "Shakai kagakusha, Suehiro Izutarō," in *Hōritsu Jihō*, vol. 23, no. 11 (Nov., 1951), 751
12. Hirano, *Shakai kagakusha*, op. cit., 751
13. Ibid.
14. Ibid. For a personal recollection, some 75 years after the fact, by a student involved with the Suehiro-led efforts, see Ōmachi Hiroshi, archived at http://www.t-shinpo.com/751/751_10.html

15. See Ono Kenjin, "Teito daishin kasai keitō chizu, Tōkyō Teikoku Daigaku risaisha jōhōkyoku chōsa (hen)," *Tokyo Nichi Nichi, Osaka Mainichi* (Dec., 1923).
16. Regarding Suehiro's "literally self-sacrificial" efforts to bring material and medical relief to the hardest-hit survivors, see Ōnishi, *Seikyō undō*, op. cit., 53 ff.
17. This was later reprinted in part in the Tokyo Teikoku Daigaku student newspaper, no. 57.
18. Soseki's first novel, *Gubijinsō* ("The Poppy"), serialized in 1903 when he began working at the *Asahi Shimbun*, is partly about class conflict and societal discord. See, e.g., Angela Yiu, *Chaos and Order in the Works of Natsume Sōseki* (Honolulu: University of Hawai'i Press, 1998).
19. Quoted in Hirano, "Shakai kagakusha," op. cit., 751
20. See Shichinohe, "Suehiro Izutarō no seishun," op. cit.
21. Hirano, "Shakai kagakusha," op. cit., 751
22. Ibid. The area remained a low-income tenement district through at least the 1980s. See, e.g., http://furoyanoentotsu.com/dojyunkaisarueuramachi19860930.html For information on the Dōjunkai project, see Manō Yōsuke and Sato Shigeru, "Sarue uramachi furyō jūtaku chiku kairyō jigyō to shinsai fukkō tochi kukaku seiri jigyō to no kanren nit suite: Dōjunkai ni yoru shūgō jūtakuchi keikaku no keikaku gijutsu ni kansuru kenkyū sono ichi," *Nihon Kenchiku Gakkai Keikakukei Ronbunshū*, vol. 62, no. 499 (1997), 105-112.
23. Hirano, "Shakai kagakusha," op. cit., 751.
24. Ibid.
25. Azuma Toshihisa, in Ishidō Kiyotomo and Tateyama Toshitada, *Tōkyō Teidai Shinjinkai no kiroku* (Tokyo: Keizai Ōraisha, 1976), 142
26. Ishidō and Tateyama, *Shinjinkai*, op. cit., 141-142.
27. For a detailed consideration of the taxonomy of "Settlement," and the work that Settlement entails, see Shiga Shinajin, "Setsurumento jigyō no keitai: keiei keitai ni tsuite," in *Shakai Jigyō* (June, 1930) (Settlement issue), 46.
28. This list of seven departments largely paraphrased from Ishidō, *Shinjinkai*, op. cit., 141-145.
29. See Henry DeWitt Smith, II, *Japan's First Student Radicals* (Cambridge: Harvard University Press, 1972).
30. Ishidō, *Shinjinkai*, op. cit., 142. It was the involvement of the Shinjinkai, in part, that later aroused suspicion among the Japanese authorities and led to the closing of the Settlement House project.

31. See, e.g., Kurotaki Chikara and Itō Tadahiko, eds., *Nihon kyōiku undōshi, dai ni kan, Shōwa shoki no kyōiku undō* (Kyoto: San'ichi Shobō, 1960).
32. Ishidō, *Shinjinkai*, op. cit., 142-143. See also Kawakami Takeshi, *Iryō shakaika no dōhyo: 25nin no shōgen* (Tokyo: Keisō Shobō, 1969).
33. Ishidō, *Shinjinkai*, op. cit., 144.
34. But see also Edwin R. A. Seligman and Alvin Johnson, eds., "Social Settlements," in *Encyclopaedia of the Social Sciences* (New York: The Macmillan Company, 1930), cited in Mutō Chōzō, "Setsurumento no haha Toinbii kan: sono sōritsusha Samyueru Bānetto fusai to Ānorudo Toinbii," *Shakai Jigyō* (June, 1935), for an example of a Western-language source placing the Japanese Settlement Houses in the Toynbee Hall tradition. (Toynbee Hall was founded by Samuel A. Barnett in 1884.) Also J.H. Covell, et al., "Twenty Years in Tokyo's East Side—The Kobokan," *Japan Christian Quarterly* 14 (July, 1939), cited in Manako Ogawa, "'Hull-House' in Downtown Tokyo: The Transplantation of a Settlement House from the United States into Japan and the North American Missionary Women, 1919–1945," *Journal of World History*, Vol. 15, No. 3 (Sep., 2004), 359–387.
35. Ōnishi, *Seikyō undō*, op. cit., 53. See also, e.g., Mutō, "Setsurumento no haha," in *Shakai Jigyō* (1935), op. cit., 38-44. The initial impetus behind the Settlement's founding and the founding of Toynbee Hall were very similar: namely, to bring the blessings of elite upbringings, as embodied by membership in the new social clubs fostered by attendance at the top universities in a given country, to those whose circumstances precluded access to such privileges. Jane Addams modeled her Hull Houses on Toynbee Hall.
36. See Konomi Imai, "The Women's Movement and the Settlement Movement in Early Twentieth-Century Japan: The Impact of Hull House and Jane Addams on Hiratsuka Raicho," *Kwansei Gakuin University Humanities Review*, no. 17 (2013), 85-109.
37. See, e.g., Anthony Anghie, "Colonialism and the Birth of International Institutions: Sovereignty, Economy and the Mandate System of the League of Nations," *NYU Journal of International Law and Politics*, Vol. 34, No. 3 (2002), 513-633.
38. "Legal Order," in Akira Iriye and Pierre-Yves Saunier, eds. *The Palgrave Dictionary of Transnational History* (New York: Palgrave Macmillan, 2009), 650.
39. Iriye and Saunier, *Transnational History*, op cit., 650.

40. See also Peter Oblas, "Naturalist Law and Japan's Legitimization of Empire in Manchuria: Thomas Baty and Japan's Ministry of Foreign Affairs (Part One)," *Diplomacy and Statecraft*, Vol. 15, No. 1 (2004), 35-55.
41. Iriye and Saunier, *Transnational History*, op. cit., 651-652. Almost unmentioned in any of the legal history literature in either Japanese or English is the affinity between the fall of the Pandekten, German Idealist, Comtean-positivist, highly abstracted code model and the rise of the case method, on the one hand, and the decline of static anthropology and the rise of psychology (which begins with cases) and phenomenology. Cf., e.g., Franz Brentano (1838-1917), as sketched in Roger Scruton, *From Descartes to Wittgenstein: A Short History of Modern Philosophy* (London: Routledge and Kegan Paul, 1981), esp. Ch. 18, "Phenomenology and Existentialism," 255-270.
42. For a specific comparative example, see Charles T. Tackney and David Kettler, "Light from a Dead Sun: The Japanese Lifetime Employment System and Weimar Labor Law," *Comparative Labor Law and Policy*, 19:101 (Fall, 1997), fn 14 ff.
43. Tadokoro Yūji, *Chi'iki shakai kyōiku shisetsu no rekishiteki kenkyū: kōminkan e no keishō to danzetsu* (PhD dissertation, Meiji Daigaku, 2014), 63-64.
44. The Kenseikai, or Association for Constitutional Government, was formed in 1916, making it among the first political parties in Japan. The Kenseikai was generally populist, favoring labor unions and universal male suffrage. See Sheldon Garon, *The State and Labor in Modern Japan* (Berkeley: University of California Press, 1987).
45. Tadokoro, *Chi'iki shakai*, op.cit., citing Kojita Yasunao, *Nihon kindai toshishi kenkyū yosetsu* (Tokyo: Kashiwa Shobō, 1991), 280.
46. Tadokoro, *Chi'iki shakai*, op. cit., 65.
47. Ibid.
48. Tadokoro, *Chi'iki shakai*, op. cit., 65, citing fn 192.
49. Tadokoro, *Chi'iki shakai*, op. cit., 65.
50. Ibid.
51. For a discussion of the relative merits and shortcomings of publicly-run Settlement houses, see Shiga Shinajin, "Kōei Setsurumento no tokuchō to ketten," in *Shakai Jigyō* (July, 1932), 8-11.
52. Tadokoro, *Chi'iki shakai*, op. cit., 77. See also following pages in Tadokoro for pictures of Koishikawa.

53. But see Ōbayashi Munetsugu, *Settsurumento no kenkyū* (Tokyo: Keibunsha, 2008), 194, for a conflicting view on the primacy of Tokyo in the Settlement race.
54. See Shiga, *Shakai Jigyō*, op. cit., 8.
55. The meaning of "complete" (*kanzen*) is not elaborated upon in the original.
56. Shiga, *Shakai Jigyō*, op. cit., 8.
57. The total given in Shiga is 114, not 117.
58. Shiga, *Shakai Jigyō*, op. cit., 8.
59. Again, Shiga gives figures different than the sum of the numbers of Settlement Houses in each location. See Shiga, *Shakai Jigyō*, op. cit., 8.
60. The population in Yokohama in 1923 was 446,600. After the earthquake, the population fell precipitously, to 389,700 in 1924, and then began to rise again steadily thereafter: 405,888 in 1925, 511,500 in 1926, and 529,300 in 1926. See http://www.city.yokohama.lg.jp/ex/stat/jinko/ayumi/pdf/01.pdf By contrast, Tokyo's population in 1922, before the earthquake, was 3,984,200; in 1923, after the earthquake, 3,859,400; in 1924, 4,185,500; in 1926, 4,485,144; and in 1926, 4,694,400. See www.toukei.metro.tokyo.jp/jugoki/2011/ju11qc0900.xls The population ratio between Tokyo and Yokohama held steady over this period. Tokyo's population was 8.92 times that of Yokohama's immediately before the earthquake, and was 8.86 times that of Yokohama's in 1926.
61. Miyata Shinpei. *Darega kaze wo mita deshō: boranteia no genten, Tōdai Setsurumento monogatari* (Tokyo: Bungei Shunjū, 1995), 91; see also photograph on 93.
62. Azuma Toshihisa, in Ishidō, *Shinjinkai*, op. cit., 144.
63. Ibid., 145.
64. Miyata, *Darega kaze wo mita deshō*, op. cit., 91-92.
65. Miyata, *Darega kaze wo mita deshō*, op. cit., 92. A seal gives the bearer complete access to all of the seal's owner's accounts, and even allows the bearer to obtain credit, buy and rent property, and notarize legal documents like wills and deeds in the owner's name. The man had effectively pawned his identity, mistakenly believing that he could reclaim it unblemished whenever he had sufficient funds to do so.
66. Miyata, *Darega kaze wo mita deshō*, op. cit., 92-93.
67. Ibid.
68. See previous chapter in the present volume.
69. Miyata, *Darega kaze wo mita deshō*, op. cit., 91-92.
70. *Hōritsu Jihō* (June, 1973), 110.

71. Miyata, *Darega kaze wo mita deshō*, op. cit., 90. Other sources give one to nine pm, Tuesdays and Thursdays. See, e.g., Fukushima, et al., *Kaisō no Tōkyō Teidai Setsurumento* (Tokyo: Nihon Hyōronsha, 1984).
72. Miyata, *Darega kaze wo mita deshō*, op. cit., 90-91.
73. Miyata, *Darega kaze wo mita deshō*, op. cit., 91.
74. See Andrew E. Barshay, "Postwar Social and Political Thought, 1945-90," in Bob Tadashi Wakabayashi, ed., *Modern Japanese Thought* (Cambridge: Cambridge University Press, 1998), 307. See also Maruyama Masao, tr. Ivan Morris, *Thought and Behavior in Modern Japanese Politics* (London: Oxford University Press, 1969).
75. See, e.g., *Shibusawa Ei'ichi zenshū* (Tokyo: Heibonsha, 1930).
76. *Toku wa konarazu, kanarazu tonari ari.* From the *Li Ren* section of the *Analects* of Confucius. See *Hōritsu Jihō* (June, 1973), 109.
77. *Tomi wa sekimu wo shōzu*, lit., "wealth engenders responsibility." Kainō Michitaka, Nihon Hōshakaigaku Kai, "Hozumi hōgaku, Suehiro hōgaku no bunseki to hihan (zadankai)," in *Hōshakaigaku 2* (1952), 54-55.
78. See *Hōritsu Jihō* (June, 1973), 109.
79. Hirano, "Shakai kagakusha," op. cit., 751.
80. See Yoko Hayashi, "Women in the Legal Profession in Japan," *US-Japan Women's Journal*, English Supplement, No. 2 (1992), 16-27.
81. Hirano, "Shakai kagakusha," op. cit., 751-2.
82. Yakushinfushi, Sunbibeibushi, and Koeteyo wakabito, in *Ryūkō kayō shū* (roku) (July, 1937) Suehiro credited as "lyricist" (*sakushi*), National Diet Library, ndljp/pid/3569902, and Koeteyo wakabito (Orinpikku haken senshu ōenka) (May, 1936) (Suehiro again credited as "lyricist"), National Diet Library, ndljp/pid/1323110. For "Yakushinfushi" see: https://www.youtube.com/watch?v=olLSIaodwDs
83. "Hōgaku to wa nanika (1)," *Hōritsu Jihō*, Vol. 23, No. 4 (April, 1951), 12-15, and *2*, Vol. 23, No. 5 (May, 1951), 3-7.
84. See esp. Kawaguchi Yoshihiko. *Kindai Nippon no tochihō kan'nen: 1920 nendai kosaku rippō ni okeru tochi shihaiken to hō* (Tokyo: University of Tokyo Press, 1990).
85. *Hōritsu Jihō* (June, 1973), 108-109.
86. Ibid.
87. *Hōgaku Kyōkai Zasshi*, Vol. 44, No. 4.
88. *kansoku*, which connotes scientific observations.
89. Kawashima Takeyoshi, ed., *Hōshakaigaku kōza 2, hōshakaigaku no genjō* (Tokyo: Iwanami Shoten, 1972). 211, citation from Suehiro original source.

90. See esp. Hiromi Mizuno, *Science for the Empire: Scientific Nationalism in Modern Japan* (Stanford: Stanford University Press, 2009).
91. *Hōritsu Jihō*, vol. 15, no. 4 (1942). The portrait picture on the frontispiece of this issue is of Konstantin Hierl (1875-1955), director of the *Reichsarbeitsdienst* for the National Socialists. Prior to that, Hierl had headed the *Freiwilliger Arbeitsdienst*, which was similar to the Yūaikai. See, e.g., Angela Vogel, *Das Pflichtjahr für Mädchen. Nationalsozialistische Arbeitseinsatzpolitik im Zeichen der Kriegswirtschaft* (Frankfurt am Main: Lang, 1997). See also Tawara Shizuo, "Nachisu gyōsei no senji taisei: tokuni senji ni okeru gyōsei saiban seido ni tsuite," in *Hōritsu Jihō*, Vol. 12, No. 10 (Oct., 1940), 39, ff.
92. Sagara Iichi letter to American authorities, in GHQ/SCAP Records (RG 331), Box no. 2275 0, Folder title/number (32), SUEHIRO, Izutaro, Nov. 1946 – Apr. 1950, Classification 021, Type of record z, National Archives of the United States, accessed in microfiche version at National Diet Library, Tokyo, Japan.
93. Roger Scruton, "How to be a Nonliberal, Antisocialist Conservative," from *Intercollegiate Review*, Vol. 28, No. 2, 1993, quoted in Mark C. Henrie, ed., *Arguing Conservatism: Four Decades of the Intercollegiate Review* (Wilmington, DE: ISI Books, 2008), 768-769. See also Scruton, in Henrie, ed., *Arguing Conservatism*, op. cit., 766, ff.
94. *Twenty Years at Hull-House: With Autobiographical Notes* (New York and Scarborough, Ontario: Signet Classic/ Penguin, 1961), 160-161. Addams gave the Modern Lear speech in Chicago in 1896; it was eventually published in *Survey*, vol. 29 (Nov. 2, 1912), 131-137.
95. Monbushō, ed., *Saishin kōminka shiryō seisetsu* (Tokyo: Monbushō Gakumukyoku, Nov., 1931).
96. Suehiro also wrote on citizenship education as part of a much broader and lengthier consideration of the social problems that needed fixing. For Suehiro, the myth of the fair contract between labor and management, and the need to reclaim private property by force if necessary, were essentials to long-lasting equity in Japanese society. See Monbushō, ed., *Saishin kōminka shiryō seiryō seisetsu*, op. cit., 817-819.
97. "Dai kyū setsu: kojin to dantai seikatsu," in Monbushō hensan, *Saishin kōminka shiryō seisetsu*, op. cit., 54-55 (500-501).
98. Ibid.
99. Ibid.
100. "Shinsai ni tsuite no kansō," 148, collected in *Hōsō kanwa*, op. cit., 398.

101. "I saw with my own eyes that it was, after all, a human effort, moving on a grand scale, that was responsible for creating a new legal order and a new world order." (*Suehiro Lectures*, 21) Quoted in Segawa Nobuhisa, "Suehiro Izutarō no minpō kaishaku to hō riron," in Rokumoto and Yoshida, eds., *Suehiro Izutarō to Nihon no hōshakaigaku*, op. cit., 218.
102. "Rōdō kyōyaku to hōritsu" (1925), 318, cited in Segawa, "Suehiro Izutarō no minpō kaishaku to hō riron," op. cit., 216.
103. "Rōdō kumiai hō ron," 14. See also *Minpō kōwa* (Vol. 1) (1925), op. cit., 7-11. Both cited in Segawa, "Suehiro Izutarō no minpō kaishaku to hō riron," op. cit., 216.
104. Segawa, "Suehiro Izutarō no minpō kaishaku to hō riron," op. cit., 216-217
105. Ibid. See also Harold Joseph Laski, *The Foundations of Sovereignty and Other Essays* (London: George Allen & Unwin, 1921), as well as Isomura Satoshi, *Shakai hōgaku no tenkai to kōzō* (Tokyo: Nihon Hyōronsha, 1975), 78, both cited in Segawa, "Suehiro Izutarō no minpō kaishaku to hō riron," op. cit., 216-217.
106. Seki Kazuo, *Sainō wa tsukurareru: jishin wo tsuke tenbun wo nobasu manabikata* (Tokyo: Mirion Bukkusu, 1964) 185.
107. *Rōdōhō kenkyū*, op. cit., 309.
108. Segawa, "Suehiro Izutarō no minpō kaishaku to hō riron," op. cit., 219.
109. Ishidō, *Tōkyō Teidai Shinjinkai*, op. cit., 145.
110. Ishidō, *Tōkyō Teidai Shinjinkai*, op. cit., 145-146.
111. Cf. Segawa, "Suehiro Izutarō no minpō kaishaku to hō riron," op. cit., 219 ff.
112. *Rōdōhō kenkyū*, 309, cited in Segawa, "Suehiro Izutarō no minpō kaishaku to hō riron," op. cit., 219.
113. *Hōritsu Jihō*, vol. 12 no. 10 (Oct., 1940), 49, cited in Rokumoto Kahei, "Suehiro hōshakaigaku no shiza: sengo hōshakaigaku to no taihi," in Rokumoto and Yoshida, eds., *Suehiro Izutarō to Nihon no hōshakaigaku*, op. cit., 240-241, and Segawa, "Suehiro Izutarō no minpō kaishaku to hō riron," op. cit., in ibid., 219-220.

Chapter 5

Minoda Muneki, Tanaka Kōtarō, and the Shibboleth of the Kokutai

The State and the Law

For Suehiro in the early 1920s, influenced by the living-law ideas of Eugen Ehrlich, the state was a passive adjunct to society. The primacy of society meant that each state could be home to any number of different societies, each with its own internally binding regulations and mores. Suehiro pushed the state to remain pliant before these differing social norms, with case law as the vehicle for disrupting and decentering the state's monopoly on the use of force. In deciding case law, judges, responding to the immediate needs of communities under their jurisdiction, supplemented the lacunae left behind by legislatures at the state level. Not only was the state not transcendent, then, for Suehiro in the 1920s it wasn't even solidly in control of its own basic legislative functions. As Hirohama Yoshio points out:

> *Ubi societas ibi jus* ["wherever there is society, there is law"] means that, within a given nation, there will be multiple legal orders in addition to the state legal order. Interpretive jurisprudence was brought about as a discipline whose aim was to understand legal orders as normative systems, logically and without contradiction. Interpretive jurisprudence which takes as its subject the state legal order must see statutory law as the only source of law, and must take no account of things such as customary law or cases. This is because, in all likelihood, the actual authority of customary law and case law is not preserved by state power. The traditional stance of interpretive jurisprudence has been that there is but one legal order existing within the society in a given state. The reason for this direct formation of the state legal order was the absence of purely legal investigation. However, on the question of whether customary law and case law can be sources of law within state-law interpretational jurisprudence, interpretational jurisprudence borrows customary law, based on the practical scientific nature of service to the government, and sees case-law analogously as an original source of law.[1]

Eugen Ehrlich also used the maxim *ubi societas, ibi jus* to explain and justify his insistence on the multiplicity of legal orders under any given state framework. This advocacy for a spontaneously arising societal law independent of the state was one of the hallmarks of the law-and-society movement in both Europe and Japan.

Suehiro was at first even more explicit about the limits of the state. In a stance that Yoshida Katsumi calls "Suehiro's negative evaluation of the actual state at that time,"[2] Suehiro wrote in *Kaizō* in 1923:

> One of the most remarkable features of the Meiji Period was that the state [*kokka*] was trying to lead the people in every facet of their lives. And, not only did most people accept this position [of the state], they relied on the state's directives, were devoted to them—and the state was able to accomplish anything. The Meiji state took it upon itself to issue directives to the populace not just on matters of economics and material concerns, but even on

> spiritual questions. What's more, the state was quite successful in all of this. If a government official said something was beautiful, the people said it was, too. And if an official said something was ugly, the people also said so. That's what kind of an age it was. Furthermore, the state became a font of morals and mores, and even made plans to unify religion within the state's grasp. And hardly anyone thought any of this to be out of the ordinary. It was thought that the state and the law were omnipotent, and the highest good. Thus, as everything was accomplished in the name of the state, the people, in general, lost all power to critique the state. Sober reflection will reveal how strange a phenomenon that was. But it was all just like that. But all phenomena arise from some kind of cause, correct? [...] Does the state really have the ability to act in a directive capacity? Is it not a cause for concern when the state assumes such a stance?[3]

Two years later, Suehiro continued this line of thought: "According to state philosophy today, the state exists for the mutual benefit of us citizens. The law and the courts and the other government agencies all exist for the purpose of protecting the citizens' welfare."[4]

Suehiro's early views on the nature of the state thus ran directly counter to Minoda Muneki's understanding of the inviolability, and unquestionability, of the kokutai. Minoda was especially troubled by Suehiro's demotion of the state to the level of helpful referee. In Suehiro's estimation, the state should play only an auxiliary, ancillary role (*sewayaku toshite no kokka*):

> The state must exist in an ancillary role as long as we human beings live in groups. The state as a mechanism for the rulers and the ruling class, may, perhaps, eventually disappear. But the state in an auxiliary role will carry on forever.[5]

As Yoshida explains, "Obviously, this [ancillary state] will not be adopting a stance of issuing directives to the people from a position of superiority over them."[6] Yoshida sees Suehiro as trying to overcome the self-declared transcendent and all-powerful state by pointing out that the state was a subject of its citizens and also by emphasizing problems with the state as it actually existed at the time, all with an eye to "attempting to limit the state's functions" (*kokka no kinō gentei wo hakaru*).[7]

Minoda, outraged by Suehiro's publications, did more than just critique Suehiro for these anti-kokutai views. He actually filed suit against him, on the charge of *lèse majesté*, with the prosecutor's office of the Tokyo District Court on June 6, 1934. Minoda reprinted the text of his lawsuit in its entirety in *Genri Nippon* (the journal Minoda edited) in an article titled "The Violent Thought of Suehiro Izutarō."[8] Minoda's main complaint was that Suehiro had openly advocated for a violent overthrow of the national polity, thereby offending the dignity of the kokutai. Minoda shows this partially by selectively quoting from Suehiro's writings and then comparing those excerpts with similar quotations from the works of Karl Marx, Friedrich Engels, and Vladimir Lenin. Underlying this insinuation that Suehiro, like the Marxists and Communists, was inciting armed revolution is the much more fundamental premise that Western ideals, such as individual rights, are incompatible with the Japanese ethnos and ethos, and, ultimately, pose an affront to the unique political arrangement of the Japanese archipelago.

Minoda's lawsuit leads off with an indictment of Suehiro's argument, as Suehiro set it forth in "Fundamental Principles for Compensation Following Erroneous Court Decisions,"[9] that the state must exist in an ancillary role as long as people live in groups.[10] Suehiro, possibly following Engels, also thought it possible that the state as a mechanism of the ruling class would eventually disappear. For Minoda, this emphasis on the "state as a mechanism of the ruling class" (*shihai kaikyū no kikan toshite no kokka*) bore a striking similarity to a passage from Lenin's *The State and Revolution*, which Minoda cites in full, in English (without Japanese gloss), immediately after citing Suehiro's offending phrase:

"The authority of the government over persons will be replaced by the administration of things and direction of process of production. The state will not be 'abolished'; it will wither away."[11] Minoda goes on to quote Suehiro making an explicit appeal to violence as being the *sine qua non* of "subjectivity": "Because I believe that subjectivity is nothing more than a concept, a hypothesis meant to supplement those areas lacking in physical force, I cannot conceive of a subjectivity divorced from military power—whether such power is in the hands of the bourgeoisie or the proletariat."[12] This seeming call to use force to uphold subjectivity, according to Minoda, constituted a desire to "alter the kokutai" (*kokutai henkaku*) in direct violation of Article One of the Imperial Japanese Constitution—Minoda's "solemnity clause" (*genshuku jōshō*)—that states: "The Empire of Japan shall be reigned over and governed by a line of Emperors unbroken for ages eternal."[13]

This is not all. Minoda also uses Suehiro's criticism of the military to argue that Suehiro has committed a second instance of *lèse majesté*. Suehiro writes: "In essence, the military . . . is perhaps nothing more than a nuisance encountered in the course of average, everyday living. But it's a nuisance that one has no choice but to keep around in anticipation of [...] when something extraordinary happens. That is to say, [the military] is a 'necessary evil.'"[14]

This slight against the military, according to Minoda, violated the principles set forth in the Imperial Japanese Constitution, sections 11 through 14, inclusive, as well as the *Imperial Rescript to Soldiers and Sailors* (*Gunjin ni okuritaru chokuyu*) (1882), which called for a unified sincerity (*ichi no seishin*) among the Emperor's military.[15] By extension, Suehiro's slight therefore impinged upon the Emperor's military prerogative.[16] Minoda spells it out as showing "intent of heinous treason" (*kyōgyaku ishi*), which, again, is the illicit desire to effect the alteration of the kokutai.[17]

Suehiro issued a carefully-worded *mea culpa* in response to Minoda's attacks:

> While engaged in the high-minded activity of seriously lamenting for one's country, the flip side is that there are ways in which it is

> easy to lapse into rogue behavior, and as an educator it is felt that this is a point on which one should very much take responsibility.[18]

But as might have been expected, Minoda did not relent. If anything, Suehiro's apology only emboldened him, and Minoda pressed for more:

> If Suehiro is sorry for what he has done, then he shouldn't need to be told how to give shape to his feeling of responsibility and clearly express [his regret].[19]

Minoda then listed all the positions that Suehiro still held—at Tokyo Imperial University and elsewhere—adding that it was "lamentable" that he continued to occupy such positions of authority.[20]

These charges of seeking to alter the kokutai and the ferocity of the attacks against those who were alleged to be tampering with it beg the question: what, for Minoda, *was* the kokutai? In the same essay in which he attacks Suehiro and lays out his lawsuit against him, Minoda offers a brief gloss of the kokutai:

> The Japanese national polity calls for a spirit of vassalage, expressed as "the lords do as the august sovereign commands," and "to receive an imperial command is to obey it." It is for this reason that we may be sure that it is an expression of a desire to alter the kokutai to express the willingness to contradict the sublime pronouncement made by His Majesty in a rescript proffered upon the promulgation of the Imperial Japanese Constitution: "Our Ministers of State, on Our behalf, shall be held responsible for the carrying out of the present Constitution, and Our present and future subjects shall forever assume the duty of allegiance to the present Constitution."[21]

The kokutai, for all intents and purposes, lay beyond interrogation. Suehiro had made himself an easy target with his criticisms of the military and the use of state force to maintain "subjectivity."

More specifically, one of the reasons why Minoda thought that Suehiro's appeal to "subjectivity," however enforced, would not work was that it was an artifact of Western science and political philosophy and therefore a priori inimical to the Japanese kokutai: "It is obvious that the justifying pronouncements of liberal research on *Geisteswissenschaftlich* universal rights must not be applied as a model for research into the national polity or the national Constitution of Japan."[22] For Minoda, the kokutai was out of bounds. It could be used as a cudgel for enforcing obedience or as a spotlight for discovering enemies among the people, but it could never be placed under a microscope and examined objectively. Suehiro's quest for apolitical equity had brought him up against a wall of totalizing politics. The kokutai, as the essence of the Japanese polity, was the means that Japanese imperial politics infiltrated and politicized all attempts to find non-political solutions to problems with Japanese society.

Minoda was also exercised by Suehiro's having brought his theoretical speculations to bear upon a particular question of pressing political import. In a 1933 essay titled "Violence and the Rule by Law" (*Hōchi to bōryoku*),[23] Suehiro expounded upon the theoretical reasons for the need for occasional violence in order to overturn laws. This work was a clear reference to Suehiro's advocacy for tenant farmers,[24] an advocacy that Minoda and many of his colleagues saw as helping open the door to communist revolution in Japan.[25] In a later essay, Suehiro touches directly on the tenant farmers' struggle, allowing, again, that violence in the name of righting perceived injustices is not always forbidden. In the text of his lawsuit against Suehiro, Minoda quotes Suehiro: "Just as, in the past, a theological worldview corresponding to rule by theocratic despots was in broad control of society, the modern democratic state, which champions rule of people by people, has concomitantly established a jurisprudential *Weltanschauung* which has substituted the state for God, and law for the divine will. This worldview is nothing but the 'vulgarization of the theological worldview', just as Engels said."[26] What Minoda found especially troubling was that, for Engels—and, by extension, presumably for Suehiro, too—class conflict was inevitable and perennial, ending only when the oppressed classes took up arms and violently overthrew their bourgeois oppressors.[27]

Up to this point, Minoda's attacks may perhaps be dismissed as circumstantial, based on equivocations between terms and phrases found in Suehiro's works and the works of communist agitators and Marxist philosophers. But Suehiro goes further in his insistence that violent struggle is the very essence of the modern capitalist state. For example, in an essay titled "Legal Conflict and Actual Conflict,"[28] Suehiro explicitly adopts the Marx/Engels line on the centrality of class conflict and concomitant violent struggle to the modern state:

> Real society is always the scene of a conflict of actual force.[29] [...] It has always been the case that the tenant farmer disputes were like labor disputes in that neither were suitable for resolution in a court of law. From the beginning, these were disputes that transcended the law, and were also ways of settling disputes.[30] [...] Most likely, he who has social power will awaken to that fact and will then demand a position within society in accord with his power. When he makes the effort to carry through his demands by force, the dispute that will arise because of it can be resolved only through a forceful struggle. [The resolution of such disputes] is altogether impossible for the state [to effect].[31] [...] Therefore, class-based struggles of force, like labor disputes and tenant farmer disputes, will certainly never be resolved by applying state power or through the law courts. The state must deal with such things by first recognizing the reality that they are struggles of power, and then must resolve them as precisely what they are: power struggles.[32] [...] It should be obvious that tenant farmers would tend toward the use of violence as their weapon of absolute last resort.[33] [...] It is eminently natural that tenant farmers should exhaust every ounce of their strength in a fight to the death in order to resist this [threat to their livelihood]. The Kizakimura Incident[34] and all the other tragedies happening in farming villages are nothing but a consequence of this perfectly natural [drive to defend one's own livelihood].[35]

Suehiro is clearly not opposed to the tenant farmers' use of force in resolving their disputes with the state. Not only this, but, as Minoda remarks in his comments on the string of Suehiro quotations just given,

Suehiro, in his essay titled "Tenant Farmers and Land Ownership Rights,"[36] argues in favor of the uncompensated confiscation of [landlords'] land.[37] For Minoda, these were not even veiled threats against the kokutai—they were direct assaults.

Gnosticism and Conflicting Interwar Ideologies

Japan in the 1930s was a whirlpool of absolutisms (including absolute relativisms) all vying for control. Much of the centralized Japanese state's efforts to suppress communist and socialist activity were grounded in the need to defend against the totalizing nature of those ideologies. Minoda's zealous support for the kokutai was in many ways a response to the Comintern's program for world revolution that had also proven itself unwilling to brook any kind of dissent. Between the Japanese imperial kokutai and the dictates of Third International communism, there could be no common ground. The ideologies themselves precluded compromise.

In this sense, both Comintern communism and Minoda's philosophy were nearly perfect examples of what Eric Voegelin would later diagnose as "Gnosticism." For Voegelin, Gnosticism was "a purported direct, immediate apprehension or vision of truth without the need for critical reflection; the special gift of a spiritual and cognitive elite."[38] As a closed system, Gnosticism relied on some kind of prophetic insight, usually by a charismatic founder, which was prevented in some way from being accessed by those outside the system.[39] Assenting to a founder's totalizing organizing principle was typically the passe-partout into the Gnostic scheme. Those outside the scheme were, by definition, incapable of accessing and understanding the intellectual or spiritual riches available to initiates. Minoda's hermetically sealed definitions and tautologies offered in support of the kokutai make it clear that Minoda was most certainly a Gnostic in the Voegelian sense of the term.[40]

What about Suehiro, though—was he a Gnostic, too? The answer is "no." A hidebound pragmatist and intellectual bowerbird, Suehiro almost never, in his sheaves of writings, appealed to an overarching principle in justification of a proposed course of action. If it works, do it; if not, do something else—this seemed to be the one lodestar of Suehiro's philosophical cosmos.[41] If Voegelin's diagnosis of Gnosticism applies to Marx and Minoda, then by the same measure it falls short of fully encompassing Suehiro's philosophical outlook and jurisprudential approach. The living law did, in fact, have a guiding principle beyond muddling trial-and-error tactics in a Polanyian sense of being rooted in a particular culture, a network of mores, memories, and shared assumptions about the way the world should work. As such, both Suehiro's Ehrlichianism and Minoda's kokutai find their heft in the particularities of Japanese cultural and historical life. But for all of his Ehrlichian influence, Suehiro's brand of equity was ad hoc and fundamentally apolitical and only incidentally Japanese. Suehiro, in that sense, was the antithesis of Minoda and of the communists and Marxists, for Suehiro subscribed to no overarching ideology at all.

It also militates against Suehiro's having been a Gnostic that the Taishō Period, before the raised imperial stakes of the 1930s, had been a relatively apolitical age. Politics as a totalizing episteme simply was not a factor of early Taishō intellectual life. As philosopher Miki Kiyoshi later recalled:

> Even though we experienced the tremendous event of the First World War, we were utterly uninterested in politics. We had contempt for politics and valued culture, meaning we exhibited both anti-political and apolitical tendencies. This was a culturalist way of thinking. The thought known as "refinement" was literary and philosophical. Which is to say that we placed a particularly high premium on literature and philosophy, but looked down on science and technology as being subordinate to culture and civilization.[42]

According to Miki, at least, the Taishō Democracy milieu out of which Suehiro emerged was not a place likely to foster political or ideological Gnosticism.

Voegelin's insights thus allow us only to go so far in splitting Minoda and Suehiro. Is there nothing that allows us a view of the divide from a higher, more permanent remove? The answer lies in Tanaka Kōtarō's criticisms of his contemporaries' neo-Kantianism. In other words, whereas Suehiro's antinomian pragmatism slips through the net of Voegelin's Gnosticism rubric, which assumes an active attempt to enclose contingency under a philosophical paradigm (precisely what Minoda did with his complete devotion to the amorphous idea of the kokutai), Tanaka's critique of neo-Kantianism reveals a deeper layer of contradictions underlying not only Minoda's political fervor, but also Suehiro's pragmatic avoidance of organizing principle.

In a revealing essay,[43] Kevin Doak highlights Tanaka's principled critique of several Japanese thinkers. For example, Tanaka criticized Miki Kiyoshi's "technological reductionism."[44] As Doak explains:

> By the early Shōwa period, [...] the greatest threat to universalism and moral philosophy was Miki's own technological positivism that eschewed both metaphysics and a religious outlook in favor of a socially deterministic ideology of technological positivism. As Tanaka astutely observed, such positivism led to the view that 'there is no science other than the recognition of the conventional morals and laws (*jittei-teki dōtoku mata wa jitteihō*) of a given society. This is a negation of the very ideas of ethics and jurisprudence'. Tanaka saw such positivism as the greatest threat to the moral good of Japanese society, and he emphasized that this positivism informed movements on both wings of the political spectrum.[45]

While other groups and individuals, such as those associated with the quasi-Marxist journal *Under the Banner of the New Science*, were more explicit in their attempts to "[r]eject nature as a constraint," Suehiro, in his often-repeated emphasis on social science as the key to understanding and overcoming social problems, as well as in his neo-Ehrlichian call to privilege the organically arising living law as a challenge to the rigidity of the logic of the state, falls squarely within the bounds of criticism against the "socially deterministic ideology of technological positivism" leveled by Tanaka Kōtarō.[46] Tanaka saw that the unifying thread connecting all of the disparate attempts to reject the given order of things in favor of one form of social or political re-engineering or another—be it Minodian statism or Suehiroian pragmatism—was the wholesale adoption by most Japanese thinkers and political philosophers, whether they realized it or not, of neo-Kantianism.[47] It was in the shadow of this neo-Kantianism, prominent in Japanese intellectual life since the 1913 publication of a Japanese translation of *Prolegomena zu einer jeden künftigen Metaphysik die als Wissenschaft auftreten können*, that subsequent Japanese philosophers would have to work out their moral and political philosophies.[48]

Even Nishida Kitarō—the mentor of Miki Kiyoshi and arguably the greatest Japanese philosopher of the twentieth century—ultimately espoused a consonance between subject and object in the entity of the state.[49] Nishida's radical neo-Kantian relativism left him unable to find transcendence to human nature as particularized in the individual. Therefore, the individual finds identity in the state. In *Zen no kenkyū* (An Inquiry into the Good), Nishida writes:

> We individuals, conversely, have developed as cells within a single society. The substance of the state (kokka no hontai) is the expression of the communal consciousness that is the basis of our spirit. We can achieve significant growth in character (jinkaku) within the state. The state is a single, unified character, and the system of laws of a given state is, in this way, the expression of the will of the collective consciousness. The reason we give our all to the state is to complete the development of this great character. And the reason the state punishes people is not revenge, nor for social tranquility. It is because it possesses a dignity whose character must not be violated.[50]

Nishida, eschewing his earlier advocacy of a Buddhist-Christian universalism, began to anchor his philosophy in the particularity of the Japanese nation-state.

Catholicism at the Center of the Debate

Despite these seeming affinities, Nishida and Minoda disagreed on how, and whether, the Japanese state should be universalized. While Minoda advocated a pan-Asianist transformation and liberation of Japan's Asian neighborhood by means of the ancient Confucian notion of the "kingly way" (*ōdō shugi*), Nishida was in favor of *hakkō ichiu*, or the joining of the entire world under one roof of rule by the Mikado, which was a distinctly Japanese—in contradistinction to Christian, Buddhist, or even kingly—way of universalizing his surroundings.[51] This was too universalistic for Minoda, though. Japan might work on behalf of her Asian neighbors, but Minoda saw it as heretical, and even nonsensical, to suggest extending the kokutai out to those unable, by their very nature, to understand it.

Minoda Muneki's true adversary was not Nishida, however, but Tanaka. What especially riled Minoda was Tanaka's Catholicism, and in particular Tanaka's advocacy of a globalist instantiation of the natural law that Tanaka called "world law." In *The True University Problem*,[52] Minoda criticizes Tanaka's "stateless globalism."[53] As Minoda quotes Tanaka:

> Law premised on the state system is nothing but an immoderation. . . . We believe that the time has arrived for us to break apart this stubborn shell by means of the problem of world law.[54] For the sake of the academic consciousness of law, it is sorely needed to liberate law from the state, in doing so overturning the old way of thinking according to which the commands of the sovereign were accepted, and establish law on the basis of mankind's social life itself.[55]

Minoda does not quote unfairly here. If anything, he has left out the most strident of Tanaka's points from the cited *Sekaihō no riron* section[56] that ends on an unequivocal note entirely consistent with the rest of the book: "In summary, the single most urgent task before us for the sake of affirming world law is to liberate law from the concept of the state."[57] Whether intentionally or not, this posed a direct challenge to the very heart of Minoda's kokutai ideology.

The timing of Tanaka's book's release, in February of 1932, also seemed calculated to increase Minoda's anger. Just three months after Tanaka's book was published, Colonel Kitahara Hitomi, an army officer assigned to the Catholic Sophia University (*Jōchi Daigaku*) in Tokyo for training purposes, took sixty sophomores from Sophia's college preparatory school to Yasukuni Shrine in Kudanshita, Tokyo. When two or three (reports disagree on how many) students refused to bow at the Shintō shrine to the war dead, Col. Kitahara reported the incident, which immediately made national news.[58] In May of 1932, Tanaka serialized a long essay titled "Fascism and Catholicism" in the *Yomiuri Shimbun*.[59] Minoda mentions this briefly in "Motive and Objective in Censuring the Tokyo Imperial University Law Faculty: Impressions Concerning Tanaka Kōtarō and Yokota Kisaburō's Lawless Anti-Japan Thought, and on the Communist Party Lynching Incident [of Obata Tatsuo],"[60] noting with disapproval that Tanaka's attitude had remained defiant since the Sophia Affair.

Despite Minoda's fixation on Tanaka's Catholicism, the issue at question was not essentially a theological one. Minoda did not necessarily take umbrage at particular points of Catholic dogma, but with the very fact that Catholicism is not a political system and in fact claims to transcend politics entirely. Tanaka put this succinctly in his initial column for the Yomiuri serialization: "Catholicism is not a political ideology. For this reason, generally speaking it is not possible for Catholicism to mount a direct attack on any kind of political ideology whatsoever."[61]

Minoda's disagreement with Tanaka, then, was not really about Catholicism as a religion per se, but about whether Catholicism can claim to go beyond the ethno-chthonic nationalism of Minoda's kokutai.

The *casus belli* for Minoda's full-scale attack on Tanaka and Catholicism was, of all things, a tiff over weights and measures. Tanaka had critiqued one Okabe Nagakage (1884–1970), a diplomat and minor politician who opposed the overturning of Japan's Meiji-era decision to maintain the older Japanese system of measurement.[62] Minoda disagreed with Tanaka's opinion that Japan would benefit by adopting the metric system, finding the old, native system of measurement more suited to Japanese use. But it was really Tanaka's obiter dicta on this issue that provoked a strong reaction from Minoda and others in the Genri Nipponsha. As Tanaka points out in his critique of Okabe, "We live today in a realm wherein nationalism is omnipotent," which Minoda immediately links to what he calls "The Red Professors at the Imperial Tokyo University and their Common Thread of Lawless, Anti-*Volk*, Treasonous Thought."[63] As with Nishida, Minoda objected here to a competing universal encroaching on the sacred particularity of the kokutai.

In his essay on the weights and measures issue, Minoda quickly dispenses with the pretext and gets to the meat of the dispute, launching into a lengthy mockery of Tanaka's Catholic-informed world law: "Tanaka is completely unrepentant that his own Roman Catholic revivalist thinking and his 'Theory of World Law' based thereon have fallen into Western medieval theologico-metaphysical errors of both time and place." For nearly a full page thereafter, Minoda gives a history of the divisions of Christianity, starting with Martin Luther, John Wycliffe, John Calvin, and Huldrych Zwingli to show that the former "Crusader" (Minoda's term) idea of a unified Christianity is now a "story from the past," the principle of national unity having long since outstripped and overwhelmed the ability of Christianity to organize political units on any sizeable scale.[64]

> In the modern age, during which political and economic activities and the common citizens' culture that supports those activities have become the unified center of the life of mankind, a nominally world religion—Christianity—is a private, individual affair that, insofar as the question of actual community in the social life of the nation is concerned, has nothing positively to do with anything.[65]

Minoda is not saying that Catholicism is a false religion as such, only that it isn't bigger than the state and has no business influencing the distinct national polity of Japan.

After criticizing Tanaka's apparent denial of the nation-state in favor of an abstract scheme of social organization strategies, Minoda cites Tanaka again: "Besides the *Volk*, there are the individual, the family, cities, villages, the state, international society, and the society of all humankind. Each of those has their own inherent functions. I can understand somewhat the emphasis on the significance of the *Volk vis-à-vis* a globalism arising out of individualism."[66]

In response to this, Minoda returns to his theme of the primacy of the nation-state in forming the individual and giving society a context in which to develop and thrive.

> Tanaka sees the *Volk* and the individual—and, *a fortiori*, even the state—in an oppositional, disjunctive relationship. But this view is an anachronism of eccentric medieval thought even as Western thinking goes. Tanaka is missing or has otherwise lost that common sense of a Japanese which sees the land of the gods, Japan, as one timeless and perfectly inwardly-indivisible relationship of *Volk*, state, and individual, all actually forming one living body, coeval with the creation of heaven and earth and as eternal as they, and making one divine, naturally generated cooperative, communal, *gemeinschaftlich* body. But where do the "individuals, families, cities, and villages"—which each have their "own inherent functions" "separately from the *Volk*, the citizens, and the state"—exist? Tanaka should think about the reality of the human and social values impinging upon that existence, for example the Chinese as a "disunified people scattered like sand"; Tanaka should also try considering how the Chinese are fulfilling their "own inherent functions"![67]

Minoda then avers that Tanaka cannot possibly know the meaning of the "international society"[68] that he (Tanaka) advocates, as "international" implies the interacting of nation-states (which Tanaka's theory presumably denies). Nor can Tanaka know the meaning of "a society of mankind," as "the global history of the human race is nothing other than the history of the rise and fall, emergence and disappearance of ethnic nations."[69] Minoda's conclusion is that Tanaka, who has accused Japanese nationalists of "cultural imperialism" (and here one strongly suspects that

Minoda has taken the liberty of including himself among those Tanaka has criticized), is, in point of fact, a Catholic cultural imperialist.[70]

The Problem of Denatured Western Philosophy

Interestingly, one of the main references in the long chapter of *Sekaihō no riron* from which Minoda cites above is Eugen Ehrlich. Tanaka is understandably eager to grandfather Ehrlich in as a member of the natural-law camp. The living-law approach, which Suehiro appropriated as technique but which Tanaka attempted to evaluate as philosophy and method, does indeed bear affinities with the natural law. For example, legal positivism sees law as merely the end product of legislation, which in turn is founded on state sovereignty backed up by force. But Ehrlich's living law, if seen as an embrace of spontaneous social ordering based on the innate human ability to know and live out the basic demands of justice, is a profound, albeit tacit, admission of the existence of the natural law. Tanaka writes:

> In both [ancient] Rome and in recent times, the authority of the state has expanded greatly and there has been a transformation into a despotic polity. The state is attempting to monopolize the law and is doing its utmost to suppress all sources of law that do not originate either directly or indirectly in state power. This is a situation one can find in both imperial Rome and in Western Europe during the sixteenth century.[71]

But then, in the corresponding footnote, Tanaka admonishes Ehrlich for not having seen either the historical antecedents to, or the philosophical ramifications of, his (Ehrlich's) own insights:

> I must say that it is regrettable that on this point Ehrlich had in view only the natural law of the seventeenth and eighteenth centuries, and was ignoring the strongly-rooted tradition of Scholastic natural law, which began in [ancient] Greece and Rome and continued through the middle ages and up to the present time. However, Ehrlich makes some noteworthy points in the text, such as that

> the natural law scholars are forerunners in the legal-historical view, and that the pioneers of the legal-historical viewpoint are those who perfected the natural law movement.[72]

It is difficult to discuss the living law, Tanaka is reminding his readers, without taking into consideration the natural law in its fullest historical complement.

Tanaka makes these points even more clearly by showing that Ehrlich had sided with Friedrich Carl von Savigny and Georg Friedrich Puchta against those who sought to elevate the state to near omnipotence:

> Ehrlich finds it regrettable that recent theories on the German common law have gone against Savigny and Puchta in moving toward a statist view of law and returning to the old path of theories of customary law, jurisprudence during the age of Imperial Rome, and the old common law. On the outstanding theories of Zitelmann on these points Ehrlich writes: "For this reason, over and against Savigny and Puchta, the old theories have again been used on the key points of customary law. [The old-theory revivalists argue that,] because, in principle, law is a manifestation of state power, it is necessary to have state authority's permission, approval, and consent, whether explicit or implicit, in all of [law's] various forms. Even if, following Savigny and Puchta, we were to attempt to create a foundation in general legal custom (*allgemeine Rechtsübung*) for the binding force of customary law, this would be nothing more than an attempt to add one special element to the statist theory of law. The real meaning of this theory is that all law begins with the state, and the state acknowledges extra-state law under certain conditions; as in standard legal belief, the state stops at saying that a law belongs to one of those [aforementioned] conditions. Zitelmann proved convincingly that these theories are baseless. He attributed customary law's effectiveness to the simple fact of customary law's being put into practice (*Geltung*). 'They are valid precisely because they are carried out.' ("*Es gilt eben deswegen weil es gilt.*") Within this tautology there at least lies dormant the deeper awareness that customary law exists separately from the state (*Ausserstaatlichkeit*). It is tantamount to

> saying that a law may be established with no respect of the state so long as that law is carried out in society."[73]

Later, Tanaka avers that customary law was largely ignored as a scholarly subject during the latter half of the nineteenth century as scholars were much more concerned with commenting upon, and finding the boundaries of, existing law, a process occurring in tandem with the promulgation of constitutions worldwide.[74] Ehrlich, according to Tanaka's quotes of him, noted this relative indifference to the customary law. Before long, legal theorists began to notice that court cases and administrative actions came to be interpreted within the realm of "universal human action."[75] The natural progression, then, had been towards Tanaka's "world law." Ehrlich and Tanaka thus both arrived at a version of the natural law despite starting from very different places.

Tanaka does not stop with Ehrlich, however. In his endnote to the passage quoted above, he also turns his attention to Suehiro, singling him out for sharp correction:

> On the one hand, Prof. Suehiro has emphasized the intimate relationship in Japan between law and social reality. On the other hand—not in his scholarly labors, to be sure, but limited strictly to his explanations for laymen—[Suehiro argues that] law is not the standard for human action, but rather the standard for courts. (See *Hōsō kanwa*, 5, 9, 20, and *Minpō kōwa*, vol. 1, 8 ff.) This is not only extraordinarily contradictory, but also, as I have pointed out before (in my book *Law, Religion, and Social Life*, 235 and 278), when law is divorced from the social life of humanity, it robs the law of its life force. Law is order (*Ordnung*). It is clearest in the realms of the Constitution and in administrative law that law does not stop with trial norms (*Entscheidungsnorm*)—which, according to Ehrlich, are a variety of law determined to rest on the foundation of trials as legal struggles (Ehrlich, *Die Tatsachen des Gewohnheitsrechts*, 1907, S. 26). Trial norms are nothing more than one kind of legal norm. (On this point, see Ehrlich, *Grundlegung*, SS., 15 ff., 33.) One cannot avoid the criticism that to see law as

> trial norms is to lapse into an Austin-type legal viewpoint which sees the state as omnipotent.[76]

From the natural law perspective, Tanaka argues, Suehiro's engagement with Ehrlichianism had been fundamentally flawed. Suehiro and Ehrlich had method but lacked substance. They had a program for bridging law and society but nothing beyond that to guide them. Their dialectic was at the mercy of whatever terms they were given.

In his critique of Suehiro's appropriation of Ehrlich's ideas, Tanaka presciently foresaw much of what Suehiro would actually do when faced with growing state power. Suehiro saw Ehrlich's *lebendesrecht* as a methodology useful for achieving particular results. But Tanaka understood that this methodology was deeply rooted in Christianity, and that without the ballast of faith the methodology of sociological jurisprudence could easily devolve into statist neo-Kantianism.

In a broad sense, Tanaka was in agreement with Minoda that Western concepts could not be separated from the culture that had produced them. Ironically, it was Minoda who assumed that all Western ideas were tainted with the culture of their origin, while Tanaka lamented that Western philosophies had apparently been cut off from their roots and imported piecemeal into Japan. For Tanaka, the Western concepts of individualism, nationalism, capitalism, socialism, and communism were bound to produce societal and intellectual anarchy in Japan because those who had imported those concepts had failed to import their Christian foundations:

> Earlier, Japan imported Western materialist civilization with no limits. But the most socially influential political and economic leaders, at the very least, did not accept Christianity, which forms the foundation for that [materialist civilization] and counteracts the damage [that it causes], and which parallels [that civilization] and is organically linked to it. It is understandable that the political and economic leaders of Japan wanted to emulate the great politicians of foreign countries, but the Japanese leaders thought—completely

> unrealistically—that they could cut out only those politicians' achievements and study them in isolation, paying no attention to their character and belief. Scholars studied the theories of Pascal and Pasteur, but demurred when it came to their orthodox Catholic faith. Thus, many of the professional politicians, the scholars who have caught the "professional disease," and the industrialists who are men of pure economics are crippled when it comes to being human beings. And yet it is these men who control the politics, the academy, and the business world in Japan. I don't know about the politicians of the early Meiji years, but many of their successors were lacking in moral training, whether that came from Confucianism or Buddhism or *bushidō*. The early Meiji politicians may have had such training, but many of the later politicians didn't. As a result, there was an absence of ideals and moral reflection that one finds in society and in a human life.[77] The vast majority of politicians were much more concerned with getting and keeping power, prestige, and wealth for themselves than they were with the farmers and laborers who wandered about at starvation levels. Industrialists were shamelessly brazen in following the dictates of their economic natures, and were unscrupulous about exploiting workers in order to line their own pockets. The endlessly repeated bribery scandals involving elite government officials in the bureaucracy, the fact of corruption of people in the political parties, and the embezzlement scandals involving the top management in the big corporations happen despite the fact that those who do those things have all received a top-class education, and have gained the trust of society and of the state. But [these scandals] show that that education has been limited strictly to materialist knowledge, and has been utterly lacking in moral training. Without moral training, education, talent, and especially legal knowledge all conversely become calamities. Today, we are now reaping the harvest of that Meiji Era education which aimed only at the importation of materialist civilization.[78]

Apart from indirectly complicating Minoda's insistence on the purity of the kokutai—for how can Shōwa Japan be purely Japanese if Meiji Japan was so enthusiastically Western, especially when the emperor system was established by such cosmopolitan elites?—Tanaka's critique also exposes the dangers inherent in Suehiro's own appropriation of Ehrlich's legal pluralism.

Minoda, for his part, rightly saw that the fundamental question for Tanaka was that of Catholicism, without which Japanese society was unable to make sense of any of the philosophical concepts it had adopted from the West piecemeal. Hence Minoda's insistence on breaking down Christianity and subjugating it to the nation-state. For Minoda, the state was the ontological ground of being and the epistemological filter of experience. Suehiro, likewise, although not an overt proponent of the kokutai, nevertheless backed into statism as a way to overcome the social chaos engendered by Ehrlichian social pluralism in a time of global crisis. Against both, Tanaka argued in opposition to the primacy of the state and in favor of the natural law.

In light of Tanaka's religious-based critique of statism, it becomes clear that Minoda Muneki and Suehiro Izutarō were not diametrically opposed in their philosophies. Minoda saw the state as a kind of ineffable demiurge greater than the sum of its parts (i.e., individual people). Suehiro, for his part, was what Tanaka elsewhere criticized as a neo-Kantian technocrat, possessing no principles on which to base moral judgments and so unable to resist the siren call of the state when it sought to put technical expertise in the service of imperial expansion.[79] As such, despite beginning from such seemingly different philosophies, Suehiro and Minoda were virtually bound to end up in the same place.

CONCLUSION

Already by 1920, Suehiro began to fear that disputes over the government's monopoly on the use of force (*kenryoku rōdan*) would split the nation-state up along class lines. By the 1930s, Suehiro had begun to privilege "stability" (*antei*) over liberty, and the state over society, as ways around the "dead-end of a liberal economy" (*jiyū keizai no ikizumari*).[80]

In 1933, Suehiro was writing warmly about the special paternalistic character of the Japanese labor market—a paternalism he had previously criticized—advising that semi-feudal labor relations should be made use of proactively in order to prevent the damage that might arise from those relations if left to themselves.[81] Thus, by the beginning of Japan's fifteen-year war in Asia, Suehiro, the founder and leader of the law-and-society movement in Japan originally rooted in the Ehrlichian attempt to treat the state and society as two semi-autonomous entities, had merged his jurisprudential revolution with the imperial expansion of the increasingly autarkic and apotheosized Japanese state. While Suehiro never embraced the worship of the kokutai as Minoda did, Suehiro did enthusiastically participate in the administration of new imperial conquests, putting his law-and-society project fully at the disposal of the centralized state as it pushed outward into the Asian continent and beyond.

This essential harmony between Minoda and Suehiro in terms of their relationship with the state was predicted by Tanaka Kōtarō even before Minoda sued Suehiro for *lèse-majesté* in Tokyo District Court in 1934 for allegedly besmirching the kokutai. The absence of an organizing philosophical principle bigger than the state doomed both men, Suehiro and Minoda, to embracing the state as a *faute de mieux* retreat from, and also concretization of, neo-Kantian relativism.

The Japan of the Shōwa Period was not the Japan of Meiji, high-minded political thinking or freewheeling Taishō experimentation with the full range of Western modernist philosophy. The world situation had worsened to full-blown crisis by the early 1930s, and political groupings on every inhabited continent scrambled to find some way to stave off the collapse of the liberal world order, often by turning to dictatorial expediencies and the wholesale intervention of a centralized state elevated to mythical, romantico-aesthetic, or even quasi-divine status. The law-and-society movement in Japan had struggled to compete with kokutai absolutism, but had failed. The divorce between law and society had been settled in favor of neither. The state—the broker called in to heal the rift—had simply nullified all previous arrangements and declared itself to be the solution to every other problem henceforth. As Catholic philosopher Tanaka Kōtarō repeatedly warned, law without natural law—government without God—could never have ended in anything but the denial of human dignity and the wholesale worship of the state.[82]

Notes

1. Joint review: *Hōgaku Kyōkai gojū shūnen kinen ronbunshū, gōhyō, Tōhoku Teikoku Daigaku Hōbungakubu* (npd), 57 (1868 in running pagination).
2. Yoshida Katsumi, "Shakai hendōki no Nihon minpōgaku–Hatoyama Hideo to Suehiro Izutarō," *Hokkaidō Law Review*, vol. 52, no. 5 (2002), 1665-1704.
3. Suehiro Izutarō, as reprinted in "Kaizō mondai to Meiji jidai no shōsatsu," *Uso no Kōyō*, op. cit., 62 ff.
4. Yoshida, "Shakai hendōki," citing Suehiro, *Gohan baishō no konpon genri* (1924), in *Hōsō kanwa*, op. cit., 87.
5. Yoshida, "Shakai hendōki," op. cit., 275 (1679), citing Suehiro, *Gohan baishō*, op. cit., 94–95.
6. Yoshida Katsumi, "Shakai hendōki," op. cit.
7. Yoshida Katsumi, "Shakai hendōki," op. cit., 275 (1679)
8. *Suehiro Izutarō no bōryoku shisō*. See also John David Person, *Philosophizing Japan: The Genri Nippon Society and the Question of Japaneseness* (PhD dissertation, University of Chicago, 2012).
9. Suehiro, *Gohan baishō*, op. cit.
10. Page 95 in original, cited in Minoda Muneki, *Zenshū* (Complete works), 271, in *Kokka to daigaku*, 243.
11. Lenin, 17, cited in Minoda, 244 of *Genri Nippon*, 272 of *Zenshū*.
12. Minoda, *Zenshū*, 244/272, citing Suehiro, *Hōsō kanwa*, 398. (Page numbers separated by a slash indicate page in original/page in Minoda, *Zenshū*.) The citation is taken somewhat out of context, as Minoda shifts suddenly to a completely different Suehiro essay in which Suehiro offers his "disorganized" (*muchitsujo*) thoughts in the immediate aftermath of the Great Kantō Earthquake in the October 1923, edition of *Kaizō*. Suehiro is critiquing bourgeois subjectivity, with a broader reference to the global competition of capitalism which seemed to necessitate militarism in Japan, and is furthermore concerned that this militarization has been accepted entirely too easily by ordinary Japanese citizens, especially the fact that military was deployed to keep the peace in Tokyo following the Great Kantō Earthquake. Suehiro says plainly that he is not attacking the military as such, and is grateful for their quick help after the natural disaster. His concern is that the "state of emergency" that prompted

the military's deployment is gradually becoming a permanent affair, and could be used to justify full-fledged militarism in the future. See also Giorgio Agamben, *State of Exception* (Chicago: University of Chicago Press, 2010).

13. Minoda, 244/272. For the complete English translation of the Meiji Constitution, see https://history.hanover.edu/texts/1889con.html.
14. Suehiro, *Hōsō kanwa*, op. cit., 399, cited in Minoda, 244/272.
15. Article 11. The Emperor has the supreme command of the Army and Navy. Article 12. The Emperor determines the organization and peace standing of the Army and Navy. Article 13. The Emperor declares war, makes peace, and concludes treaties. Article 14. The Emperor declares a state of siege. (2) The conditions and effects of a state of siege shall be determined by law.
16. Minoda, 244–45/272–73.
17. Minoda, 245/273.
18. Minoda, op. cit., 255.
19. Minoda, op. cit., 256.
20. Ibid.
21. Minoda, 247/275. Translation of Constitutional preamble from https://history.hanover.edu/texts/1889con.html.
22. Minoda here renders "universal rights" so literally—i.e., as "rights of the universe"—as to raise doubts that he did not fully understand the term. See Minoda, 247/275.
23. Published by Nihon Hyōronsha on January 20, 1933, in *Hōsō manpitsu*.
24. Suehiro's advocacy went beyond general theorizing to include pointed critiques of specific political figures. For example, on February 10, 1926, Suehiro took to the *Asahi Shimbun* newspaper to blast the Wakatsuki cabinet for a bill that Suehiro claimed would restrict the activities of labor unions. Suehiro accuses the bill's researchers of ideologically-driven ignorance, and the political parties and the politicians themselves of malfeasance. Cited in Harukata Takenaka, *Failed Democratization in Prewar Japan: Breakdown of a Hybrid Regime* (Stanford: Stanford University Press, 2014), 117.
25. One of Minoda's colleagues at the Nippon Genri organization, Mitsui Kōshi, was personally involved in the tenancy disputes in Matsushima, Yamanashi Prefecture, and had seen firsthand how communist ideas, including the call for full-scale revolution, had come to influence the mostly uneducated tenant farmers in the region. Minoda's broadside

against Suehiro was almost certainly influenced by Mitsui's experiences and subsequent journalism on the subject.

26. Suehiro, "Violence and Rule by Law," 101, cited in Minoda, 247/275.
27. Minoda, 276/248, citing Kaizōsha, *Marukusu Engerusu zenshū*, Vol. 22 (1928 et seriatim), 101–03 passim.
28. *Hōritsuteki tōsō to jitsuryokuteki tōsō* (1930), in *Hōsō zatsuwa*.
29. Suehiro, *Hōritsuteki tōsō to jitsuryokuteki tōsō*, op. cit., 95.
30. Ibid., 115.
31. Ibid., 97.
32. Ibid., 98.
33. Ibid., 116.
34. The Kizakimura farming village in Niigata Prefecture was the scene of a violent uprising of tenant farmers in 1922. The farmers' complaint was that when the prefectural authorities instituted more stringent quality control measures in 1907 in an attempt to improve the Niigata rice product, the farmers, and not the landlords, bore the burden of implementing the measure without receiving any of the increased revenues that resulted from the better rice. The problems in Kizakimura quickly spread to other farming villages in Niigata Prefecture. See, e.g., Inoki Takenori, ed., *Senkanki Nihon no shakai shūdan to nettowāku: Taishō demokurashii to chūkan dantai* (Tokyo: NTT Press, 2008).
35. Suehiro, *Hōritsuteki tōsō*, op. cit., 115; cited in Minoda, 250/278.
36. *Kosakujin to tochi shoyūken* (Minoda mistakenly cites it as *Tochi shoyūken to kosakujin*), in *Hōsō kanwa*.
37. *Tochi mushō bosshū seitōron*, in Minoda, 250/278. Suehiro's essay first appeared in the *Asahi Shimbun* on New Year's Day, 1925. In the brief introduction to the essay as reproduced in *Hōsō kanwa*, Suehiro writes, in a possible oblique reference to Minoda, that he was continuously criticized after the publication of the tenant farmer essay in the *Asahi*, with some accusing him of the extreme position of advocating the forced appropriation of land for the tenant farmers in spite of the [landlords'] rights of land ownership. However, Suehiro goes on to argue, his position is simply one in favor of recognizing the reality of disparate strength of rights among farmers and landowners, even as rights-talk grows more prevalent throughout Japan as a whole. Suehiro ends his introduction with a plea that his essay not be criticized or thought dangerous solely from the limited viewpoint of the landholders. Suehiro, *Hōsō kanwa*, op. cit., 152.

38. Eugene Webb, *Eric Voegelin: Philosopher of History* (Seattle: University of Washington Press, 2015), 282.
39. See, e.g., Michael Franz, *Eric Voegelin and the Politics of Spiritual Revolt: The Roots of Modern Ideology* (Baton Rouge: Louisiana State University Press, 1992).
40. See Minoda, *Zenshū*, op. cit., editorial postscript.
41. For a history of pragmatism in Taishō Japan, see, e.g., Funayama Shin'ichi, "Puragumateizumu no juyō to tenkai," in *Taishō tetsugakushi kenkyū* (Kyoto: Hōritsu Bunkasha, 1965), 215, ff.
42. Funayama Shin'ichi, *Taishō tetsugakushi kenkyū*, op. cit., 2–3, citing Miki Kiyoshi, *Dokusho to jinsei* (1942) (Tokyo: Shinchosha, 2008), 35.
43. "Romanticism, conservatism and the Kyoto School of philosophy," in Christopher Goto-Jones, ed., *Repoliticising the Kyoto School as Philosophy* (Oxon: Routledge, 2008).
44. Doak's phrase, "Romanticism," op. cit., 139.
45. Ibid., 139–40, citing Tanaka Kōtarō, "Gendai no shisō taikei anākii to sono gen'in no kentō," in Hayashi Kentarō, ed., *Shin hoshushugi*, in *Gendai Nihon shisō taikei*, 35 (Series) (Tokyo: Chikuma Shobō, 1963), 235–63 (248).
46. Doak, "Romanticism," op. cit., 146–47.
47. See also Doak, "Nationalism as Dialectics: Ethnicity, Moralism and the State in Early Twentieth-Century Japan," In James W. Heisig and John C. Maraldo, ed., *Rude Awakenings: Zen, the Kyoto School, and the Question of Nationalism* (Honolulu: University of Hawaii Press, 1995), 174–96, and Doak, "Under the Banner of the New Science: History, Science, and the Problem of Particularity in Early Twentieth-Century Japan," in *Philosophy East and West*, 48:2 (4) (1998), 232–56.
48. Immanuel Kant, *Prolegomena to any Future Metaphysics That Will Be Able to Present Itself as a Science*, first published 1783. Doak, 143, citing Robert William Adams, *The Feasibility of the Philosophical in Early Taisho Japan: Nishida Kitarō and Tanabe Hajime* (PhD dissertation, University of Chicago, 1991), 123–24.
49. See Gereon Kopf, "Between Identity and Difference: Three Ways of Reading Nishida's Non-Dualism," *Japanese Journal of Religious Studies*, vol. 31, no. 1 (May, 2004), 73-103.
50. Nishida, *Zen no kenkyū*, 253, tr. Kevin Doak and cited in Doak, "Romanticism," op. cit., 140.
51. Doak, "Romanticism," op. cit., 155. Even the possibility of a Minoda attack was enough to force Nishida to hew closer to kokutai orthodoxy.

For example, Nishida had advance warning that Minoda was planning to criticize him for a three-part speech Nishida was to present at Kyoto University on April 25, May 2, and May 9, 1938. Nishida was therefore particularly careful when using words like "world," "universal," and "cosmopolitanism," as well as anything hinting, at the opposite end of the spectrum, at liberalism, individualism, or "atomis[m]." See Michiko Yusa, *Zen and Philosophy: An Intellectual Biography of Nishida Kitarō* (Honolulu: University of Hawai'i Press, 2002), 292, ff.

52. *Shin no daigaku mondai*, op. cit., 65, in Minoda, *Zenshū*, 1073.
53. *Mukokka sekaishugi*, Minoda, *Zenshū*, 65/1073.
54. *Sekaihō no riron*, Vol. 1 (Tokyo: Iwanami Shoten, 1932), 144.
55. Ibid., 142.
56. "Dai ni shō: hō no gainen to kokka no gainen."
57. Tanaka, *Sekaihō no riron*, op. cit., 153.
58. *Sophia University newsletter*, no. 40, 100th Anniversary of Sophia University (2013), 1. See also "Jinja reihai kyohi mondai: Jōchi Daigaku wa jinja no gimu tokezu to iu," *Yomiuri Shimbun* (October 13, 1932).
59. "Fashizumu to Kasorishizumu no tachiba"
60. "Tōdai hōgakubu dangai no dōki mokuteki: Tanaka Kōtarō, Yokota Kisaburō shi no futei hai-Nichi shisō to rinchi Kyōsantō jiken no shokan tō" (1933).
61. *Yomiuri Shimbun* (May 10, 1932), 4.
62. See Hashimoto Takehiko, "From Traditional to Modern Metrology: The Introduction and Acceptance of the Metric System," in *Historical Essays on Japanese Technology* (Tokyo: University of Tokyo Center for Philosophy, 2009), 87–106.
63. Minoda, *Zenshū*, 22/1110.
64. Ibid., 22–23/1110–1111.
65. Ibid., 23/1111, citing Minoda, *Gakujutsu ishin Genri Nippon*, 542–43.
66. From the June 15, 1933, *Tokyo Asahi Shimbun*. Cited in Minoda, *Zenshū*, 1111/23.
67. Minoda, *Zenshū*, 23–24/1111–1112.
68. For a much more detailed background to the question of nationalism versus internationalism in Japan, see Kevin M. Doak, "Liberal nationalism in imperial Japan: The dilemma of nationalism and internationalism," in Dick Stegewerns, ed., *Nationalism and Internationalism in Imperial Japan: Autonomy, Asian brotherhood, or world citizenship?* (London: RoutledgeCurzon, 2003), 17-41. See also Doak, "The Place of National Identity in World Law: Reflections on Tanaka Kōtarō's Theory of *Min-*

zoku," in Urs Matthias Zachmann and Christian Uhl, eds., *Japan und das Problem der Moderne: Wolfgang Seifert zu Ehren* (München: Iudicium, 2015), 441-48.

69. Minoda, *Zenshū*, 24/1112.
70. Ibid., 24/1112.
71. Tanaka, *Sekaihō no riron*, vol. 1, op. cit., 117, citing Ehrlich, *Grundlegung der Soziologie des Rechts* (1913), 8: 11.
72. Tanaka, *Sekaihō no riron*, vol. 1, op. cit., 118–19.
73. Ehrlich, *Grundlegung*, op. cit., 379 ff., cited in Tanaka, *Sekaihō no riron*, op. cit., 123–24.
74. Tanaka, *Sekaihō no riron*, op. cit., 127.
75. Ibid., 127.
76. Ibid., 128–29.
77. Tanaka makes virtually identical arguments in an English essay published in 1957. See Tanaka Kōtarō, "What is Necessary to Make Democracy Work in Japan?" in Paul K.T. Sih, ed., *Democracy in East Asia* (Taipei: China Culture Publishing Foundation, 1957), 50–56.
78. "Gendai no shisōteki anākii," 243–44.
79. See, e.g., "Kachi no sōtaisei," in Funayama Shin'ichi, *Nihon no kan'nenronsha* (Tokyo: Eihōsha, 1956), 256 ff.
80. Ishida, in Rokumoto Kahei and Yoshida Isamu, eds., *Suehiro Izutarō to Nihon no hōshakaigaku* (Tokyo: Tokyo University Press, 2007), 169–70, citing Suehiro, "Shina kankō chōsa no kaishi wo yorokobu," in *Hōritsu Jihō*, vol. 11, no. 1 (Jan., 1939), 3, and Suehiro, "Antei genri no rōdō seisaku to rōdōhō," in *Hōritsu Jihō*, vol. 10, no. 9 (Sep., 1938), 4 ff.
81. Rokumoto and Yoshida, eds., *Suehiro Izutarō*, op. cit., 168, fn. 17, citing Suehiro, "Onjōshugi no botsuraku," in *Hōritsu Jihō*, vol. 2, nos. 5 & 6 (1930), 5, and Suehiro, "Kiro ni tatsu waga rōdōhō," in *Chūō Kōron*, vol. 50, no. 1 (1935), 22.
82. See Kevin Doak, *Tanaka Kōtarō and World Law: Rethinking the Natural Law Outside the West* (London: Palgrave MacMillan, 2018).

Chapter 6

Defeat, Purge, and Rehabilitation

Much of Suehiro's work to find equity during the Taishō Period centered on Tokyo Imperial University. It was there that he founded the Minpō Hanrei Kenkyūkai upon his return from studying abroad in the autumn of 1921; there that he established the Settlement House project, including the laborers' education guild and legal consultation clinic, in the wake of the Great Kantō Earthquake in 1923; and there also that he wrote the sheaves of pamphlets, articles, essays, books, and speeches that precipitated Minoda Muneki's lawsuit against him. Suehiro's core group of law-and-society colleagues were at the Tokyo Imperial University, and the law-and-society movement itself grew out of the bevy of conferences and writings produced by Suehiro and his closest ally in the movement, Hozumi Shigetō, also a Tokyo Imperial University professor of law. Suehiro's and Hozumi's pupils, too, naturally congregated around their teachers in Tokyo and launched their own law-and-society careers from there. Tokyo Imperial University—with Suehiro Izutarō as oracle and Hozumi as resident sage—was the omphalos of the law-and-society movement in Japan.

But as Japan's war with the West approached, the search for equity without politics had gotten bogged down in the administration of empire, and Suehiro had begun to look to "rationalization" (*gōrika*) far beyond Tokyo as a way to break free of the constraints of politics. Japanese society extended across the sea to include North China, the Korean Peninsula, and Manchuria.[1] Proclaiming the rendering of jurisprudence as a scientific pursuit, with statistical data to be used in both legislation and interpretation of laws,[2] Suehiro proposed strengthening the command economy by carrying out surveys of places that had recently come under the control of the Japanese Empire:[3]

> Suehiro's law-and-society studies theories took shape amidst the North China Farming Village Customs Surveys, which were surveys of occupied territory carried out between 1940 and 1944. The surveys were part of the "China Customs Surveys" carried out mainly under the auspices of the TōA Kenkyūsho (East Asia Research Office),[4] with the South Manchuria Railway Research Department (Mantetsu Chōsabu) lending local support. Suehiro was in charge of the TōA Kenkyūsho's Sixth Research Committee, Section One, and as the survey leader he would form his own law-and-society studies theories during the process of formulating survey policies. [...] It was Suehiro Izutarō himself who called for the survey. After the so-called "China emergency" [i.e., the beginning of the Second Sino-Japanese War], Suehiro was concerned with Japan's situation, and called for a survey [of China] in the October, 1938, issue of *Hōritsu Jihō*.[5]

Suehiro attempted to justify these surveys as necessities arising from *faits accomplis*, but he had proposed the surveys some two years before they were actually carried out and had further been preparing the rhetorical ground for putting the law and society movement at the service of the empire since long before 1938.[6]

In the same October, 1938 issue of *Hōritsu Jihō* cited above, Suehiro laid out the justifications for the North China surveys, noting that:

> Henceforth, the most important thing that we can do for the sake of Japan's political contact with the Chinese masses is first to learn what legal customs are current among those masses. [...] The most important preparation that we can make is to respect those [legal customs] and to continue using them, thus regulating our relations with them [i.e., the Chinese]. [...] Even if, for instance, we refuse to do this on the grounds that this kind of survey would have no political value, it would still have a tremendous scholarly significance to do this kind of large-scale survey of the legal customs current among the Chinese masses, as such a survey should have been carried out before but so far has not sufficiently been undertaken.[7]

However, the order of the justifications is significant. As Ishida argues:

> It is noteworthy here that [Suehiro's] emphasis on the political significance of the surveys comes before [his emphasis on] their scholarly significance. From the very beginning, Suehiro called for this survey with a clearly political intention to contribute to the control of occupied territory[8] in the aftermath of the start of the Second Sino-Japanese War.[9]

Hans Kelsen, Eugen Ehrlich's intellectual nemesis, foregrounded the state as a factor in law. The earlier, Ehrlichian Suehiro would have couched seeking out the "social facts of law" (*Rechtstatsachen*) as they prevailed among a non-state setting.[10] However, the Suehiro of 1938 foregrounded the fact that one of his express goals in proposing, organizing, and completing the survey was to aid in the Japanese government's administration of recently conquered Chinese territory. In the introduction to a work on his 1930s and 40s China surveys, Suehiro wrote:

> Of course, neither economic nor social laws are absolutes. In whatever way, the dictates of political disingenuousness stand to change [these laws] quite extensively. This goes without saying. Nevertheless, we must very severely admonish [those who would] fall into the way of thinking which ignores completely the authority of [economic and social] laws, and hold that political power should

> be given free rein to shape everything. While I think that, in order to prevent the damage that would result [from such an approach], we must make preliminary efforts to separate and set in opposition the state, which is the symbol of political power, and society, which is the symbol of social laws, I also think that the scientific method is the most suitable for studying the state, politics, and law.[11]

The scientific method notwithstanding, Suehiro wrote these words as an introduction to a report on surveys carried out for the more efficient administration of areas of China conquered by the Japanese Imperial Army.

However Suehiro conceived of his project, the breadth and detail of the surveys provided rich material for the state's exercise of political power over, and through, local custom. When listed out in the first volume of the survey report, the topics to be studied fill nearly twelve pages. Every conceivable aspect of society and law is touched. Some examples of items to be researched include:

> a/ Land ownership patterns as restricted by relationships of status or sanguinity[12]
> b/ Taxes and public dues in China, differing from systems of state taxation in modern states, conform to systems inherited from the Ming and Qing dynasties, and have brought about no small amount of accumulated damage; paying attention to how this has prevented the development of farming village economies, [prepare a comparison of] the Chinese tax system and modern land taxation[13]
> c/ Household wealth—what it comprises, whether it is based mainly in rights or in stewardship (in particular in the event of wealth held in common after the death of the household ancestor), legal relationship when disposing [of commonly-held wealth] (whether the family has the right of consent, right of first refusal)[14]

Despite Suehiro's protestations to the contrary, the surveys were in reality a detail-thicketed celebration of imperial efficiency and of the superiority of Japanese scientific culture.

Like surveys, sports in interwar Japan also illustrates the impossibility of the apolitical. Indeed, for Suehiro at least, public involvement in sports was political from the beginning. In 1922, some members of the intercollegiate swim squad at the University of Tokyo had grown dissatisfied with functionaries within the swimming section of the physical education cooperative (*Taiiku Kyōkai Suieibu*). The student swimmers thought that Suehiro would be able to effect a solution, so they went to knock on his door one night to seek out his guidance. Suehiro resolved the dispute, and then was invited to stay on as advisor, finding financial support for the swim team, which included writing checks out of his own funds.[15]

Such internal politics quickly took on national and then international ramifications. In August of 1927, for instance, Suehiro circulated a public letter threatening to leave the Meiji Jingu athletic association and even forego the Far East Meet (*Kyokutō Taikai*) out of disgust over a political battle in the Diet between the Ministry of Education (*Monbushō*) and the Ministry of Foreign Affairs (*Gaimushō*).[16] But the significance of sports for building a strong national body and increasing national prestige abroad was not lost on those cobbling together the empire. As swimming coach, Suehiro helped lead the Japanese cohort to victory in the 1932 Los Angeles Olympics. This was attributed not only to Suehiro's strength as a coach, but also to his tireless advocacy for the team in Japan, including his having insisted that a pool be built for them despite the economic downturn of 1930.[17] As Suehiro grew his adopted organization to greater success, though, he inevitably began to slip into the political currents that flowed through nearly every institution in interwar Japan.

Suehiro's involvement with the Japan swim team's Olympic appearance in Berlin in 1936 marked a turning point in the transition from his role as swim coach teaching young people discipline and seeing to their healthy physical development, to a new and much more complicated role as swim coach teaching discipline and seeing to physical development for the sake of the Japanese Empire. While Suehiro was under outside pressure to understand the political expectations incumbent upon him as an ambassador of Japan on the world stage, he also was proactive about fulfilling his new and expanded role, eventually going far beyond the rather modest requests made of him by the government to embrace and elaborate upon the possibilities of sports as a means to equip young people with the tools necessary to navigate the perils of a Japanese society beset by a world in crisis. The 1936 Olympics were thus not only a landmark event in twentieth-century history—they also were a milestone in Suehiro's life and thought. By the time Suehiro traveled with his swim team to Germany for the Olympic Games, he had already shed his former liberal leanings and come fully to embrace a National Socialist-style marriage between the technocratic state and a physically fit, well-ordered citizenry.[18]

In a September, 1944 pamphlet titled, "War and Physical Culture" (*Taiiku to sensō*), Suehiro set forth his ideas on the interconnectedness of sports and soldiering. This pamphlet, partially translated by SCAP staff, was included in Suehiro's SCAP file and contributed to the Occupation authorities' decision to purge him from Tokyo Imperial University. In the pamphlet, Suehiro recounts his experiences surrounding the 1936 Berlin Olympics:

> I got to hear of it [i.e., the army's attempt to co-opt sports for military purposes] for the first time in June, 1936 when on my way to the Olympics in Berlin, from Lieutenant General Oshima who was at that time the Managing Chief Director of the Great Japan Phys[ical] Culture Assisting Assoc[iation] (Dai Nippon Tai Iku Kyo [sic] Kai). What his Excellency Oshima told me at that time was: "You are going to the Olympics in this brilliant summer. The general public too, not knowing anything, hustle about to see you off. As long as you win in Berlin, they are simple enough to believe that that shows the excellence of our people's Physical Culture. But what the results of the latest examination of the conscripts show is something to be anxious about. I am Managing Director General of the Phys[ical] Culture Assisting Assoc[iation] + as such I have great anxiety about the future of our country. What I want you to do when you arrive in Berlin is win in the

> Olympics by all means. That goes without saying. But more than that—starting with Germany see how physical culture in every country is doing. Particularly note + see whether the general public in foreign countries are in ecstasy as in our country over the principle of Olympics. I want you to note + study this point carefully + look at it as a means of nat'l defense.["] Even England (where Suehiro sojourned in the autumn of 1936 on his way home to Japan from Berlin) was deadly in earnest on the viewpoint of defense + was making phys[ical] strength of the people her objective. And being made to see this, I secretly felt the anxiety for my country's slowness on this point.[19]

Suehiro says that a military officer ordered him to scout Europe for ways to integrate sports and empire in Japan, but in the end concurs with Lt. Gen. Oshima, "secretly fe[eling] anxiety" for Japan's "slowness on this point."

As with his decision to call for surveys of newly conquered territory on the Asian mainland, Suehiro cites the China Incident in 1937 as one of the key factors influencing his gradual turn toward embracing the Japanese imperial project in the realm of national sports:

> In 1937, the China incident broke out accompanied by the Olympics problem. Strong controversies took place between two opposing parties, one in favor of retaining the Olympics + the other of refining it. This was accompanied by discussions as to whether or not to do away with sports in general. In conclusion the Olympics were refused + the Phys[ical] Culture Assisting Assoc[iation] became a thing of the past, liquidating the first principle of the Olympics April 17, 1942. [triple underlining in the handwritten English translation] At the same time the Great Japan Physical Culture Assoc[iation] of today was established. Since liquidating the first principle of Olympics that has sports as its basis, connecting it to the Peoples' Phys[ical] Culture representing its object—the perfect fighting power [triple underlining in the handwritten English translation]—the Japan Physical Culture

> Assoc[iation] has been steadily working for the success of the new mission under military and government leadership.
>
> The whole nation's fighting power is found in its people's physical force. All people of the country must display full vigor otherwise we cannot fight out the war. To reach this object—what sort of physical culture is required? — First of all—give all the youth who will shortly become soldiers the kind of phys[ical] culture which would abundantly give physical force suited to a soldier such as: —Healthy people's training, soldier's training, soldiers all swim training + flying physical training.[20]
>
> All must do physical culture, not that based on sports. That is your first duty in these times.[21]

After the Japanese military became fully engaged in China in July of 1937, Suehiro encouraged "all people of the country" to "display full vigor" under the "Great Japan Physical Culture Assoc[iation]," which was "steadily working for the success of the new mission under military and government leadership."

Suehiro was visited monthly by the Kempeitai "throughout the war," so there is a possibility that he was playing up to a very particular audience.[22] And in many letters to the American authorities during the Occupation, Suehiro strenuously denies the charges against him, pointing out his own attempts, and powerlessness, to resist the "militarists" and "ultranationalists" in the organizations with which he had been associated. Suehiro also argued that the charges against him were politically motivated: Tanaka Kōtarō and Suehiro had clashed over a faculty appointment at Tokyo Imperial University in 1943 and had been on bad terms ever since. It was Tanaka who designated the Nippon Hōri Kenkyūkai as a dangerous organization and Tanaka who recommended that Suehiro be purged, even though then-Tokyo Imperial University president Nambara Shigeru vouched for Suehiro, writing to GHQ that he thought it "rather severe" to purge him. Suehiro's "chief weakness," Nambara allowed, "is that he follows the current of the times." But Suehiro's actions did not justify a purge, Nambara went on to argue.[23]

But another of Suehiro's acquaintances, Vice-Minister of Education Yamazaki Kyōsuke [Yamazaki Tadasuke], also wrote to say that, yes, Suehiro had accepted money as the head of the Nippon Hōri Kenkyūkai (Yamazaki says 400 to 500 yen a year; other accounts give 4,000 to 5,000) and had been an influential and leading member of the group.[24] And the overall tenor of Suehiro's oeuvre, beginning around the time he was sued by Minoda Muneki in Tokyo District Court in 1934 for having impugned the *kokutai*, provides very little reason for questioning the sincerity of Suehiro's publicly expressed sentiments. Indeed, as early as January of 1941, nearly one year before the bombing of Pearl Harbor, Suehiro took to the pages of his own magazine, *Hōritsu Jihō*, to express his admiration for the National Socialist method of government:

> At the party rally held at Nürnberg, Hitler and the other Fascist leaders declared that our government is a government which is most suitable to the name of democracy. Now, for the first time, I have begun to understand what he had meant.[25]

And, perhaps most revealing of his true feelings, in a private postcard to his wife in Japan mailed from Berlin in 1936, Suehiro recalled meeting Hitler in person during a personal audience between the German leader and the Japan swim team. Suehiro wrote glowingly about shaking hands with Hitler, who praised Japan's efforts in the pool.[26]

The Purge

On October 6, 1947, a certain Yoshiaki Kamei wrote in English to the Government Section at GHQ in part to recommend that Suehiro be purged. "He always changes his opinion to cope with the circumstances," Kamei wrote, and "is known to be an opportunist since his school days." Kamei lists as the first cause for Suehiro's recommended purge Suehiro's work with the "Nippon Taiiku Kai (Japan Athletic Union)":

> Dr. Izutaro Suehiro [...] during the war closely collaborated with Army people and as a matter of fact, he, as managing director of Nippon Taiiku Kai (Japan Athletic Union) ordered such games as baseball, lawn tennis, foot balls [sic] to be ousted because of their being foreign origin and adopted some new games such as army's fencing and others which were considered useful in war in all schools. If Butoku Kai officials should be purged, he has a great deal more reasons to be purged.[27]

Suehiro had therefore not only embraced the martial and calisthenic aspects of sports, but had also taken the cultural significance of sports—their names, their origins, their ability to cause association with particular habits of being—into account when using sports as a means to strengthen empire.[28]

Suehiro had other detractors, too. For example, Sagara Iichi (1910–1987), a Catholic educator and bureaucrat who had been a student of Minobe Tatsukichi and Tanaka Kōtarō at Tokyo Imperial University, took the trouble to write to SCAP to inform them that "Dr. SUEHIRO was originally a liberalist, but [...] the outbreak of the China Incident found him an opportunist to the backbone." The *Yomiuri Shimbun* was similarly anti-Suehiro immediately after the war, and SCAP duly took notice of this for their Suehiro files:

> As son-in-law of the late Dr. KIKUCHI Dairoku, he is brother-in-law of Dr. MINOBE Tatsukichi and the late Dr. HATOYAMA Hideo. He had such a conviction in his theory that he did not try to stand by Dr. MINOBE, when the latter became a target of criticism for his emperor-organ theory, and that he lived up to the policy of wartime physical education as the leader of the Physical Culture Association. [...] Dr. SUEHIRO was certainly looked upon as a persona non grata by the liberalists and democrats during wartime. Since the suspension of hostilities he made a left-turn apace. Labor problems in which he is a specialist were in favor of his volte-face. Taking advantage of the chance when he was appointed chairman of the Metropolitan Labor Committee for

> the settlement of the first Yomiuri dispute, he veered to the left, keeping himself abreast of the trend of the time."[29]

The immediate event which prompted Kamei to write to GHQ in October seems to have been the decision GHQ officials reached on September 17, 1947, not to purge Suehiro on the basis of his activities with the Butokukai, or Greater Japan Martial Virtue Society (*Dai Nippon Butokukai*). By the time the decision was made, Suehiro had already been "disqualified for assuming any educational post because of his having been an influential member of the Japan Jurisprudence Research Society," but Suehiro's appeal of this other judgment was working its way through GHQ.

The Dai Nippon Butokukai, founded in Kyoto in 1895 and disbanded on October 31, 1946, was a significant site for the intentional overlapping of sports and empire. As with the swimming federation, whose members knocked on Suehiro's door late one night to ask him to mediate an acrimonious internal dispute, the Butokukai members, too, called on Suehiro to restore order to their organization when their director, Gō Takashi, died in April of 1944. The background to the confusion surrounding the role of the Butokukai was the attempt, by both the Ministry of Welfare (*Kōseishō*) and the Army, to co-opt sports and sporting institutions for the purpose of "quasi-militaristic" training and recruitment.

Writing in September of 1947, to defend himself against the charges of collaboration and opportunism being leveled at him from various quarters, Suehiro gave a different interpretation of his involvement with the Butokukai:

> As both of the Great Japan Physical Training Association and the Butoku Kain [sic] have received the subsidies from the Welfare Ministry, they, with a view to obtaining full informations [sic] of business, particularly accounting, of the other so that both sides will abide by the demarcation line between their business, have concluded an agreement, at the time of the ex-chairman GO, Takashi of the Physical Training Association, that the chairman of

> board of directors of the one will be appointed as a director of the other. In April, GO, Takashi passed away and the subject person [i.e., Suehiro] who succeeded the chairman ship [sic] was neither based upon his willingness nor upon his contribution for the promotion of the Budo. [...] The subject person has tried to prevent the militarization—With reference to the problem to transfer the 'shooting division' of the Physical Training Association to the Butoku Kai, the subject person was positively opposed to it contending that, while, once transferred, the shooting would be militarized under the influence of the military officers, it should be kept, as it had been withing [sic] the Physical Training Association as one of the international sports.[30]

In a petition to the SCAP authorities dated February 20 of the same year, Suehiro provided more details on the government's insinuation into the inner workings of the various athletic boards:

> 1/ My connection with the Japan Amateur Athletic Association
>
> This JAAA was founded in 1911 mainly with the object to become the National Olympic Committee, and kept on growing as a purely civilian organization until 1942 when it was ordered by the Government to reorganize with a new name of Dai Nihon Taiikukai.[31] Officers of the Dai Nihon Taiikukai were to be appointed by the Government. Among the officers of the former JAAA four or five members were added to the new board of trustees as representatives of civilian groups. As I was chairman of the board of trustees of the JAAA at the time of the reorganization, I was made a trustee on the new board. [Suehiro then relates the death of Chairman Gō and his own succession to his post, the latter event of which Suehiro puts in April of 1944, conflicting with the SCAP document quoted above, in which Suehiro is said to have assumed the post in June of that year.] I am the founder and president of the Japan Swimming Association which had become an influencial [sic] organization among the athletics circles. It was natural, therefore, that I, chairman of the Japan Swimming Association, was asked to become a trustee of the JAAA in 1924. That was the beginning of my connection with the JAAA.

2/ The relation of the Dai Nihon Taiikukai with the Butokukai

The JAAA and the Butokukai were entirely separate civil organizations. But in April, 1942, by the order of the Government these two organizations were put under the control of the Social Welfare Department [Kōseishō], and were given the same amount of subsidy from the Government.[32] [Suehiro's undated petition continues:] After the reorganization, in spite of the interferences by the Koseisho and the Army, we, old patrons of the Taiikukai, fought hard and tried our best to maintain the real spirit of sportsmanship. This attitude was very much different from that of the Butokukai which was easily militarized from the very reason of its own nature.

After the reorganization, these two organizations came under the control of the Koseisho and began to receive government subsidy, and it was natural that there came out a necessity of connection and negotiation between the two in order to decide how much they should receive from the government. [...] The Taikukai [sic] and various sports organizations under it were drawing their necessary money from the admission fees and the contributions from the public. But since the outbreak of the war this source of income became very insignificant and they had to rely upon the government subsidy more and more.

However, the Butokukai's main income was the fees they charged when they granted "grades" and this source of income continued to come in without any change even after the war was started. Compared with our financial situation the Butokukai was much better off, but they always wanted the same amount of the government subsidy as that of ours, and it was the cause of many unpleasant matters between the two. [...] I made a strong protest against the fact that the sport shooting which had been organized in the Taiikukai was transferred to the hand of the Butokukai and was changed to military shooting. The shooting section of the Taiikukai was in accordance with the Olympic system, as the Taiikukai was organized for the Olympic Games. Even during the war we thought of the time when Japan could send men to the

> Olympic Games, and we wanted to continue this kind of sport shooting. But the Butokukai changed the nature of this section and put more emphasis on march than on shooting. I made a strong protest to Mr. Genzo Moroo who encouraged and pushed this tendency very strongly in the Butokukai. [To this statement is appended several testimonials by witnesses attesting to the truth of various claims Suehiro makes.][33]

In these lengthy missives, Suehiro portrays himself as a civic-minded outsider fighting militarists entrenched in civilian sports organizations.[34]

These postwar protestations of pacifism are difficult to square, though, with many passages from Suehiro's 1944 "War and Physical Culture," quoted in SCAP's English translation earlier in this chapter. For example, at the end of the 1944 essay, Suehiro writes:

> It goes without saying that the fighting force of a nation lies in the physical force of its entire people. Officers and soldiers on the front lines must, as a matter of course, be in robust and tough physical condition. We will not be able to fight this war through [to victory] if all of the citizens laboring on the homefront do not devote themselves 120% to keeping themselves physically fit so as to maximize labor efficiency. This is not all. Even regular citizens—young and old, male and female alike—not directly involved in production must be fit enough to survive this trying wartime production in good health. If we accept this as true, then it is clear that a regimen of physical education suited to the goal of cultivating this kind of physical fitness will be needed. This is precisely the kind of citizens' physical cultivation that we actually need today, and is the kind of citizens' physical cultivation for which we advocate. [...] But what sort of physical cultivation should one do in order to achieve these goals? [...] First and foremost, it must be a physical cultivation suitable to soldiering provided to every growing young male, without exception, who will later go on to join the ranks. Training in healthy citizenship, training for young men of conscription age, swim training for all young men of conscription age, aerial physical cultivation—all of these are physical education [examples] along the lines [of

> what we propose]. [...] I am therefore of the view that everyone individually must awaken to their primary duty as citizens at this time, which is none other than to cultivate, always and on a daily basis, that bodily strength that will allow them to carry through with distinction whatever contribution is deemed necessary during wartime, including serving in the military.[35]

These passages, and others like them in "War and Physical Culture," undermine Suehiro's postwar claims to have been against the militarization of sports. As demonstrated above, Suehiro was convinced of the necessity of sports to preserve Japan by at least as early as the Berlin Olympics of 1936.

Suehiro's writings on sports were similarly conflicted before his first excursion to the Olympics. In August of 1932, for example, on the occasion of the send-off party for the Japan men's swim team, Suehiro wrote in *Bungei Shunjū* that winning was much less important than sportsmanship, and that luck would determine much more of the outcome than would will.[36] But one year earlier, in 1931, Suehiro cited Theodore Roosevelt's views on sports, which were that some amount of "sacrifice" (*gisei*) on the field of play was necessary, even if it meant losing lives to the violence of sport, in order to cultivate "fighting spirit" (*fuaichingu supiritto*) among young men.[37] The picture that emerges is of Suehiro, turning "by slow degrees"—as Suehiro's denouncer Sagara put it—to put the political winds at his back.

Nippon Hōri Kenkyūkai

In their final report recommending that Suehiro be purged from all educational activity, the SCAP authorities, although aware of Suehiro's views on the usefulness of sports to empire and fully apprised of his conflicting statements on the nature of his involvement with the Dai Nippon Butokukai, nevertheless focused on Suehiro's involvement with the Nippon Hōri Kenkyūkai (Japan Jurisprudence Association).[38] The Nippon Hōri Kenkyūkai, originally founded in 1940 by former Minister of Justice and suspected "war criminal" Shiono Suehiko "to create a system of laws adequate to the establishment of a highly armed state in accordance with the national policies [for] the emancipation of East Asia from the yoke of Western Powers."[39] In the eyes of the SCAP authorities, it was this involvement, however secondary to Suehiro's other activities, that placed him "under Item 6, Paragraph 1, Annex 1 of the Ministry Ordinance Attached to the Imperial Ordinance 'as lacking in constancy of thought as an educator'."[40]

The same Sagara Iichi who wrote to GHQ to inform them that Suehiro had been "an opportunist to the backbone" wrote again to denounce Suehiro in more detail:

> As he admits, Dr. SUEHIRO was personally responsible for the Guidance [sic] of business concerning the Civil Code, especially the Status Act. [...] It was Dr. SUEHIRO who dr[ew] up the synopsis [of the Status Act, with] special emphasis laid on the following points:
>
> The Japanese Status Act must be looked upon with the Emperor —who holds the throne unbroken for eternity—as the focus, like the sun of the system. Properly speaking, all Japanese laws are derived from the Illustrious Virtues of the Emperor, who, as an incarnation of Divinity, is of a piece with His Divine Ancestors. [...] In strict observance of this Imperial Spirit, Japanese subjects should play their respective part in the field of politics, economy, learning and other walks of life. [...] The Japanese Status Act is derived from the Illustrious Virtues, the one fountain-head—being at once an ideology of unifying law which reverts to them. [...] First and foremost of all, we are the Imperial subjects, not mere human beings.[41] The emphasis laid on opposing conflict of rights and duties between individuals by allowing ample scope to individual liberty in the various laws and regulations regarding man's status, does not fit in with the particular circumstances of Japan. It is of urgent necessity to regulate the duties of the subjects by moral laws derived from the national polity, dissociated from individualistic and liberalistic legislation. Not only must drastic reforms by made, in order to place Japanese laws where they should be, in the statutes that do not fit in with the actual circumstances

> of our country, that are against morals and that do not serve the need of national life, but the inherent spirit of Japanese laws must be brought to light by being emancipated from the yoke of the Western spirit of laws in their interpretation and application.[42]

In light of these views of the Status Act, it becomes clear why the SCAP authorities purged Suehiro primarily on the basis of his involvement with the Nippon Hōri Kenkyūkai. Whereas labor, surveys, and sports were all means for the collaboration between individuals and empire, the Nippon Hōri Kenkyūkai was the jurisprudential, philosophical, and even theological justification for that collaboration. The Status Act and the accompanying memoranda and interpretations are much lengthier than these brief excerpts indicate. As Sagara remarks at the end of his report, these excerpts alone are sufficient to show that Suehiro's later defense of weak involvement with the Nippon Hōri Kenkyūkai is entirely implausible.

With GHQ at the helm of Japan, the gap between law and society grew even wider. SCAP's decision to purge Suehiro on the most purely legal grounds available to the Occupation authorities flew in the face of Suehiro's enormous popularity with Japanese law students. The results of a straw poll published in the November 15, 1946, edition of the *Asahi Shimbun*, for instance, showed that an overwhelming majority—94.7% percent—opposed Suehiro's purge and wanted him to continue to lecture, especially on labor law. This was despite ongoing attacks against Suehiro, including a scathing October 2, 1946, article in the *Yomiuri Shimbun* that portrayed Suehiro as a shrewd opportunist.[43]

Conclusion

The members of Suehiro's law-and-society group, including Suehiro himself, both acknowledged the "inefficiency" of the empire, but were stunned by the empire's dissolution. As Suehiro's protégé, Kainō Michitaka, writes in the prologue to Suehiro's book on the Civil Code (*Minpō Kōwa*):

> As we in our generation understood it thirty years ago [i.e., around 1924], the collapse of the Great Japanese Empire was unforeseen. As the Great Japanese Empire grew increasingly irrational and inefficient [*higōriteki na mono*] with the expansion of war, it began to exert greater and greater pressure on individuals' personal lives. And yet, until we actually experienced it for ourselves, we had no idea that it was inevitable that something so irrational and inefficient would cease to exist.[44]

The arrangement of state, empire, and courts was not perfect, but it worked, and it seemed permanent, until suddenly it ended.

That Suehiro was purged for his involvement in the Nihon Hōri Kenkyūkai, but then allowed to become the head of the Labor Commission (in 1946), shows just how undecisive the shift from wartime to postwar actually was. While he was under investigation for his wartime activities by the SCAP bureaucracy, for example, Suehiro was also applying for funds to travel to the US and observe the ways in which labor unions and the labor law functioned. He was awarded those funds, and returned to Japan to write a flurry of articles and essays on what he had seen of American labor and labor law. Diagnosed with cancer, Suehiro died soon after returning from the US. Perhaps in an act of mercy, or perhaps just in a case of unintentional bureaucratic timing, Suehiro was "de-purged" on September 10, 1951, just one day before he passed away on September 11.

While the American Occupation has largely passed into history—with the important exception, especially when discussing Suehiro, of the 1947 Constitution—the caselaw method Suehiro introduced, along with his law-and-society-studies movement more broadly, continue to influence the way in which law is actually learned and practiced in Japan. In many ways, the equity that Suehiro promoted has even modified the Anglo-American case method to make it more apt to produce justice in a given case: whereas the principle of *stare decisis* can lead to a separate set of quasi-statutory law that must also be worked around when attempting to administer justice under unique circumstances, in Japan judges may consult prior cases, but are forbidden from using them as (overt) bases for their decision-making. As Suehiro advocated, judges flesh out the statutory law in an ongoing process of jurisprudential dialectics, filling in gaps in the legislated law by using natural reason, and not necessarily abstracted ratiocination meant to carry the weight of prophetic finality, to decide what is best for the parties in a given dispute.

This is the practice of Japanese law, and it has been so for a span of time in comparison with which the heady world-remakings of the Meiji Period and thereafter—including especially the New Deal refounding of the Meiji state in 1945—dwindle in significance.[45] The key to understanding the continuities that underlie post-Meiji Japanese jurisprudence is Suehiro Izutarō and the law-and-society movement that he midwifed. The Japanese empire for a time confounded the practice of equity that is the natural mode of Japanese justice, but even the empire did not outlast it.

NOTES

1. See Thomas David Dubois, "Inauthentic Sovereignty: Law and Legal Institutions in Manchukuo," *Journal of Asian Studies*, Vol. 69, No. 3 (August, 2010), 749-770.
2. Ishida, in Rokumoto and Yoshida, eds., *Suehiro Izutarō to Nihon no hōshakaigaku*, op. cit., 170, citing Suehiro, "Hōritsugaku no kagakuka," in *Hōritsu Jihō*, vol. 13, no. 9 (Sep., 1941), 61-62.
3. This was not to be the first survey of Chinese territory. See, e.g., Okamatsu Santarō (writing as "Santaro Okamatsu"), *Provisional Report on Investigations of Laws and Customs in the Island of Formosa, Compiled by Order of the Governor-General of Formosa* (1900; reprinted by Ch'eng Wen Publishing Company, Taipei, 1971). See also Uchiyama Masao, *Nihon no Chūgoku nōson chōsa to dentō shakai* (Tokyo: Ochanomizu Shobō, 2009).
4. See, e.g., Tsuge Hideomi, *TōA kenkyūsho to watakushi: senchū chishikijin no shōgen* (Tokyo: Keisō Shobō, 1979). See also Tsuge Hideomi, *Waga uchinaru Chūgoku* (Tokyo: Aki Shobō, 1971).
5. Ishida Makoto, in Rokumoto and Yoshida, eds., *Suehiro Izutarō to Nihon no hōshakaigaku*, op. cit., 170-171, citing Ishida Makoto, "Senzen Nihon ni okeru Ajia hō kenkyū no ichi danmen: Kahoku nōson kankō chōsa wo chūshin toshite," in *Nagoya Daigaku hōsei ronshū*, no. 132 (1990), 35 ff. Suehiro continued to advocate for the collection of data as a way to understand the law even after the end of the Pacific War. See, e.g., Rokumoto and Yoshida, eds., *Suehiro Izutarō to Nihon no hōshakaigaku*, op. cit., 105, ff.
6. See also Suehiro Izutarō, "Chōsa kenkyū to okusoku," in TōA Kenkyūsho Dai Roku Chōsakai, Gakujutsubu Iinkai, ed., *Shina kankō chōsa ihō* (Tokyo: not issued for sale, 1942).
7. Suehiro, "Shina ni okeru chōsa no hitsuyō," in *Hōritsu Jihō*, vol. 10, no. 10 (Oct., 1938), 2-3.
8. For a detailed history of how this occupied territory was actually administered by the Japanese police, see, e.g., Erik Esselstrom, *Crossing Empire's Edge: Foreign Ministry Police and Japanese Expansionism in Northeast Asia* (Honolulu: University of Hawai'i Press, 2009).
9. Ishida, in Rokumoto, *Suehiro Izutarō to Nihon no hōshakaigaku*, op. cit., 170-171, citing Suehiro, "Shina ni okeru chōsa no hitsuyō," in *Hōritsu*

Jihō, vol. 10, no. 10 (Oct., 1938), 2-3. See also Ishida Makoto, "Shokuminchi shihai to Nihon no hōshakaigaku—Kahoku nōson kankō chōsa ni okeru Suehiro Izutarō no baai," in *Hikaku hōgaku*, vol. 36, no. 1 (2002), 1 ff; Toshitani Nobuyoshi, "Senzen no hōshakaigaku," in Kawashima Takeyoshi, ed., *Hōshakaigaku kōza*, Vol. 2, op. cit., 236-238; and Baba Ken'ichi, "Kagakuteki chōsa to kenkyūsha no seijiteki sekinin: Kahoku nōson kankō chōsa to sono hyōka wo megutte," in *Hōshakaigaku*, no. 57 (2002), 170 ff. See also Fukushima Masao, "Chūgoku nōson kankō chōsa to hōshakaigaku: tokuni Suehiro hakase no hōshakaigaku riron wo chūshin toshite," in *Fukushima Masao chosakushū*, Vol. 6, *Hikakuhō* (Tokyo: Keisō Shobō, 1995), 351, ff. Suehiro, "Hōritsu to kanshū: Nihon hōri tankyū no hōhō ni kansuru hito kōsatsu," in Chūgoku nōson kankō chōsa kankōkai, ed., *Chūgoku nōson kankō chōsa*, Vol. 1 (Tokyo: Iwanami Shoten, 1955), 25-32; quotes taken from 27.

10. See Michel Coutu, review of Marc Hertogh, ed., *Living Law: Reconsidering Eugen Ehrlich*, in *Osgoode Hall Law Journal*, 47:3 (2009), 593.
11. Suehiro, *Hōritsu to kanshū*, in *Chūgoku nōson kankō chōsa*, op. cit., 25-32; quotes taken from 31.
12. *Chūgoku nōson kankō chōsa*, op. cit., 33.
13. *Chūgoku nōson kankō chōsa*, op. cit., 37.
14. *Chūgoku nōson kankō chōsa*, op. cit., 39.
15. Tabata Masaji, "Nihon Suiei Renmeikai kaichō, Suehiro Izutarō sensei no shi wo itamu," *Suiei: Nihon Suiei Renmei Kikan zasshi*, no. 92 (1951), 3
16. Tabata, *Nihon Suiei*, op. cit., 2-3
17. Tabata, *Nihon Suiei*, op. cit., 3
18. On the worldwide interest in National Socialist law at this time, see Wagatsuma Sakae, ed., *Nachisu no hōritsu* (Tokyo: Nihon Hyōronsha, 1937), esp. 3-4.
19. GHQ/SCAP Records (RG 331, National Archives and Records Service), Box no. 5435, Folder title/number (12) War and Physical Culture—by SUEHIRO, Gentaro (Senso To Taiiku), Sept. 1944, Classification 750,870, handwritten pages, 1-4.
20. For an alternative scan of this passage, see later in this chapter.
21. GHQ/SCAP Records (RG 331, National Archives and Records Service), Box no. 5435, Folder title/number (12) War and Physical Culture—by SUEHIRO, Gentaro (Senso To Taiiku), Sept. 1944, Classification 750,870, handwritten pages, 4-5.
22. "Throughout the war, from the China incident on, Dr. Suehiro was visited monthly by the Kempeitai (Military Gendarmerie), a total of ninety-

six times according to his estimate." Under II. Information from Japanese Sources, 3h., under Appendix I, To Check Sheet 4 October 1946, ESS to CIE thru CS, Subject: 'Purge of Dr. Suehiro'.

23. GHQ/SCAP Records (RG 331), Box no. 2275 0, Folder title/number (32), SUEHIRO, Izutaro, Nov. 1946 – Apr. 1950, Classification 021, Type of record z, National Archives of the United States, accessed in microfiche version at National Diet Library, Tokyo, Japan.
24. Ibid.
25. *Hōritsu Jihō*, Vol. 13, No. 1 (Jan., 1941), 59, English translation in General Headquarters, Supreme Commander for the Allied Powers, Check Sheet, Subject: Extracts from Articles Written by Dr. Suehiro, Date: 29 April 1947, From: ESS/LK, contained in GHQ/SCAP Records (RG 331), Box no. 2275 0, Folder title/number (32) SUEHIRO, Izutaro, Date: Nov. 1946 – Apr. 1950, Classification 021, DECLASSIFIED E.O. 11652 SEC. 3(E) and 5(D) or (E) NNDG #775012
26. Nürnberg postmark 14 9 36, postcard dated Sep. 12, addressed to "Frau H. Suehiro, Tokio, Japan"; Suehiro family collection. Scanned by Waseda University staff, summer, 2015.
27. Declassified E.O. 11652 Sec. 3(E) and 5(D) or (E) NNDG #775012, two-page handwritten letter, numbered "-12-" at bottom of first page; quote taken from page one to page two of letter.
28. Cf. Shiotani San, ed. *Rohan okina zadan* (Tokyo: Kadokawa Bunkō, 1951).
29. *Yomiuri Shimbun* (October 1, 1946). English translation in Additional Remarks, marked "Confidential," by SAGARA, Iichi (16 Oct 46), in Suehiro's omnibus SCAP file, National Diet Library. Suehiro was the second commissioner of the Central Labor Relations Commission (Chūō Rōdō Iinkai) (founded March 1, 1946) after the end of the Pacific War. Suehiro took over after Miyake Masatarō (1887-1949) resigned in October of 1947. See *Chū Rō I 15nen no katsudō, shashinshū* (1961) (no publication information listed). Suehiro was known as "one of the very few men in whom both workers and employers have confidence." Confidential, 230,033 (4 Oct 46) ESS/LA, Purge of Dr. Suehiro, SCAP archives, National Diet Library, Tokyo.
30. Screening results of former officials of the Central Office of the Butoku-Kai, SUEHIRO, Izutaro, 17 September 1947, Declassified E.O. 11652 Sec. 3(E) and 5(D) or (E) NNDG #775012, hand-numbered "-11-" at bottom of page.
31. In another, undated petition, Suehiro refers to this as the "half-forced reorganization by the Tojo Cabinet."

32. "Statement," in SCAP archives, National Diet Library, hand-numbered "-4-" at bottom of page.
33. Draft, Memorandum For: Chief, Public Service Qualification Division, Subject: SUEHIRO, Izutaro: Reason for his having fallen under the Educational Purge criteria, 12 August 1947, signed 2nd Lt. Hans H. Baerwald, Declassified E.O. 11652 Sec. 3(E) and 5(D) or (E) NNDG #775012. Hans Baerwald's papers, dealing extensively with the purge of Japanese officials, are available online at the National Diet Library: https://rnavi.ndl.go.jp/kensei/tmp/BAE.pdf See also Hans H. Baerwald, *The Purge of Japanese Leaders under the Occupation* (Berkeley: University of California Press, 1959).
34. This is the same approach Suehiro used in answering GHQ questions about his involvement on the Board of Wage Control during the war. For example: "Inasmuch as the [wage] scales were virtually 'fait accompli' [sic], SUEHIRO said, the Board did little more than rubber stamp them." In the same deposition, Suehiro blames "young bureaucrats in key positions in the Home Finance and Welfare Ministries who were largely under the influence of the Young Officer's Clique" for labor union suppression beginning in 1937. Headquarters, U.S. Strategic Bombing Survey (Pacific), Interrogation No. 13, Tokyo, 8 Oct. 1945, 1000 am. GHQ files, 10057-28, Copy 2.
35. Suehiro, *Sensō to tai'iku*, op. cit., 18-20. Translation here is by the author.
36. *Hōsō manpitsu* (Tokyo: Hyōronsha, 1933), 333-334.
37. *Chūō Kōron* (October, 1931), reprinted in *Hōsō manpitsu*, op. cit., 327-328.
38. For a detailed investigation of Suehiro's activities with this group, see Shiraha Yūzō. *Nihon Hōri Kenkyūkai no bunseki: Hō to dōtoku no ittaika* (Tokyo: Chūō Daigaku Shuppanbu, 1998), 279, ff.
39. Sagara Iichi, "Why the Japan Jurisprudence Society Was Designated by the Ministry of Education to Be an Unacceptable Organization," 10 Oct 1946, Suehiro Omnibus File, National Diet Library, marked, "Confidential".
40. Additional Remarks, marked "Confidential," by SAGARA, Iichi (16 Oct 46), in Suehiro's omnibus SCAP file, National Diet Library, Tokyo.
41. *Nihon Mibunhōri Kenkyū Yōko*, 5-6, cited in Sagara Iichi, "Why the Japan Jurisprudence Society Was Designated by the Ministry of Education to Be an Unacceptable Organization," 10 Oct 1946, Suehiro Omnibus File, National Diet Library, marked "Confidential".
42. Ibid., 22-23. Sagara Iichi, "Why the Japan Jurisprudence Society Was Designated by the Ministry of Education to Be an Unacceptable Organiza-

tion," 10 Oct 1946, Suehiro Omnibus File, National Diet Library, marked "Confidential".

43. Both articles in Suehiro's SCAP omnibus file, National Diet Library, Tokyo. The Yomiuri editorial staff may have been eager for revenge against Suehiro, as he had not arbitrated in their favor during a prominent labor dispute in 1945, in the immediate aftermath of the initial American Occupation. See, e.g., Joe Moore, *Japanese Workers and the Struggle for Power, 1945-1947* (Madison, WI: University of Wisconsin Press, 1983), 50, ff.
44. Suehiro Izutarō cho, Kainō Michitaka kaitei, Vol. 1 (Tokyo: Iwanami Shoten, 1954), 3.
45. See Theodore Cohen, edited by Herbert Passin, *Remaking Japan: The American Occupation as New Deal* (New York: The Free Press, 1987), 237-238.

Photos

Figure 1. Suehiro Izutarō.

Source: Image obtained from Hirooka (née Suehiro) Namiko. Used with the permission of the Suehiro Family.

Figure 2. Suehiro Izutarō.

Source: Image obtained from Hirooka (née Suehiro) Namiko. Used with the permission of the Suehiro Family.

Figure 3. An illness-stricken Suehiro Izutarō, April, 1951. In the garden near his home in Tokyo.

Source: Image obtained from Hirooka (née Suehiro) Namiko. Used with the permission of the Suehiro Family.

Figure 4. Suehiro at work in the garden near his home.

Source: Image obtained from Hirooka (née Suehiro) Namiko. Used with the permission of the Suehiro Family.

Figure 5. Suehiro's rendering (with slight changes) of a famous passage from the *Doctrine of the Mean* about giving ten times more effort than others.

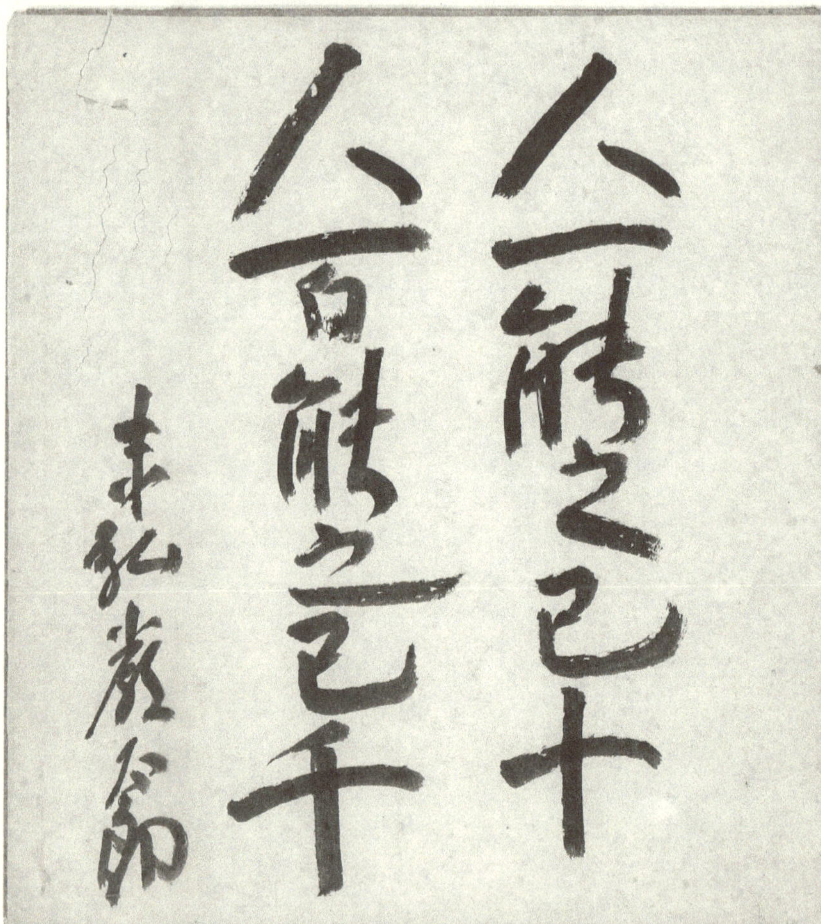

Source: Image obtained from Hirooka (née Suehiro) Namiko. Used with the permission of the Suehiro Family.

Figure 6. Suehiro Izutarō.

Source: Image obtained from Hirooka (née Suehiro) Namiko. Used with the permission of the Suehiro Family.

Figure 7. Suehiro, probably during wartime.

Source: Image obtained from Hirooka (née Suehiro) Namiko. Used with the permission of the Suehiro Family.

Figure 8. Golf was one of Suehiro's many athletic pursuits.

Source: Image obtained from Hirooka (née Suehiro) Namiko. Used with the permission of the Suehiro Family.

Figure 9. Suehiro Izutarō.

Source: Image obtained from Hirooka (née Suehiro) Namiko. Used with the permission of the Suehiro Family.

Figure 10. The Suehiro family. From left middle son Tadao, Suehiro Izutarō, Suehiro's wife Fuyuko, Suehiro's mother Fune (also listed as "Yoshi"), youngest son Shigeo, eldest son Izuo, and Izuo's wife Yasuko holding a baby Hirooka (née Suehiro) Namiko.

Source: Image obtained from Hirooka (née Suehiro) Namiko. Used with the permission of the Suehiro Family.

Figure 11. Suehiro with his ubiquitous pipe in hand.

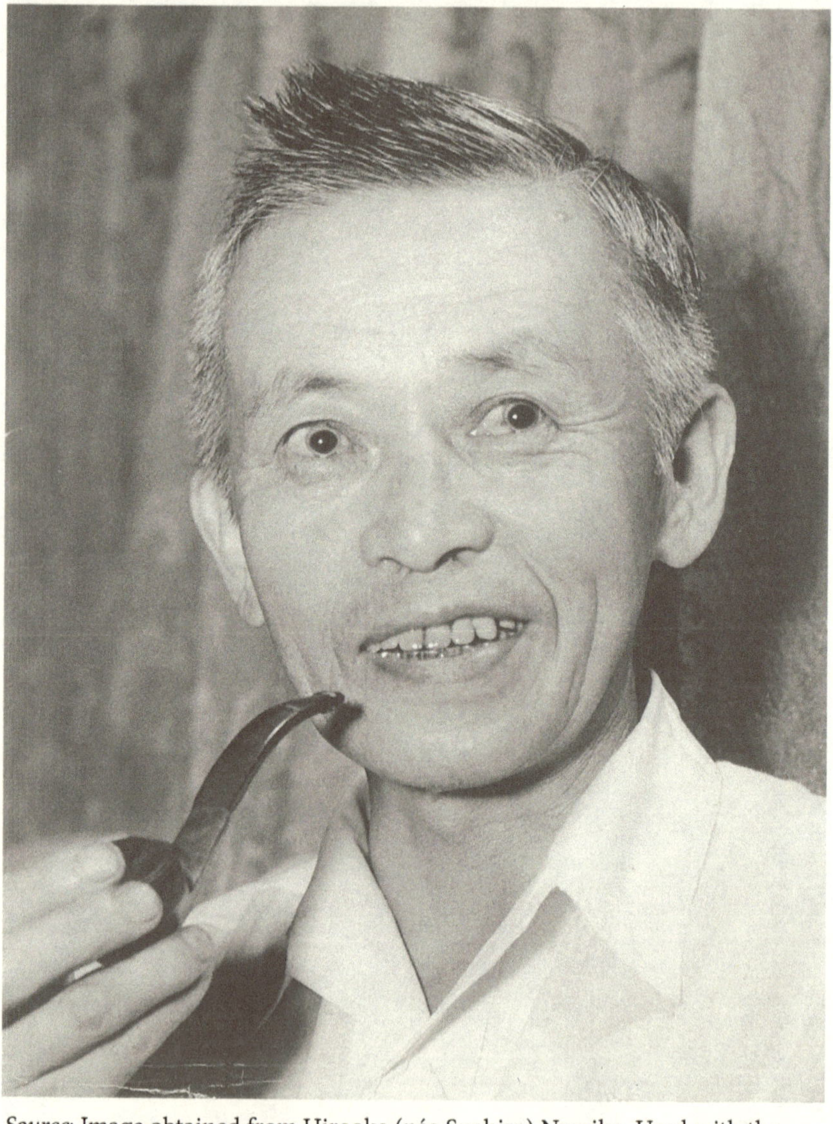

Source: Image obtained from Hirooka (née Suehiro) Namiko. Used with the permission of the Suehiro Family.

Figure 12. A young Suehiro.

Source: Image obtained from Hirooka (née Suehiro) Namiko. Used with the permission of the Suehiro Family.

Figure 13. A young Suehiro with his car.

Source: Image obtained from Hirooka (née Suehiro) Namiko. Used with the permission of the Suehiro Family.

Figure 14. An inscription bearing the name of Kikuchi Dairoku.

Source: Image obtained from Hirooka (née Suehiro) Namiko. Used with the permission of the Suehiro Family.

Figure 15. Kikuchi Dairoku, Suehiro's father-in-law and president of Tokyo Imperial University.

Source: Image obtained from Hirooka (née Suehiro) Namiko. Used with the permission of the Suehiro Family.

Figure 16. Suehiro practicing putting at a club in Tokyo. Spring, 1933.

Source: Image obtained from Hirooka (née Suehiro) Namiko. Used with the permission of the Suehiro Family.

Bibliography

Note: As this book was going to press, I discovered Shichinohe Katsuhiko's index of works by and about Suehiro. It is, to my knowledge, the most exhaustive such index available anywhere. Readers are encouraged to consult Shichinohe's "Suehiro Izutarō kenkyū shiryō sōran," listed below, for the best Suehiro research guide in any language.

Abosch, David. Katō Hiroyuki and the Introduction of German Political Thought in Modern Japan: 1868–1883 (Ph.D. dissertation, University of California, Berkeley, 1964).

Adams, Robert William. The Feasibility of the Philosophical in Early Taisho Japan: Nishida Kitarō and Tanabe Hajime (PhD dissertation, University of Chicago, 1991).

Addams, Jane. Twenty Years at Hull-House, with Autobiographical Notes (New York and Scarborough, Ontario: Signet Classic/Penguin, 1961).

Agamben, Giorgio. State of Exception (Chicago: University of Chicago Press, 2010).

Akamatsu Katsumaro. Nihon shakai undōshi (Tokyo: Iwanami Shinsho, 1952).

Amino Yoshihiko. Chūsei shōen no yōsō (Tokyo: Hanawa Shobō, 1966).

Anan, Seiichi. "Some Trends of Legal Thought and Natural Law Study in Japan: Note," Natural Law Forum, Paper 75 (1962).

Anghie, Anthony. "Colonialism and the Birth of International Institutions: Sovereignty, Economy and the Mandate System of the League of Nations," NYU Journal of International Law and Politics, Vol. 34, No. 3 (2002), 513–633.

Aomi Jun'ichi. Hō to shakai: atarashii hōgaku nyūmon (Tokyo: Chūō Kōron Shinsha, 1967/2007).

Aragaki Hideo. Sengo jinbutsuron (Tokyo: Yakumo Shoten, 1948).

Arima, Tatsuo. The Failure of Freedom: A Portrait of Modern Japanese Intellectuals (Cambridge: Harvard University Press, 1969).

Asahi Camera. (July, 1934).

Asako Hiroshi, et al. Nihon hōseishi (Tokyo: Seirin Shoin, 2010).

Avenell, Simon. "Japan and the global revival of the the 'civil society' idea: contemporaneity and the retreat of criticality," in Japan Forum, Vol. 23, No. 11 (September, 2011), 311–338.

Azuma Mitsutoshi. Rōdō kijunhō (Tokyo: Nihon Hyōron Shinsha, 1960).

Azuma Suehiko, pub. Mita mama kiita mama: meihō Doku-I ni tsukashite (not for sale, Tokyo: 1942).

Baba Ken'ichi. "Kagakuteki chōsa to kenkyūsha no seiji sekinin," in Hōshakaigaku, Hō: sono jissenteki kiban, No. 57 (2002), 170–190.

Baba Ken'ichi. Review of "Rokumoto Kahei & Yoshida Isamu, Suehiro Izutarō to Nihon no hōshakaigaku," in Hōshakaigaku, No. 69 (2008), 230–236.

Baehr, Peter. "The 'Iron Cage' and the 'Shell as Hard as Steel': Parsons, Weber, and the Stahlhartes Gehäuse Metaphor in the Protestant Ethic and the Spirit of Capitalism," in History and Theory, vol. 40, no. 2 (May, 2001), 153–169.

Baerwald, Hans H. The Purge of Japanese Leaders under the Occupation (Berkeley: University of California Press, 1959).

Balandier, Georges. "Georges Gurvitch (1894–1965)," Cahiers Internationaux de Sociologie, Nouvelle Série, Vol. 40 (Jan.-Jun., 1966), 3–5.

Banno Junji. "Kaikyū shikan no fukken," in Hon, Vol. 31, No. 12 (Dec. 1, 2014).

Banno Junji. Meiji kenpō taisei no kakuritsu: fukoku kyōhei to minryoku kyūyō (Tokyo: Tokyo University Press, 1971).

Barshay, Andrew E. State and Intellectual in Imperial Japan: The Public Man in Crisis (Berkeley: University of California Press, 1988).

Bartholomew, James R. The Formation of Science in Japan: Building a Research Tradition (New Haven: Yale, 1993).

Barton, Charles. History of a Suit in Equity from its Commencement to its Final Termination (Cincinnati: Robert Clarke & Co., 1884).

Beer, Lawrence W. "Constitutional Revolution in Japanese Law, Society and Politics," Modern Asian Studies, Vol. 16, No. 1 (1982), 33–67.

Bentham, Jeremy. "Essay on the Influence of Time and Place in Matters of Legislation," in John Bowring, ed., The Works of Jeremy Bentham (1843), Vol. I, 169–194.

Berman, Harold J. Law and Revolution: The Formation of the Western Legal Tradition (Cambridge: Harvard University Press, 1983).

Bialock, David T. Eccentric Spaces, Hidden Histories: Narrative, Ritual, and Royal Authority from The Chronicles of Japan to The Tale of Heike (Stanford: Stanford University Press, 2007).

Bluntschli, Johann Kaspar. Lehre vom modernen Stat (1875).

Borg, Dorothy. The United States and the Far Eastern Crisis of 1933–1938: From the Manchurian Incident through the Initial Stage of the Undeclared Sino-Japanese War (Cambridge: Harvard University Press, 1964).

Botsman, Daniel. Punishment and Power in the Making of Modern Japan (Princeton: Princeton University Press, 2007).

Bowen, Roger W. Rebellion and Democracy in Meiji Japan: A Study of Commoners in the Popular Rights Movement (Berkeley: University of California Press, 1980)

Braisted, William Reynolds, tr. and ed. Meiroku Zasshi: Journal of the Japanese Enlightenment (Cambridge: Harvard University Press, 1976).

Brook, Timothy. The Troubled Empire: China in the Yuan and Ming Dynasties (Cambridge: Harvard University Press, 2010).

Brown, Philip C. Cultivating Commons: Joint Ownership of Arable Land in Early Modern Japan (Honolulu: University of Hawai'i Press, 2011).

Brownlee, John S. Japanese Historians and the National Myths, 1600–1945: The Age of the Gods and Emperor Jinmu (Vancouver: UBC Press, 1997).

Budziszewski, J. What We Can't Not Know: A Guide (San Francisco: Ignatius Press, 2011).

Budziszewski, J. Written on the Heart: The Case for the Natural Law (Westmont: IVP Academic, 1997).

Burns, Susan L. Before the Nation: Kokugaku and the Imagining of Community in Early Modern Japan (Durham: Duke University Press, 2003).

Burrow, J.W. The Crisis of Reason: European Thought, 1848–1914 (New Haven: Yale University Press, 2002).

Cappelletti, Mauro. "The Significance of Judicial Review of Legislation in the Contemporary World," in Ernst von Caemmerer, Soia Mentschikoff, and Konrad Zweigert, eds., Ius Privatum Gentium: Festschrift für Max Rheinstein zum 70. Geburtstag am 5. Juli 1969, Band II: Nationales und Vergleichendes Privatrecht (Tübingen: J.C.B. Mohr, 1969).

Cassel, Pär Kristoffer. Grounds of Judgment: Extraterritoriality and Imperial Power in Nineteenth-Century China and Japan (Oxford: Oxford University Press, 2012).

Chapman, David. "Geographies of Self and Other: Mapping Japan through the Koseki," The Asia-Pacific Journal, Vol 9, Issue 29 No 2 (July 18, 2011).

Chen Hansheng, tr. Ide Kiwata. Minami Shina nōgyō mondai no kenkyū (Tokyo: Shōsanbō, 1940).

Chernilo, Daniel. The Natural Law Foundations of Modern Social Theory: A Quest for Universalism (Cambridge: Cambridge University Press, 2013).

Chūgoku Nōson Kankō Chōsa Kankō Kai, ed. Chūgoku Nōson Kankō Chōsa, Vols. 1–5 (complete set) (Tokyo: Iwanami Shoten, 1955–1958).

Chūō Hōritsu Shinpōsha, ed. Shinkō bunka to hōritsu (Tokyo: Dōjinsha Shoten, 1923).

Chūō Kōronsha. Fujin Kōron Daigaku, supōtsu hen (Chūō Kōronsha, not issued for sale; 1931).

Chūō Shakai Jigyō Kyōkai. "Settsurumento gō," Shakai Jigyō, Vol. 14, No. 3 (June, 1930) (complete issue).

Chūō Shakai Jigyō Kyōkai. Shakai Jigyō (multiple issues).

Cohen, Theodore, with Herbert Passin, ed. Remaking Japan: The American Occupation as New Deal (New York: Free Press, 1987).

Comitato Italo-Giapponese per gli Studi Scientifici. Aspetti del Giappone: Tradizioni e Realizzazioni. Vol. 1 (Tokyo: Istituto Italiano di Cultura, 1942).

Conroy, Hilary. The Japanese Seizure of Korea, 1868–1910: A Study of Realism and Idealism in International Relations (Philadelphia: University of Pennsylvania Press, 1960).

Coquillette, Daniel R. The Anglo-American Legal Heritage: Introductory Materials (Durham, NC: Carolina Academic Press, 1999).

Cotterrell, Roger. Émile Durkheim: Law in a Moral Domain (Stanford: Stanford University Press, 1999).

Cotterrell, Roger. Law, Culture, and Society: Legal Ideas in the Mirror of Social Theory (Hampshire, England: Ashgate, 2006).

Coutu, Michel. "Book Review: Living Law: Reconsidering Eugen Ehrlich, by Marc Hertogh (ed)," in Osgoode Hall Law Journal, Vol. 47, No. 3 (2009), 587–593.

Crowley, James B. Japan's Quest for Autonomy: National Securty and Foreign Policy, 1930–1938 (Princeton: Princeton University Press, 1966).

Curran, Vivian Grosswald. "Rethinking Hermann Kantorowicz: Free Law, American Legal Realism and the Legacy of Anti-Formalism," in Annelise Riles, ed., Rethinking the Masters of Comparative Law (Oxford: Hart Publishing, 2001), 70 ff.

Dahlmann, Joseph, S.J. *The Great Tokyo Earthquake September 1, 1923. Experiences and Impressions of an Eye-Witness* (New York: The America Press, 1924).

David, René. "Deux Conceptions de l'Ordre Social," in Ernst von Caemmerer, Soia Mentschikoff, and Konrad Zweigert, eds., Ius Privatum Gentium: Festschrift für Max Rheinstein zum 70. Geburtstag am 5.

Juli 1969, Band II: Nationales und Vergleichendes Privatrecht (Tübingen: J.C.B. Mohr, 1969).

Davis, Allen F. American Heroine: The Life and Legend of Jane Addams (Chicago: Ivan R. Dee, 2000).

Dean, Meryll. Japanese Legal System (2E) (London: Cavendish: 2002).

Doak, Kevin M. "Beyond International Law: The Theories of World Law in Tanaka Kōtarō and Tsuneto Kyō," Journal of the History of International Law, Vol. 13 (2011), 209–234.

Doak, Kevin M. "Liberal nationalism in imperial Japan: The dilemma of nationalism and internationalism," in Dick Stegewerns, ed., Nationalism and Internationalism in Japan: Autonomy, Asian brotherhood, or world citizenship? (London: RoutledgeCurzon, 2003), 17–41.

Doak, Kevin M. "Nationalism as Dialectics: Ethnicity, Moralism and the State in Early Twentieth-Century Japan," in James W. Heisig and John C. Maraldo, eds., Rude Awakenings: Zen, the Kyoto School, and the Question of Nationalism (Honolulu: University of Hawaii Press, 1995) 174–196.

Doak, Kevin M. "Romanticism, conservatism and the Kyoto School of philosophy," in Christopher Goto-Jones, ed., Repoliticising the Kyoto School as Philosophy (Oxon: Routledge, 2008).

Doak, Kevin M. "Tanaka Kōtarō and Natural Law," in Doak, ed., Xavier's Legacies: Catholicism in Modern Japanese Culture (Vancouver: UBC Press, 2011), 64–79.

Doak, Kevin M. Tanaka Kōtarō and World Law: Rethinking the Natural Law Outside the West (London: Palgrave MacMillan, 2018).

Doak, Kevin M. "The Place of National Identity in World Law: Reflections on Tanaka Kōtarō's Theory of Minzoku," in Urs Matthias Zachmann and Christian Uhl, eds., Japan und das Problem der Moderne: Wolfgang Seifert zu Ehren (München: Iudicium, 2015), 441–448.

Doak, Kevin M. "Under the Banner of the New Science: History, Science, and the Problem of Particularity in Early Twentieth-Century Japan," Philosophy East and West, 48:2 (4) (1998), 232–256.

Dore, Ronald P. and Ōuchi Tsutomu. "Rural Origins of Japanese Fascism," in J.W. Morley, ed., Dilemmas of Growth in Prewar Japan (Princeton: Princeton University Press, 1971).

Dreyer, June Teufel. Middle Kingdom and Empire of the Rising Sun: Sino-Japanese Relations, Past and Present (Oxford: Oxford University Press, 2016).

Dubois, Thomas David. "Inauthentic Sovereignty: Law and Legal Institutions in Manchukuo," Journal of Asian Studies, Vol. 69, No. 3 (August, 2010), 749–770.

Duff, Alexander S. Heidegger and Politics: The Ontology of Radical Discontent (Cambridge: Cambridge University Press, 2015).

Dunn, Charles J. Everyday Life in Traditional Japan (North Clarendon, VT: Charles E. Tuttle, 1969).

Duus, Peter. The Abacus and the Sword: The Japanese Penetration of Korea, 1895–1910 (Berkeley: University of California Press, 1995).

Earl, David Magarey. Emperor and Nation in Japan: Political Thinkers of the Tokugawa Period (Seattle: University of Washington Press, 1964).

Eberly, Don E., ed. The Essential Civil Society Reader: The Classic Essays (Lanham, MD: Rowman and Littlefield, 2000).

Edayoshi Isamu. Chōsaya ruten (Tokyo: Bunkasha, 1981).

Edmonds, I.G. Ooka the Wise: Tales of Old Japan (Indianapolis: Bobbs-Merrill, 1961).

Ehrlich, Eugen. "Die Erforschung des lebenden Rechts," in Schmollers Jahrbuch, XXXV, 1 (1911), S. 131.

Ehrlich, Eugen. The Fundamental Principles of the Sociology of Law (1913), trans. W. Moll (Cambridge: Harvard University Press, 1936).

Ehrlich, Eugen. Grundlegung der Soziologie des Rechts (1913).

Ehrlich, Eugen. "Law and the Inner Order of Social Associations," in Martin P. Golding, ed. The Nature of Law (New York: Random House, 1966).

Ehrlich, Eugen. Lecture at Juristische Gesellschaft, Vienna, 4/3/1903, reprinted in Recht und Leben, Berlin, 1967 (M. Rehbinder, ed.).

Ekonomisuto Henshūbu. Nihon kindai no meicho, sono hito to jidai (Tokyo: Mainichi Shimbunsha, 1966).

Elison, George. Deus Destroyed: The Image of Christianity in Early Modern Japan (Cambridge: Harvard University Press, 1973).

Emori Itsuo. Kazoku rekishi no minzokugaku: higashi Ajia to Nihon (Tokyo: Kōbunsha, 1990).

Esselstrom, Erik. Crossing Empire's Edge: Foreign Ministry Police and Japanese Expansionism in Northeast Asia (Honolulu: University of Hawai'i Press, 2009).

Ezaki Michio. Kominterun no bōryaku to Nihon no haisen (Tokyo: PHP, 2017).

Ezaki Michio. Nihon senryō to 'haisen kakumei' no kiki (Tokyo: PHP, 2018).

Farganis, James. Readings in Social Theory: The Classic Tradition to Post-Modernism, 3E (New York: McGraw Hill, 2000).

Fassbender, Bardo and Anne Peters, eds. The Oxford Handbook of the History of International Law (Oxford: Oxford University Press, 2012).

Ferrara, Christopher. Liberty, The God that Failed: Policing the Sacred and Constructing the Myths of the Secular State, from Locke to Obama (Kettering, OH: Angelico Press, 2012).

Flaherty, Darryl E. Public Law, Private Practice: Politics, Profit, and the Legal Profession in Nineteenth-Century Japan (Cambridge: Harvard University Press, 2013).

Foote, Daniel H., ed. Law in Japan: A Turning Point (Seattle: University of Washington Press, 2007).

Franz, Michael. Eric Voegelin and the Politics of Spiritual Revolt: The Roots of Modern Ideology (Baton Rouge: Louisiana State University Press, 1992).

Friedman, Lawrence M. "The Law and Society Movement," in Stanford Law Review, Vol. 38, No. 3 (Feb., 1986), 763–780.

Fuess, Harald. "Informal Imperialism and the 1879 Hesperia Incident: Containing Cholera and Challenging Extraterritoriality in Japan," Japan Review, No. 27 (2014), 103–140.

Fujii Genki, Inamura Kōbō, and Moteki Hiromichi. Nichi Bei sensō wo okoshita no wa dareka (Tokyo: Bensei Shuppan, 2016).

Fujii Shin'ichi. The Constitution of Japan: A Historical Survey (Tokyo: The Hokuseido Press (Kokushikan University), 1965).

Fujino Hiroko. "Toshi minshū sōjōki no shuppatsu, saikō: Hibiya yakiuchi jiken," in Rekishigaku kenkyū, Vol. 792 (Sep. 2004), 1–16.

Fujioka Nobukatsu. Nihonjin ga mezameta kokunan no Nihonshi (Tokyo: Bijinesusha, 2015).

Fujita Isamu and Emori Itsuo, eds. Bunken kenkyū, Nihon no hōshakaigaku, hōshakaigaku ronsō (Tokyo: Nihon Hyōronsha, 1969).

Fujitani, Takashi. Splendid Monarchy: Power and Pageantry in Modern Japan (Berkeley: University of California Press, 1996).

Fukushima Masao. Fukushima Masao chosakushū, dai hakkan (Tokyo: Keisō Shobō, 1995).

Fukushima Masao. Fukushima Masao chosakushū, dai ikkan (Tokyo: Keisō Shobō, 1993).

Fukushima Masao. Fukushima Masao chosakushū, dai nanakan (Tokyo: Keisō Shobō, 1993).

Fukushima Masao. Fukushima Masao chosakushū, dai rokkan (Tokyo: Keisō Shobō, 1995).

Fukushima Masao. "Kyōdai Hozumi hakase to kazoku seido: Meiji minpō no seitei to kanren shite," in Tōkyō Daigaku Hōgaku Kyōkai Zasshi, Vol. 96, No. 9 (Sep., 1979), 1061–1120.

Fukushima Masao, Ishida Tetsuichi, and Shimizu Makoto. Kaisō no Tōkyō Teidai Setsurumento (Tokyo: Nihon Hyōronsha, 1984).

Fukushima Masao and Kawashima Takeyoshi, eds. Hozumi, Suehiro ryō sensei to Setsurumento (Tōkyō Daigaku Setsurumento Hōritsu Sōdanbu, not issued for sale, 1963).

Funayama Shin'ichi. Nihon no kan'nenronsha (Tokyo: Eihōsha, 1956).

Funayama Shin'ichi. Taishō tetsugakushi kenkyū (Kyoto: Hōritsu Bunkasha, 1965).

Gardner, James A. "The Sociological Jurisprudence of Roscoe Pound (Part I)," Villanova Law Review, vol. 1 (1961).

Garon, Sheldon. The State and Labor in Modern Japan (Berkeley: University of California Press, 1987).

Gellner, Ernest. Nations and Nationalism (Cornell: Cornell University Press, 1983).

GHQ/SCAP Records. Dossier of Suehiro Izutarō files, listed partially under "Folder title/number 333.5: Investigations—Screening (Suehiro Case), 1946, Aug. 1941–June 1948, Classification 340, 812, Type of record e, m, t," in National Diet Library, Tokyo, Japan.

GHQ/SCAP Records (RG 331), Box no. 2275 0, Folder title/number (32), SUEHIRO, Izutaro, Nov. 1946 – Apr. 1950, Classification 021, Type of record z, National Archives of the United States, accessed in microfiche version at National Diet Library, Tokyo, Japan.

Gierke, Otto. Natural Law and the Theory of Society, 1500 to 1800 (Boston: Beacon Press, 1957).

Goodwin, Janet R. and Joan Piggott, eds. Land, Power, and the Sacred: The Estate System in Medieval Japan (Honolulu: University of Hawai'i Press, 2018).

Gordon, Andrew. "The Crowd and Politics in Imperial Japan: Tokyo, 1905–1918," in Past & Present, No. 121 (November, 1988).

Gotō Hiroshi, ed. Asu no rōdō mondai: taidan, Nakayama Ichirō, Suehiro Izutarō (Tokyo: Nihon Seihan Kabushikigaisha, 1950).

Gotō Kiyoshi. Tenkanki no hōritsu shisō (Tokyo: Mikasa Shobō, 1940).

Gottfried, Paul Edward. Carl Schmitt: Politics and Theory (New York: Greenwood Press, 1990).

Grotius, Hugo. De jure belli ac pacis (1625).

Guo Wei. Hō to jōhō kūkan: kindai Nihon ni okeru hōjōhō no kōchiku to henyō (PhD dissertation, Hokkaido University, 2014).

Guttman, Allen, and Lee Thompson. Japanese Sports: A History (Honolulu: University of Hawai'i Press, 2001).

Haines, Charles Grove. The Revival of Natural Law Concepts: A Study of the Establishment and of the Interpretation of Limits on Legislatures with special reference to the Development of certain phases of American Constitutional Law (New York: Russell & Russell, 1965).

Haley, John Owen. Authority without Power: Law and the Japanese Paradox (Oxford: Oxford University Press, 1991).

Haley, John Owen. "The Politics of Informal Justice: The Japanese Experience, 1922–1942," in Richard L. Abel, ed., The Politics of Informal Justice, Comparative Studies (New York: Academic Press, 1982), 125–147.

Haley, John Owen. "The Role of Courts in 'Making' Law in Japan: The Communitarian Conservatism of Japanese Judges," in Pacific Rim Law and Policy Journal, Vol. 22, No. 3 (June, 2013), 491–503.

Hall, James Parker. Constitutional Law (Chicago: La Salle Extension University, 1911).

Hall, John Whitney. "Tokugawa Japan: 1800–1853; Life Under the Tokugawa," in James B. Crowley, ed., Modern East Asia: Essays in Interpretation (New York: Harcourt, Brace & World, 1970).

Halpérin, Jean-Louis. "Transplants of European Normativity in India and in Japan: a Historical Comparison," in Rechtsgeschichte/Legal History, 22 (2014), 150–157.

Hammer, Joshua. Yokohama Burning: The Deadly 1923 Earthquake and Fire that Helped Forge the Path to World War II (New York: Free Press, 2006).

Hane, Mikiso. Reflections on the Way to the Gallows: Rebel Women in Prewar Japan (Berkeley: University of California Press, 1993).

Hannemann, Stacie. "Moving Beyond the 'Unequal Treaties'" (unprovenanced paper, npd).

Harada Keikichi. Shin kenpō kenkyū (Tōkyō: Yūhikaku, 1947).

Hardacre, Helen. Shintō and the State, 1868–1988 (Princeton: Princeton University Press, 1989).

Harootunian, H.D. Things Seen and Unseen: Discourse and Ideology in Tokugawa Nativism (Chicago: University of Chicago Press, 1988).

Harootunian, H.D. Toward Restoration: The Growth of Political Consciousness in Tokugawa Japan (Berkeley: University of California Press, 1970).

Hasegawa Masayasu. Hōgaku ronsōshi (Tokyo: Gakuyō Shobō, 1976).

Hashimoto Takehiko. "From Traditional to Modern Metrology: The Introduction and Acceptance of the Metric System," in Historical Essays on Japanese Technology (Tokyo: University of Tokyo Center for Philosophy, 2009).

Hata Ikuhiko, tr. Jason Morgan. Comfort Women and Sex in the Battle Zone (Lanham, MD: Hamilton, 2018).

Hata Ikuhiko. Senzenki Nihon kanryōsei no seido, soshiki, jinji (Tokyo: University of Tokyo Press, 1981).

Hatoyama Hideo, Mitsuma [sic: Mizuma] Shinzō, and Suehiro Gentarō [sic: Izutarō], comp. Zivilrechtliche Lesestücke (Tokyo: Maruzen, 1916).

Hayashi Chikatsu. Konoe Fumimaro: yabō to zasetsu (Tokyo: WAC, 2017).

Hayashi Chikatsu. Nichi-Bei kaisen rikugun no shōsan: Akimaru kikan no saigo hōkokusho (Tokyo: Shōdensha, 2015).

Hayashi Kentarō, ed. Gendai Nihon shisō taikei, 35 (Tokyo: Chikuma Shobō, 1963).

Hayashi Nobuo. Shingisoku hōgaku: minshushugi hōritsugaku no juritsu e no michi (Kyoto: Minerva, 1976).

Hayashi, Yoko. "Women in the Legal Profession in Japan," in US-Japan Women's Journal, English Supplement, No. 2 (1992), 16–27.

Hayashida Seimei. "Jissenteki suiron to puragumachizumu hōgaku: wagakuni hōritsugaku no kadai to Amerika hōritsugaku no tenkai," in Hōritsu Jihō, Vol. 64, No. 11, 6–16 (and in No. 12, and in Vol. 65, No. 1 and No. 3).

Hegel, G.W.F., tr. T. M. Knox. Philosophy of Right (Oxford: Oxford University Press, 1952).

Hein, Laura. Reasonable Men, Powerful Words: Political Culture and Expertise in Twentieth-Century Japan (Berkeley: University of California Press, 2004).

Heisig, James W. "The Religious Philosophy of the Kyoto School: An Overview," Japanese Journal of Religious Studies, Vol. 17, No. 1 (March, 1990), 51–81.

Hellyer, Robert I. Defining Engagement: Japan and Global Contexts, 1640–1868 (Cambridge: Harvard University Press, 2009).

Hirano Yoshitarō. Burujoa minshūshugi kakumei (Tōkyō: Hōsei University Press, 1968).

Hirano Yoshitarō. Hōritsu ni okeru kaikyū tōsō (Tokyo: Kenshinsha, 1948).

Hirano Yoshitarō. Meiji ishin ni okeru seijiteki shihai keitai (Tōkyō: Iwanami Shoten, 1933).

Hirano Yoshitarō. Meiji ishin no henkaku ni tomonau atarashii kaikyū bunka to shakaiteki seijiteki undō (Tokyo: Iwanami Shoten, 1932).

Hirano Yoshitarō. "Shina kenkyūsho zuisō," in Kaizō (May, 1940), 367–377.

Hirano Yoshitarō and Moritani Katsumi, eds. and trans. Karl Wittfogel, Tōyōteki shakai riron (Tōkyō: Nihon Hyōronsha, 1939).

Hiroshi Hojo, tr. Yuriko Mori. History of the Commons of Yamanaka Buraku at the Foot of Mt. Fuji (Yamanaka Sengen Jinja, 2012).

Hiroshi Hojo, tr. Nobuko Tsukui. History of the Wagokai Foundation and the Commons (History of Zaidan Hojin Wagokai and Iriai) (Wagōkai, 2011).

Hirowatari Seigo and Yoshida Katsumi. "'Shimin shakairon no hōritsugakuteki shatei' ni yosete," Shakai Kagaku Kenkyū: Tōkyō Daigaku Shakai Kagaku Kenkyujo Kiyō, Vol. 60, Nos. 5 & 6 (May and June, 2009).

Hōgaku Kyōkai Jimusho. Hōgaku Kyōkai Zasshi (complete set).

Hōgaku Seminā. Hōgaku seminā besuto serekushon (complete set).

Hogue, Arthur Reed. Origins of the Common Law (Indianapolis: Liberty Fund, 1986).

Hōjō Hiroshi. Iriai no hōshakaigaku (Tokyo: Ochanomizu Shobō, 2000).

Holtom, D.C. Modern Japan and Shinto Nationalism: A Study of Present-Day Trends in Japanese Religions (Chicago: University of Chicago, 1943).

Hoppe, Hans-Hermann. Democracy, The God that Failed: The Economics and Politics of Monarchy, Democracy, and Natural Order (New Brunswick: Transaction Publishers, 2003).

Hōritsu Taimuzu Sha. Hanrei Times (complete set).

Hōsei Daigaku. Hōgaku Shirin (multiple volumes).

Hoston, Germaine A. "Conceptualizing Bourgeois Revolution: The Prewar Japanese Left and the Meiji Restoration," in Comparative Studies in Society and History, Vo. 33, No. 3 (Jul., 1991), 539–381.

Hoston, Germaine A. Marxism and the Crisis of Development in Prewar Japan (Princeton: Princeton University Press, 1986).

Howell, David L. Geographies of Identity in Nineteenth-Century Japan (Berkeley: University of California Press, 2005).

Howland, Douglas R. Translating the West: Language and Political Reason in Nineteenth-Century Japan (Honolulu: University of Hawai'i Press, 2002).

Hozumi Nobushige. The New Japanese Civil Code, as Material for the Study of Comparative Jurisprudence, a Paper Read at the International Congress of Arts and Science, at the Universal Exposition, Saint Louis, 1904.

Hozumi Nobushige. Hōritsu Shinkaron (Tokyo: Hozumi Shōgaku Zaidan Shuppan/Iwanami Shoten, Vols. 1 & 2, 1924, Vol. 3, 1926).

Hozumi Shigetō. "Chōtei hō," in Gendai hōgaku zenshū, Vol. 38 (Tokyo: Nihon Hyōronsha, 1931).

Hozumi Shigetō. "Hanrei inkyohō shūi," Hōgaku Kyōkai Zasshi, vol. 53, no. 7 (July, 1935)

Hozumi Shigetō. Rikon seido no kenkyū (Tōkyō: Kaizōsha, 1924).

Hozumi Shigetō, corr. by Nakagawa Zennosuke. Yasashii hōgaku tsūron (Tokyo: Yūhikaku, 1963).

Hozumi Shigetō Sensei wo Shinobu Kai. Hozumi Shigetō sensei wo shinonde: Hozumi Shigetō sensei go seikyo sanjū shūnen ki'nen (not published for sale; July 29, 1982).

Hozumi Shigeyuki. "Meiji jūnendai ni okeru Doitsu hō no juyō—Tōkyō Daigaku Hōgakubu to Hozumi Nobushige," in Ienaga Saburō, ed., Meiji kokka no hō to shisō (Tokyo: Ochanomizu Shobō, 1966).

Hozumi Yatsuka. "Sosenkyō wa kōhō no minamoto nari," in Uesugi Shinkichi, ed., *Hozumi Yatsuka hakase ronbunshū* (Tokyo: Uesugi Shingō, 1913).

Ichikawa Hirokatsu. "Sanjū shūnen wo mukaete," in Seikei Kenkyū, No. 21 (Nov., 1976) (entire issue, multiple authors).

Ienaga Saburō. Ueki Emori kenkyū (Tokyo: Iwanami Shoten, 1960).

Iijima Noriaki, Shimada Kazuo, and Hirowatari Seigo, eds. Shimin hōgaku no kadai to tenbō, Shimizu Makoto sensei koki ki'nen ronshū (Tokyo: Nihon Hyōronsha, 2000).

Iimura, Toshiaki, Ryu Takabayashi, and Christoph Rademacher. "The Binding Nature of Court Decisions in Japan's Civil Law System, China Guiding Cases Project," Stanford Law School China Guiding Cases Project (June 30, 2015).

Ikeda Hiroshi. Boranteia to fuashizumu: jihatsusei to shakai kōken no kingendaishi (Kyoto: Jimbun Shoin, 2019).

Ikuta Michiko. Onnatachi no Manshū: taminzoku kūkan wo ikite (Osaka: Osaka University Press, 2015).

Im Woo-jae [Im Mun-an]. Nihon teikoku to Daikan Minkoku ni tsukaeta kanryō no kaisō (Tokyo: Chikuma Bunko, 2015).

Imai, Konomi. "The Women's Movement and the Settlement Movement in Early Twentieth-Century Japan: The Impact of Hull House and Jane Addams on Hiratsuka Raichō," Kwansei Gakuin University Humanities Review, vol. 17 (2012).

Imai Sei'ichi. Nihon no rekishi 23: Taishō Demokurashii (Tokyo: Chūō Kōron Sha, 1966).

Inada Masatsugu, ed. Meiji kokka keisei katei no kenkyū (Tokyo: Ochanomizu Shobō, 1966).

Inokawa Kiyoshi. Nihon kyōiku undōshi, dai ikkan, Meiji, Taishōki no kyōiku undō (Kyoto: San'ichi Shobō, 1960).

Inoki Takenori, ed. Senkanki Nihon no shakai shūdan to nettowāku: Taishō demokurashii to chūkan dantai (Tokyo: NTT Press, 2008).

International Labor Office, Mission of Enquiry in Russia. "Labor Conditions in Soviet Russia," cited in Amy Hewes, "Labor Conditions in Soviet Russia," Journal of Political Economy, Vol. 28, No. 9 (November, 1920), 774–783.

Iriye, Akira. After Imperialism: The Search for a New Order in the Far East, 1921–1931 (Cambridge: Harvard University Press, 1968).

Iriye, Akira. The Origins of the Second World War in Asia and the Pacific (London: Longman, 1987).

Iriye, Akira and Pierre-Yves Saunier, eds. The Palgrave Dictionary of Transnational History (New York: Palgrave Macmillan, 2009).

Ishibe Masasuke. "Daini teiseiki Doitsu no hōgaku kyōiku," in Miyazawa Setsuo and Kaminaga Yuriko, eds. Hōshakaigaku korokiumu (Tokyo: Nihon Hyōronsha, 1996), esp. 23, ff., on Eugen Ehrlich.

Ishida Makoto. "Senzen Nihon ni okeru Ajia hō kenkyū no ichi danmen: Kahoku nōson kankō chōsa wo chūshin toshite," in Nagoya Daigaku Hōsei Ronshū, no. 132 (1990).

Ishida Makoto. "Shokuminchi shihai to Nihon no hōshakaigaku: Kahoku nōson kankō chōsa ni okeru Suehiro Izutarō no baai," in Hikaku Hōgaku, Vol. 36, No. 1 (2002).

Ishidō Kiyotomo and Tateyama Toshitada. Tōkyō Teidai Shinjinkai no kiroku (Tokyo: Keizai Ōraisha, 1976).

Ishii Ryōsuke. "Enkiridera: Tōkeiji no baai," Hōgaku kyōkai zasshi, Vol. 76 (1959) and Vol. 77 (1961).

Ishii Shirō. "'Uso no Kōyō' to Ōoka sabaki," in Tosho, No. 290 (Oct., 1973), 52–56.

Ishii Shirō, ed. Nihon kindai hōshi kōgi (Tokyo: Seirin Shoin Shinsha, 1972).

Ishii Teruhisa. "Suehiro Izutarō sensei wo shinobu," in Rōdō Jihō, Vol. 4, No. 10 (October, 1951), 1–3.

Ishimoda Shō. Nihon no kodai kokka (Tokyo: Iwanami Shoten, 1971).

Isoda Susumu, Hirano Yoshitarō, Kainō Michitaka, Niida Noboru, Kawashima Takeyoshi, and Fukushima Masao. Zadankai. "Hozumi hōgaku, Suehiro hōgaku no bunseki to hihan," Hōshakaigaku, No. 2 (1952), 53–83.

Isomura Satoshi. Ērurihhi no hōshakaigaku (Tokyo: Nihon Hyōronsha, 1953).

Isomura Satoshi. "Ērurihhi no hōshakaigaku ni tsuite: taikeiteki rikai wo mezashite," in Hōgaku Ronsō (Kyōto Daigaku Hōgakkai), Vol. 57, No. 3 (Apr., 1951), 1–39.

Isomura Satoshi. Shakai hōgaku no tenkai to kōzō (Tokyo: Nihon Hyōronsha, 1975).

Ito, Ken K. An Age of Melodrama: Family, Gender, and Social Hierarchy in the Turn-of-the-Century Japanese Novel (Stanford: Stanford University Press, 2008).

Itō Masami. Hōgakusha, hito to sakuhin (multiple entries) (Tokyo: Nihon Hyōronsha, 1985).

Itō Takao. Taishō Demokurashii ki no hō to shakai (Kyoto: Kyōto Daigaku Gakujutsu Shuppankai, 2000).

Itō Takeo. Mantetsu ni ikite (Tokyo: Keisō Shobō, 1964).

Itoh, Hiroshi. "How Judges Think in Japan," The American Journal of Comparative Law, Vol. 18, No. 4 (Autumn, 1970), 775–804.

Ivy, Marilyn. Discourses of the Vanishing: Modernity, Phantasm, Japan (Chicago: University of Chicago Press, 1995).

Jamin, Christophe. "Saleilles' and Lambert's Old Dream Revisited," in The American Journal of Comparative Law, Vol. 50, No. 4 (Fall, 2002), 701–718.

Jansen, Marius. "Ōi Kentarō: Radicalism and Chauvinism," in The Far Eastern Quarterly, Vol. 11, No. 3 (May, 1952), 305–316.

Ji, Zhaojin. A History of Modern Shanghai Banking: The Rise and Decline of China's Finance Capitalism (Armonk, NY: M.E. Sharpe, 2003).

Johnson, Alan. "The Recognition of Differential Power in the Sociology of Law," Mid-American Review of Sociology, Vol. 4, No. 1 (Spring, 1979), 57–70.

Johnson, Chalmers. An Instance of Treason: Ozaki Hotsumi and the Sorge Spy Ring (Stanford: Stanford University Press, 1964).

Johnson, Chalmers. Conspiracy at Matsukawa (Berkeley: University of California Press, 1972).

Jones, Sumie. The Shirokoya Scandal: Two Ways of Looking at the Case Judged by Magistrate Ōoka Tadasuké: Baba Bunkō's "The Scandal of Okuma of Shirokoya of Shinzaimoku-chō; The Good Deeds of Kagaya Chōbei" and "The Decline and Fall of the House of Shirokoya" (1757), An Episodic Festschrift for Howard Hibbett (Bangkok: Aksornsamai Press, 2010).

Kahei Rokumoto. "Philip Selznick's Conception of Law and Legal Sociology: A View from Japan," in Kagan, Robert A, Martin Krygier, and Kenneth Winston, eds. Legality and Community: On the Intellectual Legacy of Philip Selznick (Lanham, MD: Rowman and Littlefield, 2002), 167–183.

Kai Michitarō, "Suehiro hōgakuron," Hōritsu Jihō, vol. 50, no. 13 (December, 1978), 15–21.

Kainō Michitaka. "Hōritsugaku no hōshakaigakuteki kōsatsu," in Shisō, No. 321 (March, 1951), 1–7.

Kainō Michitaka. Kainō Michitaka chosakushū (Tokyo: Nihon Hyōronsha, 1977).

Kainō Michitaka, Harada Sumitaka, Hirowatari Seigo, eds. Nihon shakai to hōritsugaku: rekishi, genjō, tenbō (Tokyo: Nihon Hyōronsha, 2009).

Kaizōsha. Marukusu Engerusu zenshū (1928 et seriatim).

Kan Tadamichi. Jidenteki jidō bunkashi: senzen, senchūki hen (Tokyo: Ayumi Shuppan, 1978).

Kan Tadamichi. "Kawa mukō no daigaku: Settsurumento de katsuyaku shita gakuseitachi," in Hōsei, Tokushū: daigaku to shakai, No. 58 (March, 1957), 14–17.

Kanno Masashi. "Hōshakaigaku," in Gakkai Kaiko, Vol. 85 (1067), No. 13, 274–281.

Kano Masanao. Taishō Demokurashii no teiryū (Tokyo: NHK Bukkusu, 1973).

Kanpō. Dai 2352 gō (June 7, 1920).

Kant, Immanuel. Prolegomena to any Future Metaphysics That Will Be Able to Present Itself as a Science (1783).

Kataoka Tetsuya. The Price of a Constitution: The Origin of Japan's Postwar Politics (New York: Crane, Russak, 1991).

Katō Hidetoshi. Amerika no chiisana machi kara (Tokyo: Asahi Shimbunsha, 1965).

Kawagishi, Norikazu. "The birth of judicial review in Japan," International Journal of Constitutional Law (2007) 5 (2): 308–331.

Kawaguchi Yoshihiko. Kindai Nippon no tochihō kan'nen: 1920nendai kosaku rippō ni okeru tochi shihaiken to hō (Tokyo: University of Tokyo Press, 1990).

Kawakami Takeshi. Iryō shakaika no dōhyo: 25nin no shōgen (Tokyo: Keisō Shobō, 1969).

Kawashima Takeyoshi. Aru hōgakusha no kiseki (Tokyo: Yūhikaku, 1978).

Kawashima Takeyoshi. "The Concept of Judicial Precedent in Japanese Law," in Ernst von Caemmerer, Soia Mentschikoff, and Konrad Zweigert, eds., Ius Privatum Gentium: Festschrift für Max Rheinstein zum 70. Geburtstag am 5. Juli 1969, Band II: Nationales und Vergleichendes Privatrecht (Tübingen: J.C.B. Mohr, 1969).

Kawashima Takeyoshi. Ideorogii toshite no ie seido (Tokyo: Iwanami Shoten, 1957).

Kawashima Takeyoshi. Kawashima Takeyoshi chosakushū (Tokyo: Iwanami Shoten, 1982).

Kawashima Takeyoshi, ed. Hōshakaigaku kōza 1, hōshakaigaku no keisei (Tokyo: Iwanami Shoten, 1972).

Kawashima Takeyoshi, ed. Hōshakaigaku kōza 2, hōshakaigaku no genjō (Tokyo: Iwanami Shoten, 1972).

Kawashima Takeyoshi, ed. Hōshakaigaku kōza 7, shakai to hō 1 (Tokyo: Iwanami Shoten, 1973).

Kawashima Takeyoshi, ed. Hōshakaigaku kōza 8, shakai to hō 2 (Tokyo: Iwanami Shoten, 1973).

Kawashima Takeyoshi, ed. Hōshakaigaku kōza 10, rekishi, bunka to hō 2 (Tokyo: Iwanami Shoten, 1973).

Kelly, J.M. A Short History of Western Legal Theory (Oxford: Oxford University Press, 1992).

Kelsen, Hans. Die philosophie Grundlagen der Naturrechtslehre und des Rechtspositivismus (1928).

Kikuchi Isao. "Shakaihō no ikkanen," in Hōritsu Jihō, Gakkai Kaiko, Vol. 2, No. 12 (Dec., 1930), 30–35.

Kim, Kyu Hyun. The Age of Visions and Arguments: Parliamentiarinism and the National Public Sphere in Early Meiji Japan (Cambridge: Harvard University Press, 2008).

Kinmonth, Earl. "The Mouse that Roared: Saito Takao, Conservative Critic of Japan's 'Holy War' in China," Journal of Japanese Studies, vol. 25, no. 2 (1999), 331-360.

Kisaki, Kiyoji. "Jean-Jacques Rousseau au Japon (1876–1983)—Bibliographie chronologique," Kyoto University Economic Review, Vol. 58, No. 1 (124) (April, 1988), 33–84.

Kishi Toshio, ed. Matsurigoto no tenkai (Tokyo: Chūō Kōronsha, 1986).

Kiss, Géza. "Equity and Law: Judicial Freedom of Decision," in Science of Legal Method: Select Essays by Various Authors, Ernest Bruncken and Layton B. Register, eds. (Boston: The Boston Book Company, 1917).

Kitakamae Tarō. "Hō jinruigaku ni okeru Ērurihhi riron no juyō to tenkai," in Miyazawa Setsuo and Kaminaga Yuriko, eds. Hōshakaigaku korokiumu (Tokyo: Nihon Hyōronsha, 1996), 127, ff.

Kitamura Kusuo. "Suehiro sensei no koto," in Kōrōi Kihō, No. 4 (Jul., 1970), 28–30.

Kitayama Shigeo. Nihon no rekishi 4: Heiankyō (Tokyo: Chōkō Bunko, 1973).

Kobayashi Naoki and Mizumoto Hiroshi. Gendai Nihon no hōshisō (Tokyo: Yūhikaku, 1976).

Kobayashi Satoshi. "Suehiro Izutarō no hanrei kenkyū hōhōron to sono genkai," in HERSETEC, Vol. 4, No. 2 (2010), 41–58.

Kodama Kōta. Nihon no rekishi, bekkan 5: nenpyō, chizu (Tokyo: Chūō Kōron Sha, 1967).

Kodama Nario. "Idéologie et utopie chez Nakae Chômin: Interprétation culturaliste de la Discussion sur la politique des trois hommes ivres," in Japon Pluriel 3: Actes du troisième colloque de la Société française des études japonaises, Jean-Pierre Berthon and Anne Gossot, publication directors (Arles: Éditions Philippe Picquier, 1999), 189–197.

Kodansha. Kodansha Encyclopedia of Japan (multiple entries) (New York: Kodansha, 1983).

Koguchi Hikota. "Chūgoku hō kenkyū ni okeru Suehiro hakase no kon'nichiteki igi," in Waseda Hōgaku, Vol. 55, No. 2 (March, 1980), 13–70.

Kojima Kōji. "Daigaku Settsurumento no sōgyō jidai: Uddu shi no Eikoku shakai undō wo yomu," in Shakai Jigyō, Vol. 10, No. 8 (November, 1921).

Kokumin Shimbun Seijibu, ed. Asu wo matsu kare (Tokyo: Chikura Shobō, 1931).

Kolakowski, Leszek, tr. Norbert Guterman. The Alienation of Reason: A History of Positivist Thought (New York: Anchor Books, 1969).

Komiya Genjirō. "Suehiro Izutarō sensei nyūmon," in Rōmu Jihō (Sep. 1, 1995).

Krebs, Gerhard. "The 'Jewish Problem' in Japanese-German Relations," in E. Bruce Reynolds, ed., Japan in the Fascist Era (New York: Palgrave Macmillan, 2004).

Kubo Hideo. "Kindai hō no furonteia ni okeru bunkateki tasha ni tsuite no chi, ichi, posutokoroniaru hihan no hōshakaigaku," in Hōgaku Ronsō, Vol. 153, No. 4 (July, 2003), 92–123.

Kubota Hayato and Yokoi Yoshihiro, eds. Gendai rōdōhō nyūmon (Kyoto: Hōritsu Bunkasha, 1988).

Kudō Kei'ichi. "Shōen," Acta Asiatica 44, Studies in Japanese Medieval Social and Economic History (Tokyo: The Tōhō Gakkai, 1983), 1–27.

Kurayama Mitsuru. Tōdai hōgakubu to iu sennō (Tokyo: Bijinesusha, 2019).

Kuriyagawa Hakuson. Zōge no tō wo dete (Tokyo: Fukunaga Shoten, 1920).

Kuroki Saburō, with Ushiyama Tsumoru. Taidan. "Watashi to hōshakaigaku," in Gendai hōshakaigaku no shomondai: Kuroki Saburō sensei koki kin'en (Tokyo: Minjihō Kenkyūkai, 1992).

Kurotaki Chikara and Itō Tadahiko, eds. Nihon kyōiku undōshi, dai ni kan, Shōwa shoki no kyōiku undō (Kyoto: San'ichi Shobō, 1960).

Large, Stephen S. "The Japanese Labor Movement, 1912–1919: Suzuki Bunji and the Yūaikai," Journal of Asian Studies, Vol. 29, No. 3 (May, 1970), 559–579.

Lasch, Christopher. The New Radicalism in America, 1889-1963: The Intellectual as a Social Type (New York: Norton, 1986).

Laski, Harold Joseph. The Foundations of Sovereignty and Other Essays (London: George Allen & Unwin, 1921).

Lazar, Joseph. "Juridical Perspectives on National Character," The Annals of the American Academy of Political and Social Science, Vol.

370, National Character in the Perspective of the Social Sciences (Mar., 1967), 16–22.

Leiter, Brian. "Legal Realism and Legal Positivism Reconsidered," in Ethics, Vol. 111, No. 2 (January, 2001), 278–301.

Lensen, George Alexander. "The Attempt on the Life of Nicholas II in Japan," in The Russian Review, Vol. 20, No. 3 (July, 1961), 232–253.

Leoni, Bruno. Freedom and the Law (Princeton, NJ: D. Van Nostrand, 1961).

Levy, David J. The Measure of Man: Incursions in Philosophical and Political Anthropology (Columbia: University of Missouri Press, 1993).

Mainichi Shimbunsha. Ekonomisuto.

Makino Ei'ichi. Hijōji rippō kō (Tokyo: Chūō Kōronsha, 1943).

Makino Ei'ichi. Hōritsugaku no kadai toshite no kami (Tokyo: Yūhikaku, 1948).

Makino Ei'ichi. "Hozumi Nobushige sensei no eisei nijūgo nen," in Kokka Gakkai Zasshi, Vol. 65, Nos. 5, 6, & 7 (1952), 319–341.

Makino Ei'ichi, ed. Hozumi sensei kanreki shukuga ronbunshū (Tokyo: Yūhikaku, 1915).

Mano Yōsuke and Satō Shigeru. "Sarue uramachi furyō jūtaku chiku kairyō jigyō to shinsai fukkō tochi kukaku seiri jigyō to no kanren nit suite: Dōjunkai ni yoru shūgō jūtakuchi keikaku no keikaku gijutsu ni kansuru kenkyū sono ichi," Nihon Kenchiku Gakkai Keikakukei Ronbunshū, vol. 62, no. 499 (1997), 105-112.

Marshall, Byron K. "Academic Factionalism in Japan: The Case of the Tōdai Economics Department, 1919–1939," in Modern Asian Studies, Vol. 12, No. 4 (1978), 529–551.

Marshall, Byron K. Capitalism and Nationalism in Prewar Japan: The Ideology of the Business Elite, 1868–1941 (Stanford: Stanford University Press, 1967).

Marutschke, Hans Peter. "Die Anfangsphase der Arbeitsrechtswissenschaft in Japan: der Beitrag Izutaro Suehiros," Kobe Hōgaku Zasshi, vol. 38, no. 2 (Sept., 1988).

Maruyama Masao. Jikonai taiwa (Tokyo: Misuzu Shobō, 1998).

Maruyama Masao, tr. Ivan Morris. Thought and Behavior in Modern Japanese Politics (London: Oxford University Press, 1969).

Matsui, Shigenori. "Constitutional Precedents in Japan: A Comment on the Role of Precedents," Washington University Law Review, Vol. 88, Issue 6, Decision Making on the Japanese Supreme Court, 1669–1680.

Matsumura Akira, ed. Nihon shihonshugi hattatsushi kōza (multi-volume set).

Matsuno Yoshitora. Wagatsuma Sakae: hito to jidai (Sendai: Gyōsei, 1993).

Matsuo Takayoshi. Taishō Demokurashii (Tokyo: Iwanami Gendai Bunko, 2001).

Matsuo Takayoshi. Takigawa Jiken (Tokyo: Iwanami Shoten, 2005).

McGinty, Sean. "From Peasant to Shareholder: Divergent Paths of Group Litigation in Tokugawa Japan and England" (unprovenanced paper, npd).

McNally, Mark. Proving the Way: Conflict and Practice in the History of Japanese Nativism (Cambridge: Harvard University Press, 2005).

Merryman, J.H. "Toward a Comparative Study of the Sale of Land," in Ernst von Caemmerer, Soia Mentschikoff, and Konrad Zweigert, eds., Ius Privatum Gentium: Festschrift für Max Rheinstein zum 70. Geburtstag am 5. Juli 1969, Band II: Nationales und Vergleichendes Privatrecht (Tübingen: J.C.B. Mohr, 1969).

Miki Kiyoshi. Dokusho to jinsei (1942) (Tokyo: Shinchosha, 2008).

Miller, Aaron L. "From Bushidō to science: a new pedagogy of sports coaching in Japan," in Japan Forum, Vol. 23, No. 11 (September, 2011), 385–406.

Miller, Frank O. Minobe Tatsukichi: Interpreter of Constitutionalism in Japan (Berkeley: University of California Press, 1965).

Miller, John J. "Football and the American Character," Imprimis, Vol. 42, No. 9 (September, 2013).

Miller, John J. The Big Scrum: How Teddy Roosevelt Saved Football (New York: Harper Perennial, 2012).

Mimura, Janis. Planning for Empire: Reform Bureaucrats and the Japanese Wartime State (Cornell: Cornell University Press, 2011).

Minear, Richard. Japanese Tradition and Western Law: Emperor, State, and Law in the Thought of Hozumi Yatsuka. Harvard East Asian series, 48. (Cambridge: Harvard University Press, 1970).

Minear, Richard. Victor's Justice: The Tokyo War Crimes Trial (Princeton: Princeton University Press, 1971).

Minichiello, Sharon. Japan's Competing Modernities: Issues in Culture and Democracy, 1900–1930 (Honolulu: University of Hawai'i Press, 1998).

Minoda Muneki. Hō tetsugaku to sekaikan: Tanaka Kōtarō shi no shisō gakusetu hihan (Tokyo: Genri Nihonsha, 1938).

Minoda Muneki. Kokka to daigaku (Tokyo: Genri Nihonsha, 1941).

Minoda Muneki. Kyōsanshugi shisō no kentō (Nihon Kyōkai Shuppanbu, not issued for sale, 1940).

Minoda Muneki. Minoda Muneki zenshū (Tokyo: Kashiwa Shobō, 2004).

Minpō Hanrei Kenkyūkai. Hanrei Minpō (Tokyo: Yūhikaku, 1921).

Minpō Hanrei Kenkyūkai. Minpō Hanrei Kenkyūroku (complete set).

Minshū no Hōritsusha. Minshū no Hōritsu (multiple issues).

Mises, Ludwig von. Human Action: A Treatise on Economics (Auburn, AL: Ludwig von Mises Institute, 1998).

Mishina Akihide. Kodai saisei to kokurei shinkō (Tokyo: Heibonsha, 1973).

Mitake Jōshi and Kokutai Yōgo Rengōkai. Gokanen wo kaerimite (Not issued for sale, 1937).

Mitani Taichirō. Taishō Demokurashii ron (Tokyo: Chūō Kōron Sha, 1974).

Mitchell, Richard H. "Japan's Peace Preservation Law of 1925: Its Origins and Significance," in Monumenta Nipponica, Vol. 28, No. 3 (1973), 317–345.

Mitchell, Richard H. Justice in Japan: The Notorious Teijin Scandal (Honolulu: University of Hawai'i Press, 2002).

Mitchell, Richard H. Political Bribery in Japan (Honolulu: University of Hawai'i Press, 1996).

Mitsui Kōshi. "Yudaya teki Marukusu shisō gekimetsu hōhō," in Kokuhon, Vol. 5, No. 11 (November, 1925), 17–23.

Miyachi Masato. Nichiro sengo seijishi kenkyū (Tokyo: Azekura Shobō, 1973).

Miyamoto, Archie. Wartime Military Records on Comfort Women: A Compilation of U.S., Allied, Dutch, and Japanese Military Documents (Amazon Digital, 2017).

Miyata Shinpei. Darega kaze wo mita deshō: boranteia no genten, Tōdai Setsurumento monogatari (Tokyo: Bungei Shunjū, 1995).

Miyazawa Toshiyoshi. Tennō kikansetsu jiken: shiryō wa kataru (Tokyo: Yūhikaku, 1970), vols. 1 and 2.

Miyoshi Sōji and Terada Shin'ya. Hitosuji no michi: gojūnen no ashiato (Osaka: Shōei Insatsu, 1983).

Mizoguchi Yūzō, Ikeda Tomohisa, and Kojima Tsuyoshi. Chūgoku shisōshi (Tokyo: University of Tokyo Press, 2007).

Mizumachi Yūichirō. Rōdōhō (Tokyo: Yuhikaku, 2007).

Mizuno, Hiromi. Science for the Empire: Scientific Nationalism in Modern Japan (Stanford: Stanford University Press, 2009).

Monbushō, ed. Saishin kōminka shiryō seisetsu (Tokyo: Monbushō Gakumukyoku, Nov., 1931).

Monbushō, ed. Saishin kōminka shiryō seisetsu, Bunbushō hensan (Tōkyō: Teikoku kōmin kyōiku kyōkai, 1931).

Moore, Joe. Japanese Workers and the Struggle for Power, 1945–1947 (Madison, WI: University of Wisconsin Press, 1983).

Morgan, Jason. Amerika wa naze Nihon wo mikudasu no ka: machigai darake no 'taiNichi rekishikan' wo tadasu (Tokyo: Wani Books, 2016).

Morgan, Jason. "Book Review: Judicial Review in an Objective Legal System," Libertarian Papers, Vol. 9 (2017).

Morgan, Jason. "Catholic Critiques of Statism in Interwar Japan: Minoda Muneki, Suehiro Izutarō, and Tanaka Kōtarō," Logos: A Journal of Catholic Thought and Culture, vol. 21, no. 3 (Summer, 2018).

Morgan, Jason. "Kumazawa Agonistes: The Right of Conquest and the Rise of Democratic Ideology," Reitaku Review, Vols. 25 & 26 (2019, 2020).

Morgan, Jason. Nihonkoku kenpō wa Nihonjin no haji de aru: Beikokujin rekishi gakusha 'me kara uroko no kankenron' (Tokyo: Gokū Shuppan, 2018).

Morgan, Jason. "No Refuge from Modernity? The Intersections of American and Japanese Conservatisms, Russell Kirk, and Shirasu Jirō," The Michigan Historical Review, vol. 41, no. 1 (Spring, 2016).

Morgan, Jason. "The Great Kantō Earthquake and Suehiro Izutarō's Shift from Institutional to Interventionist Reform Efforts in Taishō Japan," Reitaku Journal of Interdisciplinary Studies, vol. 26 (March, 2018).

Morgan, Jason. "The State, Law, Religion, and Justice in Cicero's The Republic and The Laws: An Aristotelian-Thomistic Interpretation," Studia Gilsoniana, vol. 8, no. 3 (July-September, 2019), 645-681.

Morimura Susumu. Hōtetsugaku kōgi (Tokyo: Chikuma Shobō, 2015).

Morris, Ivan. The World of the Shining Prince: Court Life in Ancient Japan (Oxford: Oxford University Press, 1964).

Morse, Ronald A. Yanagita Kunio and the Folklore Movement: The Search for Japan's National Character and Distinctiveness (New York & London: Garland, 1990), reviewed by Peter Knecht in Asian Folklore Studies, Vol. 51, No. 2 (1992), 353–355.

Mukōyama Hiro'o. "Suehiro Izutarō jutsu rōdōhō josetsu," in Kokugakuin Hōgaku, Vol. 22, No. 2 (Sep. 20, 1984), 67–98.

Mukōyama Hiro'o. Tōkyō gakusei shōhi kumiaishi (1984; no press information given).

Mutō Chōzō. "Settsurumento no haha Toinbii kan," Shakai Jigyō (June, 1935).

Mutō Hideo. "Hirano Yoshitarō no Dai Ajia shugi ron: Chūgoku kahoku nōson kankō chōsa to kazokukan no henyō," Ajia Kenkyū, Vol. 49, No. 4 (October, 2003), 44–59.

Nagao Ryūichi. Nihon Kenpō shisōshi (Tokyo: Kōdansha, 1996).

Najita, Tetsuo. Ordinary Economies in Japan: A Historical Perspective, 1750–1950 (Berkeley: University of California Press, 2009).

Najita, Tetsuo and J. Victor Koschmann, eds. Conflict in Modern Japanese History (Princeton: Princeton University Press, 1982).

Nakagawa Zennosuke. Minpō: ikiteiru hanrei (1E) (Tokyo: Nihon Hyōronsha, 1962).

Nakagawa Zennosuke. "Shinzokuteki fuyō gimu no honshitsu," Hōgaku shinpō, Vol. 38, No. 6 (1928), 1–22.

Nakagawa Zennosuke, Yonekura Akira, eds. Shinpan, Chūshaku minpō (Tokyo: Yūhikaku, 1944).

Nakajima Kiyoaki. Sensan Sasaki Rakuzō shi tsuitō gō (Ikkō Yayoikai, not issued for sale; 1941).

Nakamura Shintarō. Nihon gakusei undō no rekishi (Tokyo: Shiraishi Shoten, 1976).

Nambara Shigeru. Bunka to kokka (Vol. 2) (Tokyo: Tokyo University Press, 1968).

Narita Ryūichi. Taishō Demokurashii (Tokyo: Iwanami Shinsho, 2007).

Nihon Daigaku Hōgakkai. "Azuma Suehiko hakase tsuitōgō," Nihon Hōgaku, vol. 46, no. 2 (1981).

Nihon Hōshakaigakukai. Rōdō hōgaku to hōshakaigaku, Hōshakaigaku dai 15 gō (Tokyo: Yūhikaku, 1963).

Nihon Hyōronsha Henshūkyoku. Nihon no hōgaku: kaiko to tenbō (Tokyo: Nihon Hyōronsha, 1950).

Nihon Hyōron Shinsha. Hōgaku Seminā: Hōritsu Jihō shimaishi (complete set).

Nihon Keizai Shimbun. (selected dates).

Nihon Kōsei Kyōkai. Dai ikkai Nihon kōsei taikai hōkokusho (Not issued for sale; July 12, 1939).

Nihon Ro-maji Kai. "Nihongo no ikizumari mondai: bunka undō toshite no Ro-maji no undō," Nihon Ro-maji Kai daigo satsu, kanji kara Romaji e!! "Nippongo wo Rōmazi de! Nipponsikino Rōmazi de!" (npd, but dated "1934" with library stamp on inside cover).

Nihon Shisōshi Kenkyūkai, ed. Nihon ni okeru rinri shisō no tenkai (Tokyo: Yoshikawa Kōbunkan, 1965).

Nihon Suiei Renmei. Suiei, Nihon Suiei Renmei kikan zasshi, No. 92 (1951) (complete issue).

Niida Noboru. Chūgoku no hō shisōshi: tōyōteki shizenhō no mondai (Tokyo: Nihon Hyōronsha, 1951).

Nishi Hideaki. "Tochi wo meguru kyūkan to Taiwan shihō no kankei ni tsuite," Hōgaku Kyōkai Zasshi, Vol. 122, No. 7 (July, 2005), 1217–1281.

Nishi, Toshio. Unconditional Democracy: Education and Politics in Occupied Japan, 1945–1952 (Stanford: Hoover Institution Press, 1982).

Nishida Kitarō. Nishida Kitarō zenshū.

Nishino Tatsukichi, tr. Ōoka seidan (Tokyo: Kyōikusha Shinsho, 1989).

Nishiuchi Kiyoshi. Nihon Settsurumento kenkyū josetsu (Tokyo: Dōshinsha, 1959).

Nomura Heiji, ed. Hanrei rōdō sōgi (Tokyo: Ichiryūsha, 1957).

Nomura Heiji. Minshūshugi hōgaku ni ikite (Tokyo: Nihon Hyōronsha, 1976).

Nomura Heiji. Rōdōhō kōwa (Tokyo: Nihon Hyōron Shinsha, 1963).

Nomura Heiji. Nihon rōdōhō no keisei katei to riron (Tokyo: Iwanami Shoten, 1957).

Nomura Heiji. Rōdōhō no-to (Tokyo: Nihon Hyōron Shinsha, 1958).

Nomura Heiji. Rōdō kihonken no tenkai (Tokyo: Iwanami Shoten, 1975).

Nomura Heiji and Munemura Teruo. Hōritsugaku zenshū 48 (Tokyo: Yūhikaku, 1961).

Northrop, F.S.C. The Complexity of Legal and Ethical Experience (Boston: Little Brown, 1959).

Northrop, F.S.C. "Underhill Moore's Legal Science: Its Nature and Significance," Faculty Scholarship Series. Paper 4375, The Yale Law Journal, vol. 59, no. 2 (1950).

Numata Yorisuke. Ōoka Echizen-no-kami (Tokyo: Meiji Shoin, 1929).

Ōbayashi Munetsugu, *Settsurumento no kenkyū* (Tokyo: Keibunsha, 2008).

Oblas, Peter. "Naturalist Law and Japan's Legitimization of Empire in Manchuria: Thomas Baty and Japan's Ministry of Foreign Affairs (Part One)," Diplomacy and Statecraft, Vol. 15, No. 1 (2004), 35–55.

O'Bryan, Scott. The Growth Idea: Purpose and Prosperity in Postwar Japan (Honolulu: University of Hawai'i Press, 2009).

Odegaard, Charles E. "Legalis homo," Speculum, Vol. 15, No. 2 (Apr., 1940), 186–193.

Ogawa, Manako. "'Hull-House' in Downtown Tokyo: The Transplantation of a Settlement House from the United States into Japan and the North American Missionary Women, 1919–1945," Journal of World History, Vol. 15, No. 3 (Sep., 2004), 359–387.

Oguma Eiji. Nihonjin no kyōkai (Tokyo: Shinyosha, 2003).

Oguma Eiji. Tan'itsu minzoku shinwa no kigen: Nihonjin no jigazō no keifu (Tokyo: Shinyosha, 2003).

Oka Kunio. Kagaku to bungaku (Tokyo: Mikasa Shobō, 1936).

Okada Satoshi. "Baba Bunkō to 'Ōoka seidan': Ōoka Tadasuke shussetan wo jiku toshite," Kokugakuin Daigaku Daigakuin Kiyō: Bungaku Kenkyūka, 12 ed. (1977), 108–130.

Okamatsu Santarō (writing as "Santaro Okamatsu"). Provisional Report on Investigations of Laws and Customs in the Island of Formosa, Compiled by Order of the Governor-General of Formosa (1900; reprinted by Ch'eng Wen Publishing Company, Taipei, 1971).

Ōkawa Sumio. "Daishin'in (minji) hanreishū no hensan to Daishin'in hanrei shinsakai," Ritsumeikan Hōgaku, No. 256 (1997), 1351, ff.

Ōkōchi Kazuo. Kōtoku Shūsui to Katayama Sen: Meiji no shakaishugi (Tokyo: Kōdansha, 1972).

Ōkubo Kazushi, ed. Ana-Boru ronsō (Tokyo: Dōjidaisha, 2005).

Okudaira Yasuhiro. "Uso wo kangaeru," in Hōgaku Seminā, No. 540 (Dec., 1999), 82–85.

Ōnishi Shinji. Manshū nōson gassakusha undō no kiroku: seikyō undō gojūnen, dai nibu (Tokyo: Ryūkei Shosha, 1980).

Ōnishi Shinji. Seikyō undō gojūnen: seikyō undō hitosujini, ikita rekishi no shōgen toshite (Yokohama: Kanagawa ken Seikatsu Kyōdō Kumiai Rengōkai, 1978).

Ooms, Herman. Tokugawa Village Practice: Class, Status, Power, Law (Berkeley: University of California Press, 1996).

Oppler, Alfred C. Legal Reform in Occupied Japan: A Participant Looks Back (Princeton: Princeton University Press, 1976).

Ōtaka Toshio. 20 seiki Nihon jinmei jiten (multiple entries) (Tokyo: Nichigai Asoshiētsu, 2004).

Otani Tomohiro. "Suehiro Izutarō no hōshakaigaku," in Shakai Bunseki, Vol. 20 (1992), 1–19.

Ōuchi Tsutomu. Nihon no rekishi 24, fuashizumu e no michi (Tokyo: Chūō Kōron Sha, 1967).

Ozaki Ichirō. "Hōshakaigaku," in Hōritsu Jihō, Vol. 75, No. 13 (2003), 222–230.

Ozeki Takako. Zenkoku Tomo no Kai kenkyū: Fujin no Tomo dokushatachi ni yoru seikatsu gōrika to sono jissen (PhD dissertation, Rikkyō Daigaku Daigakuin, 2012).

Pascal, Robert Anthony, James Lee Babin, and John William Corrington, eds. The Collected Works of Eric Voegelin, Vol. 27, The Nature of the Law and Related Legal Writings (Baton Rouge: Louisiana State University Press, 1991).

Person, John David. Philosophizing Japan: The Genri Nippon Society and the Question of Japaneseness (PhD dissertation, University of Chicago, 2012).

Petrażycki, Leon, tr. H.W. Babb. Law and Morality (Cambridge: Harvard University Press, 1955).

Pittau, Joseph, SJ. Political Thought in Early Meiji Japan, 1868–1889 (Cambridge: Harvard University Press, 1967).

Pitts, Jennifer. A Turn to Empire: The Rise of Imperial Liberalism in Britain and France (Princeton: Princeton University Press, 2005).

Podgórecki, Adam. "Unrecognized Father of Sociology of Law: Leon Petrażycki: Reflections based on Jan Gorecki's Sociology and Jurisprudence of Leon Petrażycki," in Law & Society Review, Vol. 15, No. 1 (1980–1981), 183–202.

Potter, Harold. An Introduction to the History of Equity and its Courts (London: Sweet and Maxwell, 1931).

Pound, Roscoe. An Introduction to the Philosophy of Law (1922) (New Haven: Yale University Press, 1959).

Pound, Roscoe. "Law in Books and Law in Action," 44 American Law Review 12 (1910).

Pound, Roscoe. "The Scope and Purpose of Sociological Jurisprudence," 24 Harvard Law Review 591 (1911), 25 Harvard Law Review 140 (1912), 25 Harvard Law Review 489 (1912).

Radbruch, Gustav. "In Memoriam Hermann Kantorowicz," Gesamtausgabe Bd. 16 (1988).

Ramseyer, J. Mark. Japan's Political Marketplace (Cambridge: Harvard University Press, 1997).

Ramseyer, J. Mark. Second-Best Justice: The Virtues of Japanese Private Law (Chicago: University of Chicago Press, 2015).

Ramseyer, J. Mark. "The Fable of Land Reform: Leases and Credit Markets in Occupied Japan," in Journal of Economics & Management Strategy, Vol. 24, Iss. 4 (Winter, 2015), 934–957.

Ramseyer, J. Mark. "The Market for Children: Evidence from Early-Modern Japan," Chicago Law and Economics Working Paper (second series), no. 24, University of Chicago Law School (1994).

Ramseyer, J. Mark and Eric B. Rasmusen. Measuring Judicial Independence: The Political Economy of Judging in Japan (Chicago: University of Chicago Press, 2010).

Roberts, Luke S. Performing the Great Peace: Political Space and Open Secrets in Tokugawa Japan (Honolulu: University of Hawai'i Press, 2015).

Rockwell, Llewellyn. Against the State: An Anarcho-Capitalist Manifesto (Auburn, AL: Rockwell Communications, 2014).

Rokumoto Kahei. Nihon no hō to shakai (Tokyo: Yūhikaku, 2004).

Rokumoto Kahei and Yoshida Osamu, eds. Suehiro Izutarō to Nihon no hōshakaigaku (Tokyo: University of Tokyo Press, 2007).

Rommen, Heinrich A. The Natural Law: A Study in Legal and Social History and Philosophy (Indianapolis: Liberty Fund, 1998).

Roth, Guenther and Ross Wittich, eds. Max Weber, Economy and Society (New York: Bedminster, 1978).

Rothbard, Murray. Man, Economy, and State: A Treatise on Economic Principles, with Power and Market: Government and the Economy (2E) (Auburn, AL: Ludwig von Mises Institute, 2009).

Rottleuthner, Hubert. Three Legal Sociologies: Eugen Ehrlich, Hugo Sinzheimer, Max Weber (Madison, WI: University of Wisconsin-Madison Institute for Legal Studies, 1987).

Rubinger, Richard. "Education: From One Room to One System," in Marius B. Jansen and Gilbert Rozman, eds., Japan in Transition: From Tokugawa to Meiji (Princeton: Princeton University Press, 1986), 195–230.

Saaler, Sven and J. Victor Koschmann, eds. Pan-Asianism in Modern Japanese History: Colonialism, regionalism and borders (London: Routledge, 2007).

Sagers, John H. Confucian Capitalism: Shibusawa Eiichi, Business Ethics, and Economic Development in Meiji Japan (New York: Palgrave Macmillan, 2018).

Saguchi Takashi. Iryō no shakaika (Tokyo: Keisō Shobō, 1982).

Saigusa Hiroto, ed. Nihon tetsugaku zensho daigo kan: Kokugaku hen (Tokyo: Dai'ichi Shobō, 1936).

Saigusa Hiroto, ed. Nihon tetsugaku zensho dairokkan, Seiyō tetsugakuhen (Tokyo: Dai'ichi Shobō, 1936).

Saikō Saibansho. "Rōdō kankei chōseihō ihan hikoku jiken," Saikō saibansho keiji hanreishū 5 kan 4 gō (1949), 634, ff.

Sandel, Michael J. Justice: What's the Right Thing to Do? (New York: Farrar, Straus and Giroux, 2009).

Sansom, George. A History of Japan to 1334 (Stanford: Stanford University Press, 1958).

Sasa Hiro'o. Zoku jinbutsu shunjū (Tokyo: Kaizōsha, 1940).

Sasakura Hideo. Hōgaku kōgi (Tokyo: University of Tokyo Press, 2014).

Sasakura Hideo. Hō shisōshi kōgi, jō, koten kodai kara shūkyō kaikakuki made (Tokyo: University of Tokyo Press, 2007).

Sasakura Hideo. Hō tetsugaku kōgi (Tokyo: University of Tokyo Press, 2002).

Sasakura Hideo. "Suehiro Izutarō 'Uso no Kōyō' kō: awasete Kurusu Saburō hō to fuikushon ron," in Waseda Hōgaku, Vol. 90, No. 2 (2015), 41–74.

Sawada, Janine Tasca. Practical Pursuits: Religion, Politics, and Personal Cultivation in Nineteenth-Century Japan (Honolulu: University of Hawai'i Press, 2004).

Scheiner, Irwin. Christian Converts and Social Protest in Meiji Japan (Berkeley: University of California Press, 1970).

Schencking, J. Charles. "Catastrophe, Opportunism, Contestation: The Fractured Politics of Reconstructing Tokyo following the Great Kantō Earthquake of 1923," Modern Asian Studies, Vol. 40, No. 4 (October, 2006), 833–873.

Schencking, J. Charles. The Great Kantō Earthquake and the Chimera of National Reconstruction in Japan (New York: Columbia University Press, 2013).

Schmitt, Carl, tr. Jeffrey Seitzer. Constitutional Theory (Durham: Duke University Press, 2008).

Schmitt, Carl, tr. Michael Hoelzl and Graham Ward. Political Theology II: The Myth of the Closure of Any Political Theology (Cambridge, UK: Polity, 2010).

Schur, Edwin M. Law and Society: A Sociological View (New York: Random House, 1968).

Scruton, Roger. From Descartes to Wittgenstein: A Short History of Modern Philosophy (London: Routledge and Kegan Paul, 1981).

Scruton, Roger. "How to be a Nonliberal, Antisocialist Conservative," from Intercollegiate Review, Vol. 28, No. 2, 1993, quoted in Mark C. Henrie, ed., Arguing Conservatism: Four Decades of the Intercollegiate Review (Wilmington, DE: ISI Books, 2008), 768–769.

Seidensticker, Edward. Tokyo Rising: The City since the Great Earthquake (New York: Alfred A. Knopf, 1990).

Seigfried, Charlene Haddock. "Socializing Democracy: Jane Addams and John Dewey," Philosophy of the Social Sciences, vol. 29, no. 2 (June, 1999), 207–230.

Sejima Ryūzō. DaitōA sensō no jissō (Tokyo: PHP Bunko, 2000).

Seki Kazuo. Sainō wa tsukurareru: jishin wo tsuke tenbun wo nobasu manabikata (Tokyo: Mirion Bukkusu, 1964).

Sekiguchi Yūko, et al. Nihon kazoku shi (Tokyo: Kazusa Shuppansha, 1989).

Sekino Michio. Imanao habikoru WGIP no uso (Tokyo: Jiyuusha, 2016).

Sekino Michio. Nihonjin wo kuruwaseta sennō kōsaku (Tokyo: Jiyuusha, 2015).

Seligman, Edwin R. A. and Alvin Johnson, eds. "Social Settlements," in Encyclopaedia of the Social Sciences (New York: The Macmillan Company, 1930).

Sharafi, Mitra. Colonial Parsis and Law: A Cultural History (Mumbai: KR Cama Oriental Institute, 2010).

Sharafi, Mitra. Law and Identity in Colonial South Asia: Farsi Legal Culture, 1772–1947 (Cambridge: Cambridge University Press, 2014).

Sherry, Dave. Empire and Revolution: A Socialist History of the First World War (London: Bookmarks, 2014).

Shibata Kenji. Hinkon to chi'iki fukushi katsudō: Setsurumento to shakai fukushi kyōgikai no kiroku (Gifu: Mirai, 2007).

Shichinohe Katsuhiko. "Genkō minpōten wo tsukutta hitobito (14)," Hōgaku Seminā, vol. 55, no. 6 (June, 2010), 56–59.

Shichinohe Katsuhiko. "Suehiro Izutarō kenkyū shiryō sōran," Hōsei Kenkyū, vol. 85, no. 1 (July, 2018), 175–237.

Shichinohe Katsuhiko. "Suehiro Izutarō no seishun: Nitobe Inazo Ikkō kōchō haiseki jiken no sōdōsha," Hōsei Kenkyū, vol. 82, nos. 2 & 3 (Dec., 2015), 143–194.

Shichinohe Katsuhiko. "Suehiro Izutarō sekinin henshū 'Gendai hōgaku zenshū' no kenkyū," Hōsei Kenkyū, vol. 85, no. 1 (July, 2018), 31–103.

Shiga Hidetoshi. Tōkyō Teidai Yanagishima Settsurumento iryōbushi: igakusei no senzen shakai undō reimeiki no kiroku (Tokyo: Shin Nippon Igaku Shuppansha, 1979).

Shiga Shinajin. "Kōei Settsurumento tokuchō to ketten," in Shakai Jigyō (July, 1931).

Shils, Edward A. and Henry Finch, eds. Max Weber, The Methodology of the Social Sciences: Max Weber (New York: Free Press, 1949).

Shimazu, Naoko. Japanese Society at War: Death, Memory and the Russo-Japanese War (Cambridge: Cambridge University Press, 2009).

Shimonaka Hiroshi. Nihon jinmei daijiten (multiple entries) (Tokyo: Heibonsha, 1990).

Shimizu Hideo, Mori'izumi Akira, and Takakubo Sadato, eds. Hōgaku kihon sho annai (Tokyo: Nihon Hyōronsha, 1976).

Shin, Peter Yong-Shik. The Ōtsu incident: Japan's hidden history of the attempted assassination of future Emperor Nicholas II of Russia in the town of Ōtsu, Japan, May 11, 1891 and its implications for historical analysis (PhD dissertation, University of Pennsylvania, 1989).

Shiotani San, ed. Rohan okina zadan (Tokyo: Kadokawa Bunkō, 1951).

Shiōten Nobutaka. Yudaya shisō oyobi undō (Tokyo: Naigai Shobō, 1941).

Shiraha Yūzō. Nihon Hōri Kenkyūkai no bunseki: Hō to dōtoku no ittaika (Tokyo: Chūō Daigaku Shuppanbu, 1998).

Sievers, Sharon. Flowers in Salt: The Beginnings of Feminist Consciousness in Modern Japan (Stanford: Stanford University Press, 1983).

Sinzheimer, Hugo. "Wie verhält sich der para.950 BGB zu dem Satz, daß jeder Arbeiter Eigentümer des Arbeitsproduktes werden soll?" (1932), in Arbeitsrecht und Rechtssoziologie, vol. 1 (Frankfurt/Köln: Europäische Verlagsanstalt, 1976), 423–426.

Smith, Henry DeWitt, II. Japan's First Student Radicals (Cambridge: Harvard University Press, 1972).

Soviak, Eugene. "The Case of Baba Tatsui: Western Enlightenment, Social Change, and the Early Meiji Intellectual," Monumenta Nipponica 18:1–4 (1963), 191–235.

Stolleis, Michael. Juristen: Ein biographisches Lexikon Von der Antike bis zum 20. Jahrhundert (multiple entries) (München: Verlag C.H. Beck, 2001).

Suehiro Izutarō sekinin henshū. Hōritsu Jihō, complete set of journals.

Suehiro Izutarō, Suehiro Fuyu cho. Minpō zakki chō, Vol. 1 (Tokyo: Nihon Hyōronsha, 1953).

Suehiro Izutarō, Suehiro Fuyu cho. Minpō zakki chō, Vol. 2 (Tokyo: Nihon Hyōronsha, 1953).

Suehiro Izutarō, Suehiro Fuyu cho. Yakuningaku sansoku: hyōron, zuihitsu (Tokyo: Nihon Hyōronsha, 1955).

Suehiro Izutarō. "Amerika no rōdō jijō," Nihon Hyōron, Vol. 25, No. 5 (May, 1950), 65–70.

Suehiro Izutarō. "Amerika no rōdō kankei zakkan," in Seikei Chōsa Geppō, No. 18 (September, 1950), 1–2.

Suehiro Izutarō. "Amerika yori kaerite," in Tōshō, The Tokyo Chamber of Commerce & Industry Journal (npd), 4–7.

Suehiro Izutarō. "Chi'iku to tai'iku to no chōwa ni tsuite," in Ōsaka Mainichi Shimbunsha, ed., Kyokutō Orimupikku yūshō senshu no renshūhō (Osaka: Ōsaka Mainichi Shimbunsha, 1926).

Suehiro Izutarō. "Chōsa kenkyū to okusoku," in TōA Kenkyūsho Dai Roku Chōsakai, Gakujutsubu Iinkai, ed., Shina kankō chōsa ihō (Tokyo: not issued for sale, 1942).

Suehiro Izutarō. "Dantai kōshō no kibo ni tsuite," Sekitan Hyōron, Vol. 1, No. 5 (Oct., 1950), 2–3.

Suehiro Izutarō, ed. Gendai hōgaku zenshū (Tokyo: Hyōronsha, 1928).

Suehiro Izutarō. Hōgaku nyūmon (Tokyo: Nihon Hyōronsha, 1952).

Suehiro Izutarō. Hōsō kanwa (Tokyo: Kaizōsha, 1921).

Suehiro Izutarō. "Hōsō mandan," in Bungei Shunjū (January 1, 1929).

Suehiro Izutarō. Hōsō manpitsu (Tokyo: Nihon Hyōronsha, 1933).

Suehiro Izutarō. "Kaishaku hōgaku ni okeru hōgenron ni tsuite," in Tanaka Kōtarō, ed., Tōkyō Teikoku Daigaku nai Hōgaku Kyōkai (Tokyo: Yūhikaku, 1933), 377–404.

Suehiro Izutarō. "Minpō gakusei seijidai no kaiko: tokuni Kawana Kaneshirō kyōju ni tsuite," in Tōkyō Teikoku Daigaku Gakujutsu Taikan (Kokusai Shuppan, not issued for sale, April, 1942).

Suehiro Izutarō. "Minpō kaizō no konpon mondai," in Makino Ei'ichi, et al., eds. Shin Nippon no kensetsu (Tokyo: Iwanami Shoten, 1922).

Suehiro Izutarō. Minpō zakkichō (Tokyo: Nihon Hyōronsha, 1940).

Suehiro Izutarō. Minpō zakkō (Tokyo: Nihon Hyōronsha, 1932).

Suehiro Izutarō. Nihon rōdō kumiai undōshi (Tokyo: Chūō Kōron Sha, 1952).

Suehiro Izutarō. Rōdōhō kenkyū (Tokyo: Kaizōsha, 1927).

Suehiro Izutarō. Rōdō kumiai (Tokyo: Kōtsū Kyōryokukai, 1946).

Suehiro Izutarō. "Rōdō kumiai torishimari: hōan wo hyōsu," serialized in Tōkyō Asahi Shimbun (Feb., 1927).

Suehiro Izutarō. Saikin no rōdō mondai ni tsuite (Nihon Kōtsū Kōsha, not issued for sale; 1947).

Suehiro Izutarō. "Settsurumento," in Iwanami Kōza, Kyōiku kagaku (Tokyo: Iwanami Shoten, 1932), 3–25.

Suehiro Izutarō. Shin taisei to tai'iku undō (Tokyo: Taisei Yokusankai [Imperial Rule Assistance Association], 1940).

Suehiro Izutarō. Tai'iku to sensō (Dai Nippon Taiikukai, 1944).

Suehiro Izutarō. Uso no kōyō (Tokyo: Kaizōsha, 1923).

Suehiro Izutarō. "Waga kuni, rōdō kumiai undō no ayumi," in Rōdō Shichō (June, 1949), 2–4.

Suehiro Izutarō. Zoku minpō zakkichō (Tokyo: Nihon Hyōronsha, 1949).

Suehiro Izutarō and Iwanaga Nobuyoshi. Taidan. "Bei-Ei kenbun are kore," Keishisha (June 1, 1950), 10–15.

Suehiro Izutarō cho, Kainō Michitaka kaitei. Minpō kōwa, Vols. 1–3 (Tokyo: Iwanami Shoten, 1954).

Suehiro Izutarō, ed. Rōdō kyōyaku no riron to jissai (Tokyo: Takayama Shoin, 1949).

Suehiro Izutarō, ed. Sangyō shakaika to rōdō kumiai no keiei sanka (Tokyo: Takayama Shoin, 1949).

Suekawa Hiroshi. "Hanrei kenkyū ni tsuite no kokorogamae," in Hanrei Minjihō, Vol. 3 (July, 1954), collected in Nihon no minshuka to hōritsu, Suekawa Hiroshi zuisō zenshū daigokan (Tokyo: Kurita Shuppankai, 1972), 334–339.

Sugimura Shōsaburō, Wagatsuma Sakae, Kimura Kameji, Gotō Kiyoshi. Nachisu no hōritsu (Tokyo: Nihon Hyōronsha, 1934).

Sugita Chūji, Yoshimoto Yūichi, and Abe Kitarō. Suikyū (Uōtā pōro) (Tokyo: Sunnansha, 1932).

Sumitani Mikio. Katayama Sen—kindai Nihon no shisōka (Tokyo: University of Tokyo Press, 1960).

Suzuki Ichirō. "Chūgoku nōson kankō chōsa," in Tōhoku Gakuin Daigaku Ronshū, Hōritsugaku, No. 6 (July, 1973), 85–103.

Suzuki Ichirō. "Suehiro hakase no kanshūhō riron: furenzokusen riron wo chūshin ni," in Tōhoku Gakuin Daigaku Ronshū, Hōritsugaku, No. 6 (July, 1973), 33–56.

Szpilman, Christopher W.A. "Fascist and Quasi-Fascist Ideas in Interwar Japan, 1918–1941," in E. Bruce Reynolds, ed., Japan in the Fascist Era (New York: Palgrave Macmillan, 2004).

Tabata Masaji, "Nihon Suiei Renmeikai kaichō, Suehiro Izutarō sensei no shi wo itamu," in Suiei: Nihon Suiei Renmei Kikan zasshi, no. 92 (1951).

Tachibana Takashi. "Watashi no Tōdairon" (series), in Bungei Shunjū.

Tackney, Charles. "Asian Anticipations of Cosmopolis: Participation and Distribution Decisions in Japan's Industrial Relations System after World War II - Evidence of Conversion and Workplace Evangelization" (working paper), Copenhagen Business School, Institut for Interkulturel Kommunikation og Ledelse (2009).

Tackney, Charles T. and David Kettler. "Light from a Dead Sun: The Japanese Lifetime Employment System and Weimar Labor Law," Comparative Labor Law and Policy, 19:101 (1997).

Tadokoro Yūji. Chi'iki shakai kyōiku shisetsu no rekishiteki kenkyū: kōminkan e no keishō to danzetsu (PhD dissertation, Meiji Daigaku, 2014).

Taira Satoru, Umeda Tōru, Hamada Tarō, eds., Kokusaihō no furonteia: Miyazaki Shigeki sensei tsuitō ronbunshū (Tokyo: Nihon Hyōronsha, 2019).

Takahashi Shirō. Nihon ga nidoto tachiagarenai yō ni: Amerika ga senryōki ni okonatta koto (Tokyo: Chichi Shuppansha, 2014).

Takaishi Katsuo and Kimura Shōrai. Suiei Nihon (Tokyo: Kaizōsha, 1934).

Takano Yoshio. Shōwa jinmei jiten (multiple entries) (Tokyo: Nihon Tosho Sentā, 1993).

Takano Yoshio. Teikoku daigaku shusshin jinmei jiten, dai ni kan, Teikoku daigaku shusshin meikan (multiple entries) (Tokyo: Nihon Tosho Sentā, 2003).

Takayanagi Kenzō, with Thomas L. Blakemore. "A Century of Innovation: The Development of Japanese Law, 1868–1961," in Arthur Taylor von Mehren, ed., Law in Japan: The Legal Order in a Changing Society (Cambridge: Harvard University Press, 1963).

Takeda Kiyoko. "Yoshino Sakuzō," Japan Quarterly, XII (Oct.–Nov., 1965).

Takemae Eiji. Inside GHQ: The Allied Occupation of Japan and its Legacy (New York: Continuum, 2002).

Takemae Eiji. "Seisan kanri to GHQ: Kosutanchiino shōsa ni kiku," in GHQ rōdōka no hito to seisaku (npd), 47–54.

Takemae Eiji. "Senryō kaimakuki no rōdō seisaku: Karupinsukii shodai rōdō kachō ni kiku (yōyaku)," in GHQ rōdōka no hito to seisaku (npd), 63–74.

Takemae Eiji. "Senryō seisaku tenkaiki no rōdō seisaku: T. Kōen nidaime rōdō kachō ni kiku (kami)," in GHQ rōdōka no hito to seisaku (npd), 60–68.

Takemae Eiji. "Takobeya kaihō to rōdō pāji: L. Bekkā jun'i ni kiku," in GHQ rōdōka no hito to seisaku (npd), 68–77.

Takenaka, Harukata. Failed Democratization in Prewar Japan: Breakdown of a Hybrid Regime (Stanford: Stanford University Press, 2014).

Takeyama Michio. "Shōwashi to Tōkyō saiban," Seiron, Special Edition (Sep., 2015).

Tamaki, Norio. Japanese Banking: A History, 1859–1959 (Cambridge: Cambridge University Press, 1995).

Tamura Norio. Kaigai e yūtopia wo motomete: bōmei to kokugai konkyochi (Tokyo: Shakai Hyōronsha, 1989).

Tanaka Kōtarō. "Gendai no shisō taikei anākii to sono gen'in no kentō," in Hayashi Kentarō, ed., Shin hoshushugi, in Gendai Nihon shisō taikei, 35 (Series) (Tokyo: Chikuma Shobō, 1963), 235–263.

Tanaka Kōtarō. Hōritsugaku gairon (Tokyo: Gakuseisha, 1953).

Tanaka Kōtarō. Sekaihō no riron, Vol. 1 (Tokyo: Iwanami Shoten, 1932).

Tanaka Kōtarō. "Shakai rippō no shidō ri'nen to kokusai shakai kiso," (title of book not given) (Tokyo: Teikoku Kōmin Kyōiku Kyōkai, 1931).

Tanaka Kōtarō. "Sorobuiyofu no hō tetsugaku: tokuni shizenhō to jitteihō to no kankei ni tsuite," in Hōtetsugaku Shikihō (1948), 36–65.

Tanaka Kōtarō. "What is Necessary to Make Democracy Work in Japan?" in Paul K.T. Sih, ed., Democracy in East Asia (Taipei: China Culture Publishing Foundation, 1957), 50–56.

Tanaka Kōtarō. "Yuriusu Ofuneru 'Hō to shakai' (Julius Ofner, Recht und Gesellschaft (1931, Wien und Leipzig, XXII SS, 308))," in Hōritsu tetsugaku ronshū, 2 vols. (Tokyo: Iwanami Shoten, 1942–44).

Tanaka Masahiro. "Hesuperia gō jiken," in Kokushi daijiten, vol. 12 (Tokyo: Yoshikawa Kōbunkan, 1991).

Tanaka Shigeki. "Ibunka toshite no kindaihō," in Shimpojiumu, Hōchitsujo no kindai to gendai (npd), 19–29.

Tanizaki Jun'ichirō. Chijin no ai (Tokyo: Shinchosha, 1924).

Teikoku Daigaku Shimbun (complete set).

Thompson, E.P. "Time, Work-Discipline, and Industrial Capitalism," in Past & Present, No. 38 (Dec., 1967), 56–97.

Thomson, James Jr., Peter W. Stanley, and John Curtis Perry. Sentimental Imperialists: The American Experience in East Asia (New York: Harper and Row, 1982).

Tierney, Robert Thomas. Monster of the Twentieth Century: Kōtoku Shūsui and Japan's First Anti-Imperialist Movement (Berkeley: University of California Press, 2015).

Tipton, Elise. Japanese Police State: Tokkō in Interwar Japan (Honolulu: University of Hawai'i Press, 1990).

TōA Kenkyūsho Dairoku Chōsakai, Gakujutsubu Iinkai. Shina kankō chōsa ihō (Feb. 25, 1942; not issued for sale).

Tōkyō Daigaku Hanrei Kenkyūkai. Hanrei Minjihō (Tokyo: Yūhikaku, 1949).

Tōkyō Daigaku Hyakunenshi Hōgakubu Henshū Iinkai. Tōkyō Daigaku Hyakunenshi (Tokyo: Tokyo University Press, 1986).

Tōkyō Kokumin Gakkō Suiei Renmei, ed. Suiei dokuhon (Tokyo: Shimizu Shobō, 1943).

Tōkyōfu Shakai Jigyō Kyōkai Keiei. Ōji Rinpokan jigyō gaiyō, dainigō (March, 1926).

Tōkyō Shiyakusho. Tōkyō shinai ni okeru kiji no chōsa (March, 1937).

Tomba, Luigi, ed. East Asian capitalism: conflicts, growth and crisis (Milan: Feltrinelli, 2002).

Totman, Conrad. Politics in the Tokugawa Bakufu, 1600–1843 (Cambridge: Harvard University Press, 1967).

Treviño, A. Javier. "The Sociology of Law in Global Perspective," in The American Sociologist, Vol. 32, No. 2, The Sociology of Law (Summer, 2001), 5–9.

Trubek, David M. "Back to the Future: The Short, Happy Life of the Law and Society Movement," University of Wisconsin-Madison Institute for Legal Studies Working Papers, Series 4 (Madison, Wisconsin, April, 1990).

Trubek, David M. Max Weber's Tragic Modernism and the Study of Law in Society, University of Wisconsin Institute for Legal Studies Working Papers, Series 1 (University of Wisconsin-Madison Law School, December, 1985).

Tsuge Hideomi. TōA kenkyūsho to watakushi: senchū chishikijin no shōgen (Tokyo: Keisō Shobō, 1979).

Tsuge Hideomi. Waga uchinaru Chūgoku (Tokyo: Aki Shobō), 1971).

Uchida, Jun. Brokers of Empire: Japanese Settler Colonialism in Korea, 1876–1945 (Cambridge: Harvard University Press, 2011).

Uchiyama Masao. Nihon no Chūgoku nōson chōsa to dentō shakai (Tokyo: Ochanomizu Shobō, 2009).

Ueno Chizuko. Kindai kazoku no seiritsu to shūen (Tokyo: Iwanami Shoten, 1994).

Ukai Nobushige, Fukushima Masao, Kawashima Takeyoshi, and Tsuji Kiyoaki, eds. Kōza: Nihon kindai hō hattatsushi 8 (Tokyo: Keisō Shobō, 1959).

Ukai Nobushige, Fukushima Masao, Kawashima Takeyoshi, and Tsuji Kiyoaki, eds. Kōza: Nihon kindai hō hattatsushi 10 (Tokyo: Keisō Shobō, 1961).

Urabe Hiroshi and Urabe Takeyo. Michizure: atarashii hoiku wo motomete (Tokyo: Shōeisha, 1982).

Ushiomi Toshitaka and Toshitani Nobuyoshi, eds. Nihon no hōgakusha (Tokyo: Nihon Hyōronsha, 1974).

Utley, Jonathan G. Going to War with Japan, 1937–1941 (Knoxville: University of Tennessee Press, 1985).

Vaihinger, Hans. Die Philosophie des Als Ob (1911) (Aalen: Scientia Verlag, 1986).

Vanoverbeke, Dmitri. "Review of Dai-Kwon Choi and Kahei Rokumoto, eds., Judicial System Transformation in the Globalizing World: Korea and Japan," in Hōshakaigaku, No. 68 (2008), 256–263.

Vinogradoff, Paul. Villainage in England (Oxford: Clarendon Press, 1892).

Voegelin, Eric. The New Science of Politics, in The Collected Works of Eric Voegelin, vol. V (Columbia: University of Missouri Press, 2000).

Vogel, Angela. Das Pflichtjahr für Mädchen. Nationalsozialistische Arbeitseinsatzpolitik im Zeichen der Kriegswirtschaft (Frankfurt am Main: Lang, 1997).

von Mehren, Arthur T. "The Significance of Cultural and Legal Diversity for International Transactions," in Ernst von Caemmerer, Soia Mentschikoff, and Konrad Zweigert, eds., Ius Privatum Gentium: Festschrift für Max Rheinstein zum 70. Geburtstag am 5. Juli 1969, Band II: Nationales und Vergleichendes Privatrecht (Tübingen: J.C.B. Mohr, 1969).

Wagatsuma Sakae. Chūkamin kokuminhō sōsoku (Tokyo: Nihon Hyōronsha, 1946).

Wagatsuma Sakae. Hōgaku to gojūnen (Tokyo: Yūhikaku, 1967).

Wagatsuma Sakae. Hōritsu ni okeru rikutsu to ninjō (Tokyo: Nihon Hyōronsha, 1955).

Wagatsuma Sakae. Minpō kenkyū IX, 2 (Tokyo: Yūhikaku, 1971).

Wagatsuma Sakae, ed. Nachisu no hōritsu (Tokyo: Nihon Hyōronsha, 1937).

Wagatsuma Sakae, Ari'izumi Tōru. Minpō sōsoku: bukkenhō (Tokyo: Nihon Hyōron Shinsha, reissued 2009).

Wagatsuma Sakae et al. "Zadankai: shinzokuhō no kaisei (2)," Hōritsu Jihō, vol. 31, no. 11 (1959).

Wakabayashi, Bob Tadashi, ed. Modern Japanese Thought (Cambridge: Cambridge University Press, 1998).

Ward, Robert E. and Sakamoto Yoshikazu, eds. Democratizing Japan: The Allied Occupation (Honolulu: University of Hawai'i Press, 1987).

Waswo, Ann. Housing in Postwar Japan: A Social History (New York: RoutledgeCurzon, 2002).

Waswo, Ann. "In Search of Equity: Japanese Tenant Unions in the 1920s," in Ann Waswo and Nishida Yoshiaki, eds., Farmers and Village Life in Twentieth-Century Japan (New York: RoutledgeCurzon, 2003).

Waswo, Ann. Japanese Landlords: The Decline of a Rural Elite (Berkeley: University of California Press, 1977).

Watanabe Hiroshi. "Jidai no gaikan to kakushinteki hōritsugaku no kadai: sōron," in Hōritsu Jihō, vol. 60, no. 11 (1988).

Watanabe Hiroshi. Nihon seiji shisōshi: 17–20 seiki (Tokyo: Tokyo University Press, 2010).

Watanabe Soki. Nippon kaikoku: Amerika ga Perī kanchō wo haken shita hontō no riyū (Tokyo: Soshisha, 2009).

Watanabe Tsunayoshi. Hanrei kenkyū no kiso riron (Nagoya: Aichi Gakuin Daigaku Shuppanbu, 1967).

Watanabe Yōzō. Shakai to hō no sengoshi (Tokyo: Aoki Shoten, 2001).

Webb, Eugene. Eric Voegelin: Philosopher of History (Seattle: University of Washington Press, 2015).

Webb, Eugene. Philosophers of Consciousness: Polanyi, Lonergan, Voegelin, Ricoeur, Girard, Kierkegaard (Seattle: University of Washington Press, 1988).

Webb, Herschel. The Japanese Imperial Institution in the Tokugawa Period (New York: Columbia University Press, 1968).

Weber, Max. Gesammelte Aufsätze zur Religionssoziologie (1920–21).

Weber, Max. Gesammelte Aufsätze zur Soziologie und Sozialpolitik (1924).

Weber, Max. Wirtschaftsgeschichte (1924).

Weber, Max. Wirtschaft und Gesellschaft (1925).

Wigen, Kären. The Making of a Japanese Periphery, 1750–1920 (Berkeley: University of California Press, 1995).

Yamamoto, Nobuo. "Guide to Japanese Legal Literature," International Journal of Law Libraries, vol. 7 (1979).

Yanagita Kunio. Yanagita Kunio zenshū (Tokyo: Chikuma Bunko, 1989).

Yano Masahiro. "Rōdōhō no kisei kanwa to rōdōsha no hō shutaisei: A. Shupio no shosetsu kara," in Waseda Hōgaku, Vol. 75, No. 3 (March, 2000), 189–208.

Yasaki, Mitsukuni. "Legal Positivism and Authoritarianism in Japanese Legal Tradition," in Osaka University Law Review, 17 (1969), 1–7.

Yiu, Angela. Chaos and Order in the Works of Natsume Sōseki (Honolulu: University of Hawai'i Press, 1998).

Yomiuri Shimbun (newspaper), 1932.

Yoneda Shōtarō. Gendai chishiki kaikyū undō to narikin to demokurashii (Tokyo: Kōbundō Shobō, 1919).

Yonezawa Shinji cho, Suehiro Izutarō jo. Chingin chi'iki sa no kimekata (Tokyo: Chūō Rōdō Gakuen, 1949).

Yoshida Katsumi (shikai). "Kindai Minpōgaku no shikō yōshiki," in Hokkaidō Hōgaku Ronshū, Vol. 52, no. 5 (2002), 1723–1737.

Yoshida Katsumi. "Shakai hendōki no Nihon minpōgaku—Hatoyama Hideo to Suehiro Izutarō," Hokudai Law Review, vol. 52, no. 5 (2002), 1665-1704.

Yūhikaku. Jurisuto, rinji zōkan, Wagatsuma Sakae sensei tsuitō, No. 563 (June 21, 1974) (complete issue).

Zenkoku Setsurumento Rengō Shokikyoku. Onaji yorokobi to kanashimi no naka de: gakusei Setsurumento undō no kiroku (Kyoto: San'ichi Shobō, 1957).

Index

www.ingramcontent.com/pod-product-compliance
Lightning Source LLC
LaVergne TN
LVHW091526200926
848483LV00002B/320

* 9 7 8 1 6 0 4 9 7 9 9 3 0 *